THE ILLUSTRATED HISTORY OF
County Cricket

THE ILLUSTRATED HISTORY OF
County Cricket

Eric Midwinter

THE KINGSWOOD PRESS
in association with Bass Brewers Limited

First published in Great Britain 1992
by The Kingswood Press
Michelin House, 81 Fulham Road, London SW3 6RB

Copyright © 1992 Eric Midwinter

A CIP catalogue record for this book
is available from the British Library
ISBN 0 413 64080 9

Photoset by Deltatype Ltd, Ellesmere Port, Cheshire
Printed in Great Britain
by Clays Ltd, St. Ives Plc

Contents

Acknowledgements

This book owes much to the warm encouragement and wise advice of Tony Pocock throughout all the complex stages of its development: I am most grateful for his help. I must also thank Stephen Green, MCC's Curator at Lord's, Malcolm Lorimer, the Lancashire CCC's librarian at Old Trafford, and Neil Tunnicliffe for their help in researching illustrations, and the following for their kind permission to reproduce photographs: Patrick Eagar (for nos. 47, 49, 51–56, 58–60, 64, 65, 70, 82, 85–88, 94, 100, 105, 110, 111, 122, 123, 128, 134, 135, 140, 141, 146, 147, 151–153, 159, 160); the Hulton-Deutsch Collection (no. 121); Malcolm Lorimer (no. 99); the MCC Collection (for nos. 2, 4, 7, 8–10, 12–14, 25, 26, 28, 33, 37, 39, 41, 84, 108, 109, 142, 144); and the Roger Mann Collection (for nos. 1, 3, 5, 6, 11, 15–24, 27, 29–32, 34–36, 38, 40, 42, 43–46, 48, 50, 57, 61–63, 66–69, 71–81, 83, 89–93, 95–98, 101–104, 106, 107, 112–120, 124–127, 129–133, 136–139, 143, 145, 148–150, 154–158).

The photographs in the colour section are reproduced by permission of Patrick Eagar (nos. 1, 4–8) and the Roger Mann Collection (nos. 2, 3).

Eric Midwinter

Foreword

It is curious that, although there are several fine general histories that embrace county cricket, and although all counties have their own individual narratives, specific accounts of county cricket are rare, save for one or two which concentrate on the massive data-bank of statistics that has built up over the years. Needless to say, this book leans heavily on all of this huge and varied literature, and comprehensive acknowledgement is cheerfully offered.

Here is a full-scale history of county cricket, placed, as a cricket history properly should be, in the changing context of society at large. It is split into three simple sections. There is a general section, critically tracing the development of county cricket from its beginnings to the present day, and there is a section of essays on each of the seventeen first-class counties. These seventeen have practically monopolized first-class county cricket since the start, though Cambridgeshire played thirty-nine recognized first-class games between 1857 and 1871 before losing their status.

Now, dramatically, in 1992, at the other end of county cricket's story, Durham enter the first-class fray, the first movement in or out of the Championship since 1921.

The essays in Part Two of the book discuss the formation and the exploits of every county, and each essay ends, in a final flourish, with a suggested best-ever eleven for the county in question. This is done, in part, by way of summary of each county's story. It should be added that these selections are chiefly based on birth and residential qualifications and from those whose main career was with that county; generally, modern overseas signings have been excluded.

The third section of the book, an appendix to Parts One and Two, carries nine tables of selected facts and figures about the counties.

English county cricket is a long-standing and worthy institution, if, like any institution, a combination of virtues and vices. It deserves respectable historical analysis: one hopes that this study is a small contribution to that process.

Eric Midwinter

Glorious Cricket: Glorious Beer

In 1777 Hampshire scored 403 against England, the first recorded total of 400, out of which James Aylward made 167, the highest score in an important match until 1820. William Bass busied himself with more commercial matters, for it was in that year that his famous brewery was opened in Burton upon Trent. Of course, the story of beer has a much longer life than that, for there is evidence of it being brewed in Mesopotamia around 6000 BC, and it was certainly well-established in England during Anglo-Saxon times. Despite the sometimes frenetic efforts of cricket antiquarians to find an ancient vintage for their sport, cricket cannot rival this longevity.

However, cricketers have ever attempted to compensate for this discrepancy by their enthusiastic affection for beer, and there are many happy bat-beer connections. Early matches were often sponsored by publicans. A famous one was in 1854, when Mr Wintle, landlord of the Full Moon Hotel at Stockes Croft in Bristol, guaranteed, at a cost of £65, a visit of William Clarke's All-England XI to play XXII from the Bristol area on the field behind his pub. 'Jolly citizens', we are informed, enjoyed their 'tankards of home-brewed' as they witnessed the locals suffer a dreadful defeat. The six-year old W. G. Grace was in attendance – his father skippered the Bristol side – at this his first important game.

Many cricketers have become landlords, sometimes shrewdly investing their benefit money in that direction. Way back in the 19th century Fuller Pilch, that batsman of ancient fame, was tavern-owner and ground attendant at Town Malling in Kent, the Dingley Dell of *Pickwick Papers*, and later mine host of the Saracen's Head in Canterbury, something of a shrine for the annual Canterbury cricket festival. Cricketers as varied as Bobby Peel, the gifted Yorkshire left-hand spin bowler, and Maurice Tate, the nonpareil fast-medium bowler from Sussex, became land-lords in cricketing retirement. What, for example, could have been better than an evening during the 1930s at the Northumberland Hotel near Old Trafford or, later, at the King's Head, Droylesden? That original droll, Cecil Parkin, was the publican, yarning away by the hour about the game of which he was its most well-humoured exponent.

Historically, the most celebrated cricketer-innkeeper must be the same William Clarke who formed the All-England XI. Originally a brick-layer, he took up cricket and also became a publican at the Bell Inn in the Old Market Square, Nottingham. This was the centre for the town's cricket. His wife died in 1836, and, in 1837, he married Mrs Chapman who kept the inn at Trent Bridge; in 1838 the first game was played 'on Clarke's new ground at Trent Bridge'. Thus have the stories of pints and pitches intertwined, leading in 1990 to the ultimate relationship, BASS HEADINGLEY.

Cricket and cricket spectators have, on the whole, found a decent harmony in their pastime and the foaming beverage. The temperance movement could never claim to have exerted a stranglehold on a game, which, associated as it is with drowsy summer days and prolonged phases of play, requires the restorative and relaxing qualities of honest beer to complete its pleasure.

It would be pleasing to the academic mind were Harry Bass – one of only two *Wisden* obituaries of that name, longtime Canterbury groundsman and Kent occasional in the 1870s – somehow related to William Bass, he who had cleverly noted what the monks of Burton Abbey had recognized since before the Norman Conquest, that is, the mineral-rich nature of Burton well water. No matter. Nothing could be more apposite than the combine of leather on willow with pint in hand, which is why 'Rain Stopped Play' and 'Time, Gentlemen, Please' are among the most poignant of the nation's well-known phrases.

PART ONE

County Cricket

ONE

The Persistent Shire

Why *county* cricket? Some other sports have occasionally used the county model, but only cricket has been dominated by the persistent shire. It has long been synonymous with the high-level performance of the sport in Britain, whereas the town club has been the paramount agency in other sports. Although county cricket clubs plainly have connections with surrounding local clubs, sometimes using them as nurseries, they remain, in a constitutional sense, autonomous. Of course, like the tiniest bowls clubs in the tiniest hamlet, they have had their subscribing membership, with committees and election of officers, and this has made them quite unlike, for instance, the top-flight football clubs with their commercial company base.

Politically, the shire has an impressive lineage; some of them were originally kingdoms, and all of them were important administrative units. In Stuart England, people referred to their 'county' as their 'country', and the famous historian of Hanoverian England, Lewis Namier, perceptively called them 'county commonwealths'. The local history expert, A. M. Everitt, has judged the 19th-century county still to have been 'the matrix of local society in which political opinion was formed'.

Thus it may be self-evident that cricket would follow that pattern. Yet the concrete existence of the seventeen first-class counties dates much later than the high-water mark of county influence. They were established late in the 19th century, when other sports were being founded on clubs in cities and towns. It is essential to distinguish between cricket played *in* the county and *by* the county. Cricket historians have confirmed that something akin to cricket was played in almost all British counties at an early date, but this is no more than a flag of convenience, using the shires for geographic identification. When the noblemen in the south-east raised sides in the 18th

century, they sometimes labelled them by the county – often they controlled sufficient tracts of the county to lend justification to their action. And then there was the kudos. There was a social cachet in using the age-old county tag – 'county' is still deployed as an adjective redolent of rural upper-crust.

This urge to trace heritage back to what Pooh-Bah called 'a protoplasmal globule' afflicted cricket antiquarians, zealous in the neo-Darwinian pursuit of the evolutionary trace. An obscure reference or cloudy picture will be eagerly associated with cricket (or, for that matter, several other sports). Many county histories attempt the mystic linkage, beginning thus: 'Although there was no formal organization in Loamshire until 1874, there is evidence of cricket played by shepherd lads in the dales around Loamster. . . .'

Where there had been perfunctory county matches hitherto, these had been largely obliterated by the dominating activities of the exhibition XIs of the mid-19th century, so that, in a genuine sense, the tale of county cricket, played in a national context and to a national formula, began about the 1860s. However unrepresentative it often was, the emerging clubs, conscious of the enduring psychological and political influence and precedent of the county idea, grasped at the old catch-all title. It was suffused with that pastoral image which the gentlemen members of the county clubs were anxious to adopt.

In claiming a later start for the formation of county cricket than some would allow, it is imperative to emphasize the 'folk' nature of most games until well into the 19th century. There was 'play', with servants and young people snatching some respite from chores in the highly localized game that had evolved according to available terrain, implements, tradition and the intercession of charismatic individuals. The notion of fixtures, as opposed to the picking up of 'sides' in one's own community or school, was a long time in being widely accepted. There was, therefore, an ever-undulating condition of 'games', as evidenced by the overlaps apparent – charging the would-be catcher, for example – as versions of cricket emerged from this pulsating ruck of pastimes. Such 'disportment' endured until after the Industrial Revolution in many areas.

Even when the nobility took a restraining hand, their need for regulation – often, initially,

CRICKET.

A GRAND MATCH

Was played on WINDMILL DOWNS, Hants,

On *WEDNESDAY, July 13th, 1791, and two following Days,*

For a THOUSAND GUINEAS.

Hampshire. with Ring and Aylward, against *England.*

Hampshire.	1st	Innings.	2d	Innings.
John Small	0	b. Boxall	0	c. Beldam
Ring	20	c. Fennex	4	c. H. Walker
Aylward	1	b. Boxall	0	b. J. Walker
Colonel Lenox	12	b. ditto	22	b. ditto
Scott	3	b. ditto	13	run out
Small, sen.	36	b. ditto	0	c. John Wells
Purchase	19	run out	3	b. Boxall
T. Taylor	1	c. John Wells	0	c. John Wells
Annett	20	run out	13	not out
Freemantle	30	not out	13	run out
Collins	0	b. Boxall	9	b. Boxall
Byes	1		- - - - -	
	143		77	

England.	1st	Innings.	2d	Innings.
John Wells	3	c. Small, sen.	28	b. Annet
Crawt	10	c. Ring	0	b. Purchase
Beldam	5	run out	38	b. Collins
Fennex	5	run out	16	not out
H. Walker	9	b. Taylor	0	c. Purchase
T. Walker	22	run out	21	b. ditto
John Walker	3	c. Purchase	2	b. ditto
G. Louch, Esq.	39	b. Collins	0	c. Taylor
Pitcher	26	c. J. Small	25	b. ditto
Bullen	3	not out	2	b. Purchase
Boxall	11	b. Taylor	11	b. Taylor
Byes	1		- - - - -	
	137		143	

T. CANE, Printer, Earls Court, Leicester Fields.

---

1 'Gambling, not cricket, was the
major hobby of the Georgian peerage . . .'
Hampshire play England in 1791 for 1,000 guineas.

---

for the particular game in question – was to avoid dispute over the big money at stake. For gambling, not cricket, was the major hobby of the Georgian peerage, who treasured horse racing, cock fighting and prize fighting for the same reason. This, rather than more romantic theories about defeated Royalists, at the time of the Civil War, slinking home and starting cricket on their estates, is the chief explanation of the aristocratic influence. And cricket had one valuable advantage over most other sports then. It allowed the rakish nobleman to participate in a virile pastime, and to share this, without sullying the escutcheon, with his inferiors. These underlings might undertake most of the bowling duties, with their superiors enjoying most of the batting – and that dichotomy of amateur batsmen and professional bowlers lasted well into the present century – but cricket provided a surprisingly harmonious compromise.

Thus it was that, on the large estates, noblemen employed men in farming occupations who performed for the estate XI. Thomas Waymark, sometimes known as the father of cricket professionals, was probably groom to the Duke of Richmond. In much the same way a speedy footman might have made his mark in the 'pedestrian' races of the age, although, needless to say, the jobs were occasionally sinecures, just as, today, a cricketer might be offered an undemanding post to wile away the winter months in economic comfort. Nevertheless, this capacity to tolerate a two-class structure within the actuality of the game itself was to prove an enormous bonus, and was to be crucial in the coming emergence of county cricket proper.

All this said, it is useful to scrutinize the spread of cricket across the counties, even when bearing in mind that its incidence was exceedingly sporadic and that the format of the game probably varied eccentrically from one end of the country to the other. From various sources, it is possible to trace the expansion of cricket not so much by, as throughout, the counties. Formally recorded games called cricket had, predictably enough, taken place in Kent, Sussex and Surrey by 1700, and, by 1800, it is clearly right to believe that recognizable cricket matches had been played in almost all the English and many of the Welsh shires. More important, it is likely that, by the start of the 19th century, the game would have been recognized uniformly as such across most of England. At the same time, there remained an enormous imbalance. By the last decade of the 18th century, four-fifths of known games had occurred in the five south-eastern counties, with only about 350 of the then recorded 2000 or so fixtures having been located outside Kent, Surrey, Sussex, Middlesex and Essex. What is more, these matches remained highly localized in arrangement and interest; for instance, the famed Hambledon games were not much reported in the provincial press away from that immediate area.

In his *Cricket: A History of its Growth and Development throughout the World*, Major Rowland Bowen catalogued the year when a match was played bearing, however loosely, a county's banner. It must be repeated that this signifies no existence of a county organization. Frequently, if not one of the sporting peerage, then an ambitious club might have arbitrarily adopted the label for additional kudos or because they had been strengthened by the recruitment of players from other local clubs. Of the first-class counties, Surrey and Kent appear to have played in 1709, but there is vigorous dispute as to the status of the teams. Sussex (1728), Middlesex (1730), Essex (1737) and Northamptonshire (1741) follow, with Hampshire (1766) and Leicestershire (1791) later in the century. Somerset, Yorkshire and Nottinghamshire crowd around 1798. The rest played first in the middle sector of the last century: Warwickshire (1826), Gloucestershire (1839), Worcestershire (1844), Lancashire (1849), Glamorgan (1861) and Derbyshire (1870). Throughout the 18th century there were occasional inter-county games of this brand although the first of which we have a proper record – Surrey v. Kent – did not take place until 1773.

If one turns more specifically to the formation of county *clubs*, the picture is very different. The late 18th and early 19th centuries formed an era when, in part because of the sustained and more sophisticated involvement of the nobility, the club as such became dominant. Hambledon, Slindon and Marylebone itself are examples of this. The place of London became critical. Much of the activity was metropolitan, and gambling continued to exert its dubious charms. Often the clubs – and Hambledon, to the despair of the sentimentalist, is an instance of this – were loose collections of players, assembled for this or that game, and with wagering a forceful element. The difference between a match and a game, for example, was that the former involved betting. When it comes to the establishment of clubs based on counties, *Wisden* is valuable. It shows that the first proposed date of a county organization was that of Essex in 1790, but the evidence for this is hazy and indistinct. Leicestershire, Northamptonshire and Warwickshire come next with starts in the 1820s, while Sussex (1836), Nottinghamshire (1841), Kent (1842), Worcestershire (1844), Surrey (1845) and Hampshire (1849) follow suit. The rest cluster in the 1860s, Derbyshire completing the list in 1870. This, of course, refers only to the present first-class counties: the first known county club was Oxfordshire in 1787.

However, few counties that began administrative life early survived without interruption. It may be helpful to list the counties in chronological sequence according to the years in which, in *Wisden*'s view, the present club was formed. In a minority of cases, there has since been a substantial revision of the club, and that year is given in brackets. In every instance, however, these amounted to a reshaping and there was no break, as hitherto, in the history:

Northamptonshire	1820 (1878)
Sussex	1839 (1857)
Nottinghamshire	1841 (1866)
Surrey	1845
Kent	1859 (1870)
Yorkshire	1863 (1891)
Hampshire	1863 (1879)
Middlesex	1864
Lancashire	1864
Worcestershire	1865
Derbyshire	1870

Gloucestershire	1871
Somerset	1875
Essex	1876
Leicestershire	1879
Warwickshire	1882
Glamorgan	1888

What is apparent is that those early essays into county clubland were frail and irresolute. Even using the occasionally spurious titling of particular games as 'county' ones, they well-nigh vanish during the opening years of the 19th century. The record lucidly demonstrates that these counties, for all their tradition, were not able, or did not wish, to become genuine and full-scale institutions. The earliest, Northamptonshire, began in 1820. If major reorganizations are counted, then the oldest of the county clubs with a consecutive tale to tell is Surrey, its story dating from 1845. It will be observed that the 1860s and 1870s were self-evidently the crucial decades for this purpose. Why is the implementation of county organization so much younger than the tradition, the idea and the pioneering of county cricket?

The explanation lies in the inherent frailty of county cricket itself. Frankly, it lacked both a rationale and a platform in pre-industrial society. The county combines (they were scarcely clubs by the later yardstick) were weak. Maybe those involved did not perceive them as regular, let alone durable and lasting. When one examines what was required to mount a county club, one realizes that the Regency ambience was not propitious. Even if they were intended to endure, they had no chance to survive.

It is sometimes argued that the killer-blow was the establishment of the professional exhibition XIs after 1846. These offered more or less permanent

2 'The establishment of the professional exhibition XIs . . .'
The All-England XI travel by coach to a fixture in 1851.

employment over a very long season to a relatively small number of cricketers. William Clarke, the Nottinghamshire maestro, was the primary begetter of this profitable activity, and, at one or another stage, there were half a dozen or so of these troupes in operation. They travelled the nation ceaselessly and intrepidly, the senior teams playing twenty-five fixtures and more a summer.

In reality, the nascent county clubs had been in no position to proffer reasonable employment to the emerging group of independent professionals. Next, these professionals, full-time and part-time, illustrate the tendency of some tradesmen to enjoy a more autonomous status, released from the chains of estate management and tenure. This was happening in many fields, and was a token of the shifting ground of the economy under the stress of industrialism. The mobile exhibition XIs took to the road alongside a host of other travelling entertainers. A parallel example might be the

3 'The emerging group of independent professionals . . .' Alfred Shaw's team which toured America, Australia and New Zealand in 1881–82.
Back row: George Ulyett, Richard Pilling, James Lillywhite,
J. Conway (manager), W. E. Midwinter, William Bates; *centre*: Arthur Shrewsbury, Alfred Shaw,
Tom Emmett, Edmund Peate; *front*: Richard Barlow, William Scotton and John Selby.
Each was a noted county player as well as being a member of these touring combines.

4 'The tendency of some tradesmen
to enjoy a more autonomous status . . .'
A splendid example was John Wisden, of
Almanack fame and other cricketing ventures.

travelling fit-up theatre companies, of which Vincent Crummles's touring repertory in *Nicholas Nickleby*, published in 1838–39, provides a fictitious illustration. It was all of a part with the crumbling disintegration of the old and mainly agrarian scene, with, in consequence, spasmodic endeavours to fill the cultural vacuum. Whatever else, the touring XIs, usually playing against odds, carried the thought and the action of uniform cricket to the farthest ends of the kingdom. It was, of course, important that local talent had a chance to match itself against the pick of the nation's paid players, and that local crowds could marvel over the expertise of high-grade cricket. What was perhaps even more significant was that it was the *same* cricket. It was a question of formula as much as standard. The professional tourists did much to guarantee that the day-by-day performance of cricket became 'nationalized', and, however much the counties complained, the exhibition XIs were helping to make a national pattern of county cricket more acceptable later.

Men were to look back for inspiration to the primitive ventures of cricket in the shires in Hanoverian and Regency times. Yet, at last, and by a wry irony, county cricket, redolent of pastoral virtue, was to be a product of the Industrial Revolution.

5 'A product of the Industrial Revolution . . .' Cricket at Trent Bridge
in 1909 with the chimneys of industry in the background.

TWO

Train Starts Play

By the middle of the 19th century, just as the first of the substantive county clubs was getting under way, Britain had become the world's first ever society in which industrialism was predominant. Queen Victoria's reign, from 1837 to 1901, witnessed a doubling of the country's population from 14 millions to 29 millions. That was dramatic enough, but there was an ever more vivid switch in terms of internal migration. At the outset of Victoria's rule, the majority of people lived in the country. At the end, they mostly inhabited the towns.

Gone were the days of the cottage industry or of farms and workshops employing just the extended family or maybe a handful of labourers and apprentices. Moreover, 200 workers per manufacturing unit was the average by the last third of the century. Of the working population 20% were still in agriculture, itself subject to increasing mechanization, and the same number remained in domestic service. But there had been an enormous shift in the occupational patterns. Half the work-force was now employed in heavy industry, such as the mills, the mines and the foundries.

Old towns mushroomed and new towns sprang into existence. The great cities, soon to be the venues for leading cricket matches, trebled and quadrupled. London itself doubled in size. When Queen Victoria died, over half her subjects lived in towns of more than 100,000 inhabitants. More people; more factories; more town-life: that was the telling equation, succinctly described as 'congregation'. 'Congregation' was to be the context for county cricket. Regular and frequent sport, in public and at a high level, was obviously dependent on the close order format of high incidences of population. In that the county clubs began as, and steadfastly remain, the vehicles of a subscribing membership, there had, first, to be sufficient middle-glass gentlemen living within easy

enough reach to make this possible. Second, and later, there had to be an adequate surrounding area from which each county could draw a reasonable paying audience.

That sequence must be stressed. The county club was initially the creation of its members, who provided the players as well as the funds and the administrative know-how. Professionals were then introduced to strengthen the local amateur talent, just as the gambling scions of the great houses had discovered and paid for extra and competent hands. Thus it was a slightly later development that paraded this array of subscribing and waged ability to the public view. The move to spectatordom grew partly from an increasing sense of identification with an important team with a national fixture-list and partly from the need to raise the wind necessary to pay the wages of the professionals.

No county cricket club evolved in the way the first football clubs did with their curious mix of origins, some from the church, such as Everton, some from the work-place, such as Manchester United. County cricket clubs were only indirectly part of the movement to save workers from the perils of idleness, a movement which produced 50,000 brass bands, as well as a host of sporting teams. They did not even have the primary bonding of the officers' mess or the old school tie, as did some of the ancient football clubs, such as the Royal Engineers or the Old Etonians. Certainly they did not become commercial companies. Rather did the resurgent county clubs, strengthened by the potent amateur revival of the second half of the 19th century, seize power from the commercialized exhibition XIs. The county formula thus was able to embrace amateur and professional in a way which the football codes were to find impossible. It may, in part, have been a question of style. The 'county' was an admirable medium for the more sedate and tortuous rite of cricket, whereas J. B. Priestley's 'grey-green tide' of cloth caps, later to be found at every Football League ground, came to represent the shorter, simpler passages of football.

All classes found a little more time for leisure. The 'short Saturday' – it was still eight hours – was introduced for textile workers in 1847, and was the prelude to the Saturday half-day. The ritual of the annual holiday became a middle-class habit in the 1860s, and the working class, with the railwaymen the first to receive holidays with pay, followed suit in the 1870s. It is no coincidence that 1871 marked both the introduction of Bank Holidays and the first use of turnstiles on cricket grounds. There was more money. Wages rose 40% between 1860 and 1875, and by 1900 they were 80% higher than in mid-century. It was also an extremely youthful population: in the 1870s almost half the population was under twenty, and three-fifths were unmarried.

No wonder there was a yearning by the ruling classes for 'rational recreation' of an uplifting kind to distract and to sublimate. County cricket, with its joint appeal to middle and working class, was a wholesome element in the fray, and, informed by its own pre-industrial origins, it managed to engage all social grades, providing a piece of integrated culture in a society riven by class. It was strictly controlled. 'Rational recreation' demanded the guarantee of concrete standardization which MCC brought to cricket, and which made a national county competition feasible. It was all of a portion with the Victorian search for regulation in every corner of life, for urban life demands the precision of binding law, where rural life might survive on custom. What the German sociologist, Max Weber, called 'rationalization' meant that, just as the Act which brought coherent administration to English towns was passed in 1835, so did that same year

6 'A reasonable paying audience . . .' A typically large crowd at Birmingham in 1909.

7 'A piece of integrated culture . . .' A long-ago picture of a Derbyshire XI,
looking, it must be said, a trifle bedraggled. The amateur captain,
hands in pockets, has placed himself just within touching distance of his charges.

8 'The proper degree of social exclusiveness . . .' An early view of cricket in the cathedral
city of Canterbury.

mark the codification of the laws of cricket. Apart from the legalization of over-arm bowling, all the major elements of the game were in place, and they soon came to be universally accepted.

So earnest and so strong was this belief in the worthiness of cricket that it became closely associated with those other corner-stones of Victorian probity – education and religion. The sanctification of cricket by the public schools and the universities served as bread and wine to county cricket, offering it a perpetual diet of young and well-coached amateurs, the county providing the proper degree of social exclusiveness for such young bloods and the amateur fulfilling the county's fervent wish to be socially acceptable. Nothing is more surprising in the social history of sport than the abrupt conversion of the educational authorities to an approval of cricket. The two extremes may be illustrated in this fashion. In 1796, the Headmaster of Eton 'soundly flogged' the XI not because Westminster had defeated them, but because the game had been sternly prohibited, a singular case of adding injury to insult. By the 1860s, 700 carriages and over 7000 spectators were attending the opening day of the Eton and Harrow fixture at Lord's, which, along with the Varsity match, had become one of the pukkah highlights of the social calendar. Cricket had become the principal element in what at Eton was believed to be the 'infallible prescription' of games. It was for many headmasters a welcome alternative to their pupils' obsession with field sports, and it was more easily controlled within the confines of the school grounds.

Moreover, it was regarded as an ideal preparation for the corridors of power at home and the building of empire abroad. No less an authority than Tom Brown was heard sturdily to say, at the behest of his creator Thomas Hughes in 1857, 'but it's more than a game. It's an institution'. His master agreed, pointing out that it was as much a 'birthright' as habeas corpus and trial by jury. All this amounts to an extraordinary alteration from a generation or so earlier when cricket, with other games, was condemned for its wastefulness and sinful gambling from many a pulpit and lectern.

Instead of allowing their pupils to bask in the enjoyment of cricket for its own sake, Victorian schoolmasters invested a splendid game in the robes of character building, believing that it prepared boys for completely different exercises of leadership and skill. W. G. Grace was to state that cricket 'cultivates the manly attributes'. The best known example was in Henry Newbolt's poem *Vitaï Lampada*, in which the ranks are rallied, when in disarray, by the officer inspired by his remembrance of a breathless hush in the Close, with ten to make and the match to win.

However fallacious that notion of the transfer of training, it was a boost for the amateur player who was to contribute greatly to county cricket. There was a further aspect. This was the first Darwinian generation, and Herbert Spencer's catch-phrase – 'the survival of the fittest' – rang authentically around the cloisters. Competition and 'emulation' were key doctrines. Samuel Smiles published *Self-help* in 1859, the same year as *The Origin of Species*. Boys were urged to exhibit their fitness as social animals and for the honour of school and self, and cricket proved to be the ideal vehicle.

County cricket received an extra bonus, for the liaison between the counties and the leading schools was very strong. Lord's was to be the venue for premier school games and MCC was to develop a regular series of fixtures with the leading schools; the universities were to become and remain domains of first-class play; the gnarled ex-professional county player was soon to be an indispensable feature as coach for the young gentlemen; and the masters, ex-Blues – often playing for a county in the summer vacation (and thereby sometimes depriving a 'pro' temporarily of his living) – all these factors counted as county cricket was at last properly under way. No other sport, not even rugby or athletics, was able to form such powerful coalitions.

As manly virtue expressed through games grew into a potent educational force, cricket received a religious gloss which placed it apart from and above other games. In turn, this affected county cricket, which shone in the reflected glory of this religiosity and was suffused with respectability. It was the era of Muscular Christianity, of which Thomas Hughes was a protagonist, and the chivalrous display at sport became the outer sign of inner grace. It really is difficult to overstate this cross-fertilization between cricket and godliness. At first sight it seems that cricket is perpetually utilized as a metaphor for Christian virtue. On closer reflection one is bound to wonder whether the reverse is true – that the church had become a medium for conceiving of the purity of cricket. It is, at least, certain that the cricket cult revived the essence of Christianity as made intelligible to middle- and upper-class youth.

The public schools and the universities churned out Anglican clerics of this disposition, and in many of the early county sides were to be found cricketing parsons. To the Pauline texts of the race run straight and the well-fought fight were added the straight bat and that eighth deadly sin, 'it's not cricket'. Gone were the gaudy sky-blue coats and nankeen breeches of the late Hanoverian MCC favours. Now all was virginal white, and the ritual was as sombre and rigid as any sacrament. Umpires, clad in long white robes, slowly walked in druidic procession to supervise the wickets, part altar, part cross.

This mystique, and its very complexity, had a special attraction for the Victorians. Because the game required detailed oversight, it took on some of the aura of the counting-house, that other characteristic institution of Dickensian England. As well as the two accountants or umpires to decide the score, there was a need for two auditors or scorers to check it. Cricket is about the only game whose ball-by-ball process can be deciphered by an absentee merely by using the score book. It is planned on strict book-keeping principles, with double entry uppermost, the batsmen's credit tallying with the bowlers' debit. It is purely and simply a ledger, of the kind Newman Noggs or Mr Wemmick pored over.

The accountancy of cricket gave it a familiar and reassuring feel for cricket's bourgeois supporters, and, with the ledger, the two threads – the priestly liturgy and the algebraic formulae of high finance – were interwoven. For the book of judgement was a favourite symbol of Christian redemption or otherwise. All three proclivities of Church, Bank and Game were succinctly compounded in the famous verse of Grantland Rice:

> For when the One Great Scorer comes
> To write against your name,
> He marks – not that you won or lost –
> But how you played the game.

Gradually, piece by piece, the jig-saw took shape. The new social fabric was ready for nationally-based sports, and it is in the last quarter of the 19th century that most sports adopted some overall national structure or standard. County cricket, blessed by tradition, political convention, education, religion and other cultural aspects, was ideally placed to take advantage of these circumstances. Somehow – and sheer luck must have had a role – county cricket happened on a strange compromise. The middle-class amateurs had rescued major cricket from the clutches of the professionals, and the time-honoured device of the county was an inviting one for cricketers and organizers ambitious to spread their wings beyond ordinary club levels. It was an harmonious coming together of ancient and modern, and, once one or two models were established, the prototype was quickly copied.

These are the reasons why county cricket was able to evolve. A major question remains. Cricket had been played in every English county by the end of the 18th century, and a team loosely representative of each county had taken the field before the middle of the 19th century. Yet only a minority became first-class counties. If county cricket was ideally suited to the situation prevailing in the last third of the last century, why did not more county clubs of this superior quality emerge?

The answer is railways. The railway system, busily constructed from the 1830s onwards but with special concentration in the 1840s, was the *sine qua non* of first-class cricket. If a county was not accessible by rail, it could whistle in vain for first-class status. The caveat of the circular argument must again be entered. Naturally, urban areas with the kind of population densities that could sustain county cricket were also the ones which demanded railway services. The fact remains that this did not always work in reverse. Some counties, with sizeable and urbanized locations, were late in being blessed with the delights of the train; these were the ones that either never reached first-class status or were extremely late in so doing.

It is often forgotten that, until the Statutes (Definition of Time) Act of 1880, Greenwich Mean Time was not legally enforceable. Until well into the century, time had varied a trifle from place to place, according to the sun's movements, rather as lighting-up time still does today. As communication between such places was dilatory, it scarcely mattered. The railways transformed that situation overnight. Their speed and reliability allowed much greater accuracy. The exhibition XIs and the early country house XIs had relied on improved road and coach conditions. However, the County Championship was made possible by the certainty of train travel, just as the first international tours were to rely on the steamship.

It was partly a matter of getting the audience to the venue, but that was not too imperative in an age when lengthy walking was regarded as normal (men like Dickens and Gladstone would hike twenty and thirty miles by way of a stroll) and when most spectators were probably living not too far distant from the grounds. What was essential was that the competing teams could complete an ever more complicated fixture-list. They had to arrive in time for an early morning start and they had to be sure of meeting their next opponents often the morning after the previous match ended. Only the railways could provide that precision of service.

Basically, the initial phase of railway building delineated an inverted T. London was, of course, the inverted T junction. The western cross-piece was from Paddington to Bristol, bringing Gloucestershire and the Graces within reach of the fray. Without the Great Western Railway it is unlikely that the unparalleled genius of W. G. Grace would have been much noticed outside the south-west. Lines tracked eastward from the capital to Folkestone and then to Canterbury, the homes of

9 'Only the railways could provide that precision of service . . .' Alfred Mynn of Kent and England tries to load his kit and himself on to an early Victorian train.

Kentish cricket, while there was an early routeway to Brighton, so Sussex was catered for. The upright of the upturned T sped northwards, branched at Rugby and fed Nottingham, Leeds, Sheffield and Manchester. The great northern triumvirate was joined into the system. In the 1840s Bristol was linked with Birmingham, so there was access northwards from the southwest. Middlesex and Surrey, as the two metropolitan counties, were ready to receive visitors or embark on their own journeys. The original eight first-class counties had railway contact in advance of the beginnings of the Championship proper.

In the 1890s seven more English counties were unequivocally admitted to the élite, one or two of them having been in and around the fringes for some time. Their main grounds were all in towns served by rail – Taunton for Somerset; Derby; Birmingham for Warwickshire; Leicester; Leyton for Essex (the club moved from Brentwood in part to ensure smoother travel); Southampton or Portsmouth for Hampshire. The seventh was Worcestershire, and the next to be admitted was Northamptonshire in 1905. Worcester and Northampton were added to the rail network only in the second period of its development.

. THE DEFEAT OF YORKSHIRE.

SAMMY.—"Better be drowned in Somerset cider than Lancashire beer. It is more southern."

10 'Taunton for Somerset . . .' Sammy Woods cartooned to celebrate a rare victory for Somerset over Yorkshire.

Two further points should be noted. Although these were supposedly *county* clubs, they frequently destroyed the romantic rural illusion by being headquartered away from the county town; indeed, only Nottingham of the original eight and Derby, Leicester, Worcester and Northampton of the second group enjoyed that connection. Cricket went where the trains went.

Then there is a negative pointer. This concerns where the central passenger railways failed to penetrate, at least in the opening phases of construction. Some great cities in the furthest reaches of the nation were, unexpectedly, left off this first trunk railway map. Newcastle, Carlisle, Edinburgh, Glasgow, Cardiff and Swansea were among them, and they had all witnessed good cricket at some form of county or equivalent level. They were initially left behind, although, of course, Glamorgan were to join the Championship after the First World War. Counties that had looked reasonably thriving, such as Cumberland,

11 'Cricket went where the trains went . . .' A modern aerial shot of Old Trafford, served for years by a railway, now part of an urban tramway system.

12 & 13 'Different classes of compartment . . .' Even the photographers played out the class
system: the Lancashire Championship team of 1904 had separate pictures taken of amateurs
(above) and professionals (below). *The Amateurs*: W. Findlay, L. D. S. Poidevin, A. C. MacLaren,
A. H, Hornby, R. H. Spooner; *the Professionals*: Heapes, Cuttle, Sladen, Tyldesley (J. T.), Hallows, Kermode,
Sharp.

Hertfordshire and especially Cambridgeshire, were also now out-classed. These and other shires housed significant towns and cities which were excluded from the earlier endeavours of the railwaymen. It is an impressive list of English urban life. It includes Oxford, Cambridge, Ipswich, Norwich, Lincoln, Bedford, Hertford, Dorchester, Hereford, Plymouth, Shrewsbury, Buckingham and Grimsby. All of them had been the scene of worthy cricket; several had populations in and around them of decent dimensions; there were fine cathedral cities and powerful administrative bases amongst them; all of them were bustling market towns for agrarian and light industrial purposes. The two universities were to play first-class cricket, but the rest never recovered from that initial lack of fast and reliable communications at the time it mattered. These were the very areas where, if the Merrie England legends of cricket's rollicking, countrified origins were to be believed, one might have expected to find major development.

Although many other factors obviously played their part, one can hardly overstate the influence exerted by the locomotive engine. By 1830, almost a hundred years of road and coach improvements had doubled the average speed of main road traffic. Inside a generation, and by the dawn of the formal County Championship, there were 10,000 miles of rail track in operation and the faster trains were touching fifty miles an hour. Communities were made and broken. Sometimes by ill luck and sometimes by blinkered management, local communities were ruined. Others prospered mightily. First-class county cricket was an instance of this, for the Championship was shaped by the rail network.

Cricket scored again. It was the game which embraced both the working-class professionals and middle-class amateurs. The railway companies were equal to the challenge. They provided different classes of compartment accordingly.

THREE

The Kingdom of the Octarchy

Thus it was that the seminal phase of modern county cricket was almost exclusively the province of eight teams, each centred on a bustling urban community, each joined easily with the others by railway. Not until the 1890s were they to find fresh companions of a regular character, as first one and then another county was formally admitted to the first-class ranks. Not until 1911, when impudent Warwickshire seized the crown from their elders and betters, was the Championship won by a county other than one of the octarchy, as the original eight counties were known to Victorian cricket buffs.

Strangely, Sussex, very much in the van and

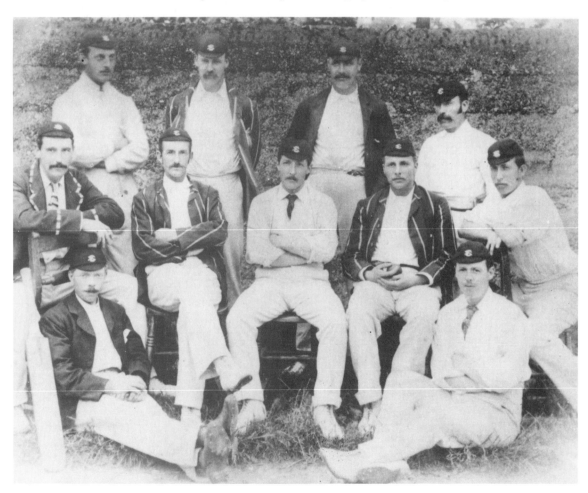

14 The strong Surrey team of 1888. *Back row*: W. P. Bowden, K. J. Key, Beaumont and Wood; *front row*: W. W. Read, Read (M), J. Shuter (captain), Lohmann and Bowley; *on ground*: Abel and Henderson.

established securely by 1839, never won the title during this period, and, indeed, the county remains one of only three teams – Somerset and Northamptonshire being the others – never to have done so. Kent, another club of lengthy and noble lineage, found the going hard and rough for many years, and it was not until the Edwardian era that they achieved any firm success, winning the coveted title four times in the immediate pre-war years.

This meant that, in terms of victory, the octet may very quickly be seen as a sextet. Surrey, with William Caffyn, H. H. Stephenson and, to the delight of those addicted to the sports quiz, Julius Caesar, were strong initially. They had an especially good season in 1857, and they won the first Championship (as recorded in *Wisden*) in 1864. Then they, too, suffered something of a lapse, winning nothing for over twenty years, before enjoying another fruitful spell between 1887 and 1899. In those dozen or so seasons Surrey won or shared the title no less than nine times, as if in rehearsal for their total domination of the County Championship in the 1950s.

Middlesex won the title early on, in 1866, but they also languished a trifle and did not win another crown until 1903. Gloucestershire, with the Grace brothers at their peak, contrived Championship successes out of somewhat meagre resources in the 1870s, four times winning or sharing the honours. The county still awaits any further beckoning from the gods, it now being well over a hundred years since Gloucestershire won the title.

Yorkshire won the Championship first in 1867; they shared the title in 1869, and they again won it outright the following year. After this perky little spell, they went into the doldrums, to emerge in the mid-1890s and enjoy considerable success over the turn of the century. Lancashire were a little slow to settle into the rigorous mode of first-class play, and it was to be 1879 before they won their first title, and a shared one at that. The next three years, with an outright win and a shared victory, also belonged to Lancashire, and they won three more titles, one shared, prior to the First World War.

The converse of the rather sporadic careers of these seven counties is, of course, the outstanding attainment of Nottinghamshire. In the early modern era Nottinghamshire proved to be far and away the greatest county XI. An auspicious litany of names attests to this: John Jackson, Alfred Shaw, Richard Daft, Arthur Shrewsbury, George Gunn. Nottinghamshire provided the early backbone for English professional cricket, and their

15 'The early backbone of English professional cricket . . .' Arthur Shrewsbury (Nottinghamshire) personified this tradition.

record is an enviable one. Put starkly, they won or shared the Championship in fifteen seasons between 1865 and 1889, a remarkable feat. Over the last hundred years they have never looked like emulating that wondrous performance, although they have won the title on four occasions. Nottinghamshire were, quite simply, the original great county.

Nottinghamshire's success was testimony to the switch of power away from the home counties, where, with aristocratic tutelage, it had long remained. With Yorkshire and Lancashire playing secondary if significant roles, Nottinghamshire emphatically illustrated the influence of industrialism. As, in the 19th century, the balance of economic power shifted northwards, so did the cultural accents change. Much of this had to do with the dominance of the professional cricketer and the seeming collapse of the amateur game. There was a concentration of competent professionals in the north midlands and this had been the backbone of the great exhibition XIs. They divided their allegiance between the county and the travelling XI, and, with William Clarke the presiding genius, Nottinghamshire always had the edge at this time. This was to carry them through the nascent years of the Championship in imposing style, at a time when exhibition and county cricket uneasily overlapped.

If evidence of early professional domination be called for, then the results of the Gentlemen and Players matches over this period should be scrutinized. From 1831 to 1865 the Gentlemen, in spite of hired help and smaller wickets and even more players on occasion, won only four games at Lord's or the Oval – and in one victorious outing they fielded eighteen men. Thereafter, the Gentlemen rallied forcefully, the Players winning only four of the next thirty-five encounters. The 'schisms' and other disruptions of the all-professional sides and the momentous presence of W. G. Grace are almost sufficient explanation, but a third reason for the amateur revival was certainly the extension of county cricket, leaning heavily, in turn, on the public schools and Oxbridge. It is no mere coincidence that the crucial date is the mid-1860s, for it was then that the

strikes and combines of the professionals were at their height; Grace began his mould-shattering career; and the senior county clubs came to prominence.

Although the amateur balance was in large part restored, solid professional diligence remained critical over the tougher travails of the Championship, most satisfactorily for Nottinghamshire. The peculiarities of industrial transformation also aided the Trent Bridge cause. The small-scale nature of the lace, hosiery and allied trades that had developed in Nottingham and its surrounds lent itself to the flexibility of broken time. Piecework at home, after the manner of Silas Marner, allowed men choice of time, so that a day away at cricket could be compensated for at another time. Neither the constant demands of agriculture, especially in the summer, nor the unceasing discipline of the full-run factory system was anything like so elastic and obliging. Many paid cricketers in these years harmonized their sporting profession with another craft of this flexible kind. The woollen industry of Yorkshire continued for some little time to offer this sort of scope to some tradesmen, unlike the scene across the Pennines, where cotton made harsh and inexorable demands on the textile workers.

This may have had an effect on the loose, never rigid, models of county clubs that emerged in the last third of the century. These were three in number.

First, there was the highly localized model, built around professionals, men of the county who earned their corn playing for their county. Mainly because of their size and the less rigid labour patterns current there, Nottinghamshire and Yorkshire were to the fore in this regard. They had the talent and confidence to take cricketing issue with the best the country had to offer without much resource to outsiders, and this was, obviously, a public relations bonus, in that they were able to command and enjoy a large measure of regional appeal.

Second, there was the predominantly amateur approach. The county club was a social club, providing cricket for its members with a paid hack or two to provide some bowling chores.

16 'The highly localised model, built around professionals . . .'
A group of suitably hard-bitten Yorkshire cricketers in 1882.

Middlesex tended toward this dispensation and so did Sussex and to some degree Kent, but the most forthright example was probably Gloucestershire. It was many years before they turned in any regular way to the professional staff. They had, of course, the advantage of having W. G. Grace among their number, although it would be misleading to categorize the 'Champion' as the *beau ideal* of amateurism. Gloucestershire, like other teams, had to find pragmatic ways and means to enable him to play. Gloucestershire's purity was also, to some extent, the innocence of the untempted. Their individual membership and general support, despite playing in the busy

city of Bristol and the charming setting of Cheltenham, was not too abundant, and they found it difficult to raise the wind for professional assistance. In fact, their first regular professional was William Evans Midwinter, distant relative of the author, and the robust pioneer who discovered that, if one had the fortitude to withstand the perils of two lengthy sea voyages annually, it was possible to become a cricketing commuter, in his case dividing his services between Gloucestershire and Victoria, Australia.

This older amateur tradition was severely upheld by E. M. Grace, W.G.'s elder brother and the Gloucestershire secretary. He was indeed an

17 'This older, amateur tradition . . .' Upheld by E. M. Grace,
seen here with his younger brother, W. G. Grace.

opponent of the County Championship: 'There ought', he proclaimed, 'never to have been one, and the sooner it is done away with the better. It simply spoils the pleasure of cricket.' He yearned for the days when the county just played a handful of games amid a pleasing volume of public enthusiasm. This was all but an extolling of the friendly virtues of the travelling country house XIs, of which I Zingari had become the best known. Indeed, these nomadic squads of young gentlemen assembling at this or that stately home had become the counterpoint of the travelling professional XIs. However, the task of the county club was to restore the alliance between the best of the professional and amateur worlds. It was a novel concept of first-class cricket and it was to withstand the rigours of a hundred years' trial. E. M. Grace, incidentally, a staunch sympathizer of the need to improve the conditions of the professionals, personified one extreme of the discussion. He feared, not without some proper justification, the worship of competition, averages and profit, and it was no doubt due to his firm influence that Gloucestershire carried the banner of a less committed approach, despite the presence of the most dedicated of all cricketers.

Third, there was the view that a county's function was to provide not so much cricket for its members to play as to watch. The purpose was to establish a successful and interesting club, which, in turn, would have a wider appeal to a public

outside the membership and which was lower middle-class if not downright plebeian in status. It is significant that Lancashire, the seat of power-based, factory-oriented industrialism, was in the van of this approach. Manchester and its surrounds were something of a socio-economic crucible in these years, with experimentation in all directions the norm. There had been and were still swarms of inventors of all sorts; and it was not out of character for Lancashire to adopt a more easy-going attitude to migrant labour than starchier Nottinghamshire and Yorkshire. Thus it was, by the early 1880s, when Lancashire triumphantly challenged for cricket honours, that Richard Barlow was their only regular professional to have been born within the precincts of the County Palatine. The others had been fostered and naturalized, and, under A. N. Hornby's strict guidance, they emerged as a strong and – very important – a coherent combine.

W. G. Grace was full of praise for that team,

18 'The best of the professional and amateur worlds . . .' The legendary Lancashire opening pair: Richard Barlow (*left*), the archetypal 'pro', and his amateur captain, A. N. Hornby.

claiming that 'it was difficult to find a weak spot in the eleven'. Acknowledging that five of the professionals were playing under residential qualifications, he argued that 'it must not be forgotten that other counties would have been only too glad to have them on similar conditions, and that it was owing to the committee of the county club and the excellent judgement of Mr Hornby that they had been originally selected and their powers developed'. Whether one regards the insistence on native-born players, adhered to by Yorkshire until 1992, as the acme of fierce loyalty or the last ditch of stultifying chauvinism, a moderate version of this third option soon became the norm for most counties. Surrey were another county to develop along such lines – significantly, a county, like Lancashire, with a less static, more swirling and cosmopolitan population for which to cater.

The argument about birthright was, in any event, more to do with poaching and excess mobility than with the deep-seated appeal of regional loyalties. Amateurs were rarely asked to show their birth certificates in those early days: they were county members, and, normally, lived locally. They might have had family connections or property in the county, or they might have found a clerical living or a schoolmastership in the vicinity. After all, Lord Hawke, the ruler of Yorkshire cricket, was not actually born on God's acre, but in Lincolnshire.

The debate more concerned the jobbing professional, keen to sell his labour to the highest bidder. Earlier, he had done so with some freedom, not least because many teams were recruited for a match or a short tour and as quickly disbanded. The settlement of first-class cricket into a more regular competition somehow made this practice seem reprehensible. Thus it was that steps were taken to bar the professional from shopping around in search of, to reverse the modern text, money for value.

It was the Surrey club which, in 1873, inaugurated a series of meetings about this intractable issue, with the Surrey secretary, Frederick Burbage, in the chair. The closeness of the debates was such that it was only on his casting vote that

19 'Lord Hawke,
the ruler of Yorkshire cricket . . .'

the proposals were adopted. They were ratified at the Oval on 9 June. The recommendations, applicable to amateur and professional alike, insisted that no one could play for more than one county in a season, a regulation that had been submitted for consideration some years before in the 1860s, chiefly at the behest of the Nottinghamshire club. Those born in one and resident in another county could choose at the beginning of the summer to which they would offer their services, while, provided it was open to him as an 'occasional' residence, the family domicile could also grant qualification.

The counties having no other formal structure of their own, MCC were asked to adopt and monitor these rules, but their attempt to allow amateurs an extra loophole via any parental property was rejected by the counties. However, half way through the 1873 season, MCC did give its approval to these regulations, and they served as the base for the competition over many years. Indeed, some historians date the County Championship as starting from the year in which that decision was taken.

In the interim MCC had entered the field with a vain and harmful experiment. They offered a silver cup to be played for on a knock-out basis on a neutral ground, and six counties were invited to participate – it was the year after the first ever FA Cup. Unfortunately, the cricketing version failed ignominiously. Just one tie was played – Kent and Sussex – on a hazardous Lord's pitch, and the notion was placed on ice for a conservative ninety years. Among several arguments against the idea was the sufficient popularity of cricket, which seemed to some to need no further encouragement, and the fear that the old-time bane of cricket – gambling – might return.

MCC was strangely reluctant to endorse the county regime. Some historians have interpreted this almost in Marxist terms as a struggle between the aristocratic, backward-looking MCC and the middle-class, progressive counties. A glance at the records suggests that MCC was not in fact overrun by the landed nobility and that many counties relied somewhat on lordly patronage. The reasons are more likely to have been stupor and indifference, coupled with a certain possessiveness.

Eventually, both sides were to need each other so desperately as to lead to amicable coalition. Playing standards at Lord's declined sharply, and the success of nearby Surrey, in terms both of playing feats and financial support, gave rise to furious thought. The secretaryship of H. A. Perkins, which began in 1876, introduced a more modern outlook, and his appointment was part of a drastic overhaul of membership and general approach. An important practical move was the agreement that Middlesex would play home matches at Lord's. Apart from bringing a much needed fillip to the Lord's fixtures, it was a transparent acceptance of the worth of county cricket.

When MCC endorsed the rules concerning players' qualifications, it insisted that these applied to all counties, for MCC was taking great care not to be dragged into the ceaseless bickering over which were first-class counties, preferring to leave that to the divination of the sporting press. In Orwellian reality, some counties were more equal than others and, apart from the eligibility of players, classification was the knottiest poser facing the nascent county competition. Opinions and press coverage differed as to which counties should be included in the reckoning. Although the well-established octet caused few problems (except when they played somebody outside their immediate ranks), there were two or three other counties which were very much on the fringe. During this period, for instance, Derbyshire were to the fore, and many commentators, then and now, count them among the great. Despite a poorish record, Hampshire were in and out like the farmer's wife on the weathercock, while, towards the end of this phase, Somerset were forcing themselves on the attention of the record-keepers. Conversely, once reputable Cambridgeshire slipped away altogether, while some other counties – Leicestershire is a pertinent example – appeared to be excluded in spite of decent results. Duration of matches, with the accent, of course, on the three-day events, was one guide, but it was by no means a foolproof one. Thus the counties ranged from the peerless triumphs of Nottinghamshire to the weak, if convivial, endeavours of some of the Scottish shires, which even MCC found it difficult to take too seriously.

Thus far, the counties had organized themselves mainly on a spontaneous, improvised basis, but, in an attempt to solve this and other problems, and in the absence of any worthwhile leadership from MCC, the county secretaries began formal annual meetings in 1882, and then in 1887 a County Cricket Council was established. A cricket 'parliament' had been mooted earlier in 1864 in some parts of the press, and, it was assumed, with the backing of some county administrators. Now it came to pass, although it did not attempt to replace MCC, as the 1864 proposal had implied. The County Cricket Council tried to operate in complement to that august body, its purpose being to standardize county cricket – then, as now, by far the smallest section overall of the game – rather than to alter the laws. The Council did useful work, but it could not contain or suppress the acrid rivalries and jealousies of its membership. The 1880s had been marred by bitter rows over those two old favourites of cricketing conflict: the poaching of players and throwing. A wrangle over the status of counties was the last straw.

The Council was officially formed at Lord's on 12 July 1887, Lord Harris, of the Kent club, taking the chair. It was agreed that the Council would consist of a representative from twenty counties, that is, the elite eight, plus Derbyshire, Essex, Warwickshire, Norfolk, Leicestershire, Staffordshire, Somerset, Northamptonshire, Hampshire, Durham, Hertfordshire and Cheshire. They resolved to alter or amend qualifications, always allowing the role of MCC as adjudicator.

In the December of 1889 the Council bravely moved to deal with classification, suggesting a logical and modern-sounding plan, which classified all active counties into three divisions, This involved promotion and relegation, and was put to a special meeting of the Council in the August of 1890. Twelve counties were represented, and the Surrey captain, John Shuter, presided.

The listing of counties makes for interesting reading. The leading eight were to form the first division, with the second division composed of Warwickshire, Derbyshire, Leicestershire, Somerset, Hampshire, Essex, Staffordshire and Cheshire. This left Hertfordshire, Northamptonshire, Norfolk, Lincolnshire, Northumberland, Durham, Glamorgan and Devonshire in the third grade. In essence, there was little quibbling over the classification. The bones of contention lay in the very complex procedure proposed to oversee promotion and relegation. The order of merit was to be determined by the current convention of subtracting wins from losses and discounting

draws, always provided that a requisite number of apposite games had been played. Then there was to be a 'qualifying series' of home and away fixtures for the relevant top and bottom teams in each division.

At their meeting of 25 October, the second-class counties had worried whether the new procedure might prove 'a sham'. At the annual meeting of the Cricket Council in December 1890, Warwickshire, on behalf of the second-class counties, thus put forward amendments less restrictive of the number and type of fixture to be undertaken and with just one qualifying match on a neutral ground. There had been much argument and press speculation about these matters, and now dissension reached its head. According to W. G. Grace, 'a very animated discussion arose, and, in unmistakable tones, the majority of the delegates declined to pledge themselves to any classification scheme that would compel them to play more matches than they wished to', or to 'the compulsion of a county to play another'. The cause of the second-class counties had been competently championed by Dr, later Sir Russell, Bencraft of Hampshire, but suddenly everything fell apart. A. J. Webbe, of Oxford University and Middlesex, moved that the Council be suspended *sine die*, and the voting was seven-all. Rather dubiously, by some standards of committee procedure, M. J. Ellison, the chairman, threw his casting vote in favour of the motion – one suspects he was frustrated by the constant bickering – and the Council came to 'an abrupt and unlooked-for termination'.

It was a sad occasion. The counties had failed to put their own house in order, and, although a form of classification was soon to be devised by MCC, no method of automatic entry to the County Championship has since been promulgated. One should note that both the cup idea and the league proposal had been suggested a year or so after its acceptance by the world of football – the Football League had embarked on its career in 1888. Neither had been agreed by the cricketing fraternity. The central issue was fixtures, for no county liked to be dictated to on that score. Although the second-class counties were prob-

20 'The cause of the second-class counties . . .'
Championed by Sir Russell Bencraft.

these affairs. W. S. Gilbert claimed to know only two pieces of music: one was the national anthem and one was not. MCC took a similarly simplistic line. It was forthrightly declared in 1894 that there were first-class counties and there were not: there was 'no need for a further sub-division'. Matches among this fraternity and with MCC, the two senior universities, the Australians, and other XIs so adjudged by MCC for the compilation of the averages, were deemed to be first-class matches. No limits were imposed nor any criteria published by which these assessments might themselves be studied. Like the Gild Merchant of medieval times, it was to be a self-regulatory mystery. MCC could beckon and it could thrust away.

It might be timely to summarize the general outcome of the debate over first-class status. Cambridgeshire, it will be recalled, had dropped out, never to be reinstated, after 1871; whereas Lancashire, from 1865, and Gloucestershire, from 1870, had been regarded as first-class along with the six old originals. Hampshire and Derbyshire had had chequered careers. The former, having not played any county matches at all in seasons 1868, 1869, 1871–74 and 1879, were not regarded as first-class after 1885, while the latter struggled from 1871 until 1887 before dropping out of the running. Somerset played against first-class counties from 1879, but were only deemed to be first-class in the seasons 1882 to 1885. Their startling success in the summer of 1890 led to their formal entry into the first-class ranks in the following year, 1891. They came fifth in the Championship at this their first attempt, and this was an important and pragmatic boost to the possibility of further admissions.

In 1894 Leicestershire, Essex and Warwickshire were granted first-class status, alongside a redeemed Derbyshire. This, incidentally, weakened the second-class competition inaugurated in 1889. All of these were playing regular three-day games against major counties, but, perhaps strangely, they were not immediately permitted to join in the revels of the Championship. However, at the end of that summer of possible probation, all four were admitted to the

ably right to have fought for a brighter place in the sun, some may have regretted not seizing the half-chance when it was offered. Of course, several of the leading second-grade counties were very soon permitted to enter the charmed circle, but that was not the same as having a device by which these matters might be properly assessed.

The classification squabble eventually ended when, in mild despair, the counties turned to MCC which, now revived and itself in better health, was ready to take over superintendance of county competition, and Hampshire regained some of its composure and its old first-class status.

Thus the Championship table sprang quite abruptly to fourteen, and, with the universities enjoying longer fixture-lists, the sheer amount of first-class cricket boomed significantly. None of the newcomers was overfaced by their daunting experience in the top flight, although it was to be many years before the top counties relinquished their grip on the title. Nonetheless, the maintenance of high levels, despite what some probably regarded as a dilution of the first-class game, is a tribute to the inordinately fine standards that cricket enjoyed in this era. Self-evidently, the counties in question were doing all the right things; playing three-day matches on pleasant grounds against first-class opposition in front of an appreciable and appreciative membership and not being pummelled too severely.

In 1895 the Minor Counties Association was formed, and, to that degree, what had been known as the second-class counties went their separate ways, although some contact obviously remained when major counties or their 2nd XIs played against them. But there was no automatic channel for movement betwixt and between, and it may also have been that some lesser counties were not too bothered about being drawn into the undue solemnity and acerbity of the senior competition. Norfolk has been quoted as an example of that cheerful spirit.

Apart from player and team qualifications, there still remained the problem of how – or even whether – to determine who were County Champions. The press had engagingly participated in its own annual coronation for many years, perhaps as early as 1825, and even in years when there were only a couple of counties involved. However, in 1864 the cricket journals decided that Surrey were the champions and that is the date which *Wisden* uses for the start of its list of champions. But the pattern is very irregular in other ways. The whole scene was bedevilled by the unevenness of fixture-making, about which, as we have noted, counties could be fiercely independent. It has to be remembered that the 'league' principle was not in wide use anywhere,

and, for example, the first national football competition based on consistent contest had to await the vigorous activities of William McGregor, the father of the Football League.

Initially, it was more a question of being the 'best' county rather than the 'top' county. It was a device that had found much favour from the tourney lists of medieval England to the conker clashes of its later school yards. The FA Cup is a 'challenge' trophy in name, and was so, originally, by intent. The idea had been that teams would play off by knock-out to find a contender to 'challenge' the holder: put another way, the previous winner had a bye to the final. The old Harrovian, C. W. Alcock, had based the scheme on a public school principle: one became 'cock' by displacing the existing cock from his midden. Alcock was secretary of the Surrey cricket club and of the Football Association – a telling example of the cross-channels of sport.

So the means of agreeing who in fact was supreme champion were controversial. Fewest defeats, most wins, or some amalgam of the two; these were favoured modes. They were typical of the Victorian ethic of forceful and manly effort, and a refusal to be pampered by the suspect namby-pambyness of over-delicate and intricate assessments. An unofficial points system was tried in 1888, and, more definitively, the Championship was officially constituted in 1890, in that the county representatives recognized its existence and agreed a method of deciding the result.

The variety of speculation is not to be underestimated. For instance, it is intriguing to compare the champions as now recorded in *Wisden* with those tabled with trenchant authority in 1891 by W. G. Grace.

Year	Wisden	Grace
1870	Yorkshire	Yorkshire
1871	Nottinghamshire	Sussex
1872	Nottinghamshire	Surrey
1873	Gloucestershire/	
	Nottinghamshire	Nottinghamshire
1874	Gloucestershire	Yorkshire
1875	Nottinghamshire	Nottinghamshire
1876	Gloucestershire	Gloucestershire

1877	Gloucestershire	Gloucestershire
1878	Undecided	Middlesex
1879	Nottinghamshire/	
	Lancashire	Yorkshire

There is a disagreement in six out of those ten seasons, with Grace, in all honesty, showing no prejudice in favour of his native heath. To take a specific illustration, Grace awards the crown in 1871 to Sussex (although, officially, they have never enjoyed that distinction) because they played and won their only four fixtures. Nottinghamshire also won four, but they played six, drawing one; but, and this was their shortcoming in the eye of Grace, losing the other one to Yorkshire. To add to the confusion, some historians hand the 1874 title to neither Gloucestershire nor Yorkshire, but to Derbyshire, whom Grace never included in any of his tables.

A semblance of order was decided upon in 1894. One point was to be awarded for a win and one point deducted for a loss, with draws, as

21 'A telling example of the cross-channels of sport . . .'
C. W. Alcock, secretary of both the Surrey Cricket Club and of the Football Association.

before, providing no more than the satisfaction of joint honour. At the end of the season, the proportion of points to finished matches was to determine the champion county. This was the same year that the classification argument was resolved, and that the competition was extended. On those three grounds, the purist might urge that the following season of 1895 - when fourteen properly classified counties contested the title

under the aegis of MCC – is the first of the modern and comprehensive dispensation. In the event, a resurgent Surrey won the Championship in both years. Although there have been myriad alterations in the formula, as well as the introduction of three other clubs, the County Championship has not, essentially, changed in construction from that time. An Advisory County Cricket Committee, with county representation, was set

22 'An attempt was made to run a London County XI, based at Crystal Palace . . .' Here the team is photographed at a match in 1902. W. G. Grace is easily recognizable in the centre; to his left is Billy Murdoch of New South Wales, Australia and Sussex.
Back row: W. Hearne, A. F. Newman, W. Smith, N. F. Norman, Carlin; *centre*: R. Powell-Williams, R. B. Brookes, W. G. Grace, W. L. Murdoch, W. G. Dyas; *front*: P. R. May, L. D. S. Poidevin, R. M. Bell.

23 'The golden age of cricket dawned . . .' And the crowds responded accordingly – Blackpool, 1909.

up in 1904, and this lasted until 1969, when the Test and County Cricket Board replaced it.

Predictably, the number of first-class county matches rose extravagantly over this phase of development, not only because of the augmentation of the league itself, but also because most counties played more matches anyway. There was, however, no acknowledgement yet of a consistent schedule of home and away games on the Football League principle. In 1873, for instance, there were only thirty-one top-class county games, but in 1892 that had more than doubled to seventy-two. In 1895 this almost doubled again to 131, close on an average of nineteen fixtures per county. It had been a remarkable expansion.

Bang on cue, the counties had had something of an administrative lift from the reform of local government in 1888. The counties had continued to be ruled, as for centuries, by non-elected oligarchies of landowners, chiefly through the quarter-sessions. As the franchise widened, especially with the extension of the vote to the rural householder in 1884, it became apparent, for this and for other reasons, that reform was needed. By the Local Government Act of 1888, sixty-two county councils were created. A severance, criticized by many, was obtained between the shires and the bigger towns, roughly those of more than 50,000 population, which became county boroughs. All this enhanced the image of the county as a natural ambit for activity, and, with an enlarged franchise (including unmarried women) it turned out to be quite a revision.

London was established as a county council, and, from 1899 to 1905, under W. G. Grace's management, an attempt was made to run a London County XI based at Crystal Palace. It was a patchy if cheerful venture, and, although some of its fixtures were declared first-class, it never aspired to join the county competition. There was probably enough first-class cricket available in the metropolis for most tastes, while the Crystal Palace authorities discovered that there was 'no partisan nucleus' around which to develop a decent membership and following.

Although the county pattern was and still is taken for granted, it was neither an inevitable nor a necessary format. Had the English bothered to look about them, they would have observed abroad quite different networks of local administration. However, the precedent of the municipal solution of some fifty years earlier was revisited on the counties and the county boroughs. They were bequeathed town rule writ large: their powers were limited and confined by parliamentary statute and official tutelage organized direct from London. This bi-partite system, sometimes uneasy in its application, and rarely to be copied outside these shores, nonetheless had the excellent advantage of having grown organically.

This curious administrative compromise was, obviously, much to the benefit of the cricketing counties, themselves the heirs of a traditional view of political geography. The reform was opportune in that it came as the county clubs were at some point of crisis and when their own attempts at modernization were in the balance. Once again, through an adroit mixture of reasonable luck and efficacious management, the cricket counties had fallen on their feet. The golden age of cricket dawned; the counties were to be irrefutably connected with that gracious era; never again would there be a serious challenge to their hegemony.

FOUR

The Gilded Lily

Cricket had reached its apotheosis. The shape of the game, after years of frantic experimentation and rapid alteration, had been resolved, certainly for the next hundred years and conceivably for ever. Blinkered commentators may talk expansively about the 'years of change' at particular points in cricket history, but they use a false perspective, or, rather, no perspective at all. There have, of course, been myriad tinkerings with cricket since the turn of the century, but, fundamentally, nothing has been altered.

For example, bowling had by this juncture successfully evolved through under-arm and round-arm and thus to the over-arm we know today. Indeed, when a season or so ago an Australian bowled an under-arm delivery for the last decisive ball of a one-day match, to avoid a boundary being scored, his captain and he were scorned for poor sportsmanship. Some semblance of a regulation about boundaries had also been agreed. In other words, the fundamentals of the game, as we now recognize them, were in place certainly by 1890 and, in most instances, ten or twenty years earlier.

The art of batting was sophisticated at this time and the styles and sciences of bowling were determined then. Fielding, not least under the pressure of one-day cricket, is now assuredly more efficient in a comprehensive sense. But, if fitness and nimbleness were less regularly to be seen in the 1890s, the techniques were mainly established, and there were specialist exponents – Jessop in the covers, MacLaren in the slips – who have not been bettered.

Perhaps the acid test, under imagination's lens, is to place the great of yesteryear in the present setting. Apart from fielding and field-placing, the advantages would stack up mostly on the ancients' side. For the batsmen, safer wickets, protective equipment, improved bats and uniformly shorter boundaries; for the bowlers, less

hours of hard toil and securer catching. All in all, it cannot be doubted that, after a decent net and a clear briefing on interim rule changes with regard to lbw or the no-ball, Grace and Arthur Shrewsbury and Ranji and Tom Richardson would, if wonderfully reincarnated, more than hold their own in present company.

It was to be of the utmost importance for county cricket that, when cricket itself was in its heyday, it was, in effect, the County Championship that provided the premier English medium. And that county cricket reached its maturity in the twenty summers prior to the First World War was to be of permanent significance.

This is perhaps an opportunity to pause and gaze on the typical county, now that fourteen of the grace-and-favour seventeen were assembled, and two more were to be recruited before the beginning of the war. The anatomy of the county clubs is strangely similar. The evolution of the first-class county, right down to some of the tiniest details, exhibits a sameness, intriguing in its very uniformity, and these parallel yarns will be traced in the sections on the individual counties in the second section of this book.

A group of gentlemen, usually under the auspices of a particular club – Montpelier CC *vis-à-vis* Surrey – and often prompted by the enthusiasm of an esteemed family or individual – the Graces of Gloucester or C. E. Green, the so-called 'originator' of Essex – foregathered, usually in some hostelry. Their purpose was to seek agreement to lift the sights of club life by establishing a combined squad under the colours of the county. It was occasionally their intention both to draw playing members and to arrange fixtures over a fairly wide area to that end, but frequently these laudable aims, especially the latter one, were thwarted. This was partly the case where one club was dominant, such as Sheffield in the Yorkshire region, or where, as also often occur-

Kent County  Cricket Club.

At the General Meeting of the Subscribers to the Kent County Cricket Club and the Beverley Kent Cricket Club, held, according to notice, at the Bull Inn, Rochester, on Tuesday, the 6th of December, 1870,

The Right Hon. LORD HARRIS in the Chair,

It was resolved—

1.—That the Kent County Cricket Club and the Beverley Kent Cricket Club be amalgamated in one Club, to be called the Kent County Cricket Club; and that Canterbury be the head quarters of the Club. Matches to be played on grounds to be named by the Committee.

2.—That the entire management ot the Canterbury Cricket Week be retained by Mr. W. de Chair Baker—the amalgamation being effected upon the basis that no change whatever take place in this Annual Meeting at Canterbury.

3.—That Mr. W. de C. Baker act as the Hon. Sec. of the Club.

4.—That a President be chosen alternately from East and West Kent; and a Committee, consisting of Ten gentlemen selected from East Kent, and Ten from West Kent, be formed to conduct the business of the Club.

A Provisional Committee to draw up rules and select the Committees from the two divisions of the County, was then formed, consisting of Mr. W. de Chair Baker, Mr. W. S. Norton, Captain Denne, Mr. E. G. Hartnell, Captain Lambert, and Mr. M. A. Troughton.

At the unanimous request of the Committee, and of those present at the Meeting, Lord Harris consented to become President of the newly-organized County Club for the year 1871.

The Provisional Committee then held a Meeting, at which a list of names was determined upon of noblemen and gentlemen in East and West Kent, who should be solicited to act upon the Committee, and others to allow their names to be added to the list of Vice-Presidents. The Secretary was also empowered to make the preliminary inquiries as to County Matches with Sussex and Surrey, and with the M.C.C., and suggestions were made as to the probability of playing the matches in the first two years, as "Kent Club and Ground," thus using the practice-bowlers, if available, without necessitating a lengthened previous residence.

It was also determined that the first Meeting of the aggregate Committee should be held at the Mitre Hotel, Maidstone, on Friday, January 6th, previous to which it is requested that any subscriber to either of the Clubs now amalgamated who may desire to alter the amount of his previous annual subscription will kindly communicate his intentions to the Hon. Sec.,

W. de CHAIR BAKER,
Beverley St. Stephen's, Canterbury.

---

24 'A group of gentlemen often prompted by the enthusiasm of an individual . . .' The notice recording the inauguration of Kent County Cricket Club, with Lord Harris in the chair.

red, there was a move to purchase or lease a ground – as when, for instance, Hampshire obtained a lease of twenty-eight years on Bannister's Park, Southampton. Once either one or both of these processes were activated, the county found itself, willy-nilly, a centripetal rather than a centrifugal organism. What, as we have seen, was a constant was the membership syndrome, and this was to remain largely unchanged. Like the local golf club or operatic society, these were members' clubs. This constitutional base was a common denominator, and a most important one for the control of the game.

A number of steps normally followed. Almost all the counties ran into some financial storm of varying strength, usually over the costs of the ground. As frequently, they were bailed out by handsome subsidies from generous patrons, sometimes businessmen, but often landed or titled gentry. For instance, C. M. Tebbutt paid the Essex debt of £3000 on their Lyttelton ground at Leyton in the 1890s. This largesse, this financial kiss of life for the ailing middle-class corpus of the county club, is an interesting illustration of the interplay of business and land, of urban and rural sectors, in late Victorian life. Some of the growing pains were the result of demands of what Ranji, in a precise usage of the word, called 'spectacular' cricket, as indicating an affair of spectacle for spectators, as opposed to the more excitable connotation it suffers today. It was the subtle balance of investment for public watching and the income which might accrue that was at the root of this difficulty. Clubs found themselves having to create public arenas without too much knowledge of how they might fare in terms of revenue.

Professional income varied, according to talent and to the club's financial position, but, by the end of the century, there was a fair amount of equality. Earlier, most county professionals were paid by the match, usually a fee of £3 to £5, with £1 travel expenses and £1 bonus for a win. This normally meant that a competent and regular servant to the county would earn between £80 and £150 a summer, at a time when the average working man's wages totalled about £85 over a year. By 1890 this overall position was substanti-

ally improved. Most professionals were on straight wages rather than match pay. This offered more security, and reduced the risks of cricketers playing with disguised injuries to assure their income. Senior paid players were earning as much as £250 a year by the onset of the Edwardian era, compared to the average of roughly £100 that constituted the manual worker's yearly wage. After the gradual rise in wages during the middle of the century, working-class incomes were beginning to level out somewhat, so that the county professional could now regard himself as one of the élite of his class, and was usually better paid than the average footballer.

The consolidation of the county team, replete with many professionals, as a basis of entertainment for others rather than a diversion for the participants, underpinned the statist position of the clubs. The place of transportation and of urbanism in the development of county cricket has already been stressed, and now these various aspects were joined together irrevocably. By 1890 the pattern was clearcut enough. A major city or town (in some counties it may have been, for particular reasons, two or three such epicentres) was at the core of the county. It tended to be the biggest town and, by that token, it was not always the county town: it was the one whose catchment area would supply most generously the subscriber members and the paying public. The effect of this was to distort, from one angle even to destroy, the sense of 'county'. In the individual county sagas one can observe some evidence of internal rivalry; perhaps not outright conflict, more a mild jockeying for position. Warwick and Birmingham; Liverpool and Manchester; Cheltenham and Bristol are examples of this. It is not an epic point, and there were no real power struggles. It is more a reminder that decisions or actions had to be taken, and this or that county might just have ended up with a different headquarters. The outcome was the predominance of a town rather than the coherence of a county region. Lancashire versus Warwickshire was, and is, in practice, Manchester versus Birmingham: one finds oneself all but muttering Manchester United versus Birmingham City.

The first-class cricket ground became an arena. From mid-18th century, and, in particular, as fuelled by the success of the exhibition XIs, cricket was the first sport to enjoy the huge bounty of large paying crowds. They sometimes took the organizers of county cricket by surprise. When, in 1878, Gloucestershire, with the resplendent Grace brothers out in force, visited Old Trafford, there were unruly and confused scenes. That match, while immortalized in Francis Thompson's verse, 'At Lord's', must also be noted for the vastness of the concourse that attended. The primitive entrances and the makeshift stands could not cope with the spectators. A crowd of 16,000 arrived on the first day and 28,000 attended overall – probably near to a provincial record for paying customers at a sporting event at that time.

Grounds became fully enclosed, turnstiles, stands and terraces were erected, and cricket telegraphs or scoreboards were introduced. Fred Lillywhite's printing press, first utilized in 1848 for the production of the 'card of the match', deserves an appreciative mention in these despatches. However, the crucial intervention of the spectator on the process of the game itself was in the matter of boundaries. Most cricket had been 'all run'. This is well worth remembering and commenting upon when immature assessors wax sniffily about the naïveté of the olden days. W. G. Grace ran the clear majority of his 99,840 runs, as recorded in all cricket. One had to be fit to bat at length, and also to field through a long innings. When cricketers spoke – as they did until after the Second World War – of 'fielding in the country', they were not joking.

It was in the 1860s, with the County Championship haltingly under way, that boundaries were properly introduced, at first by the erection of the pavilion and of other man-made edifices. As ever, there were the last ditchers to grieve the passing of deep fielding and long throwing. If, from their far pavilions, they now observe the 70-yard boundary, they would doubtless ask for the phrase 'fielding in the deep' to be expunged from cricket's lexicon on grounds of imprecision. W. G. Grace asserts that a major breakthrough

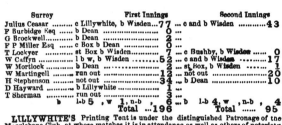

25 'Fred Lillywhite's printing press . . .
The card of the match:
Sussex versus Surrey, 1854.

occurred when, at Lord's, A. N. Hornby, the tempestuous little Lancashire captain, charged headlong into the crowd in pursuit of the ball. In the stampede, an older spectator sustained severe injuries, and, thereafter, boundaries became the accepted rule – yet another instance of martyrdom leading to legislative alteration. It was in 1884 that boundaries were first clarified in the laws of cricket, and it was 1910 before the difference between clearing the ground and the boundary for six was recommended.

County cricket, blessed by the impetus of its earlier start and by that intermix of factors that made it, supremely and peculiarly, a Victorian game, was, at this time, far and away the most popular of the spectator team sports. Around 1890 there was a first-class cricket programme, the great number of them county matches, of a hundred fixtures. About that time, too, the Football League organized roughly a hundred matches. But the support was vastly different. Whereas the football was watched by only a million in total, there was a huge turn-out of two millions for the cricket, a figure that makes today's figures look feeble and puny. There were only 2000 at the first FA Cup final at the Oval in 1872, and it was 1885 before the Cup-final crowd reached 10,000: 4000 was regarded as par for the average crowd at a League game. This state of affairs was, of course, soon to be drastically reversed, but, in those two dozen years before the First World War, cricket ruled the roost.

Not the least curious aspect of this splendid popularity was the role of the amateur. Whereas, in other countries, and, indeed, in other pastimes in Britain, it was the norm for the upper crust to relax and be entertained by paid and usually plebeian performers, in cricket this was reversed. It certainly seemed most bizarre to the untutored overseas visitor to find honest working men paying their hard earned tanners and bobs to watch an opulent Indian prince bat. Of course, many of the audience were in fact middle-class, and, it has to be affirmed, many of the purported amateurs were assisted financially. W. G. Grace and Archie MacLaren are merely the most famous of a long line of cricketers who came from a social class which made it difficult either to join the ranks of the openly paid or artisan cricketers or to self-finance a sporting career. In effect, the epithet 'gentleman', as denoting a particular social set, was much more accurate than the label 'amateur', as suggesting a voluntary activity. So, like the lords of misrule of olden times, the workers basked on the terracing while their betters drove and cut.

During this period almost all the counties were blessed with a handful of such 'gentlemen'. The Graces were followed at Gloucestershire by Gilbert Jessop, the legendary hitter, and C. L. Townsend; Yorkshire were led by Lord Hawke and boasted of the patrician arts of F. S. Jackson; Ranji and C. B. Fry graced the Sussex batting; B. J. C. Bosanquet, inventor of the

26 'Ranji and C. B. Fry graced the Sussex batting . . .'

googly, and Pelham Warner were Middlesex alumni; MacLaren and Reggie Spooner lorded it over the Lancashire ranks; R. E. Foster and his brothers held newly elevated Worcestershire together; Lionel Palairet did much the same for Somerset; Lord Harris, with amateurs such as J. R. Mason and K. L. Hutchings, was the fount of authority at Kent: from public school and university came this unending torrent of stylish talent.

Of course, they were well matched by some extraordinarily gifted professional stars, among them such names to conjure with as Tom Hayward, the first after Grace to reach a hundred centuries; the felicitous Frank Woolley; the Yorkshire masters, Wilfred Rhodes and George Hirst; Sydney Barnes, thought by many to be the best bowler of all time; and, modestly inheriting the mantle of champion batsman, the young Jack

Hobbs. Ric Sissons, in his profound and well-documented account of the paid cricketer, *The Players*, has drawn proper attention to the parlous treatment of professional cricketers until a quarter of a century ago. Their shabby conditions, when compared with the manner in which the amateurs were treated, were often scandalous, and several ended in the poor house. Drink was a frequent problem, and, all in all, they were handled, serf-like, with hauteur and awful con-descension. In this, they were no worse off than the rest of their class.

In effect, the established and capped professionals of the county circuit by now had constructed a cadre of senior support for their amateur leaders. They were the equivalent to the waged foreman or charge-hand in the factory, as aides to the salaried manager or self-employed owner. It was a very typical late Victorian and Edwardian dichotomy, for, as the industrial crucible simmered and hardened, these social patterns became likewise rigid. There are two colourful illustrations of this theme of master and servant sharing common duties according to a given formula. Literature, drama, film and television have made them familiar to us all. One was the master and butler duality, and the other was the relationship of officer and sergeant or sergeant-major. Every county team was composed, at core, of a colonel, two or three fresh-faced subalterns and a handful of battle-hardened NCOs – or, alternatively, and to borrow from television's once popular *Upstairs, Downstairs*, each county had a Hudson playing senior professional to the county captain of Mr Bellamy.

This is no idle conceit. It was not just a question of these professionals being drawn into a closed society and subjected to the kind of strict contractual agreements for which both army and servants' hall were gloomily noted, nor was it only a case of these men being treated just a shade better than their colleagues in mill and mine. The parallel goes further than this. Like the butler or the regimental sergeant-major, the senior professional often gave loyal and diligent and worldly-wise counsel to the amateur captain of impeccable pedigree. Moreover, the knowledgeable and taciturn professional was often as quick as the gentleman's gentleman or the colour-sergeant to defend the formal protocol of his tiny and confined world. They were certainly more alert than the amateur in the protection of the mechanics and manners of the game, shunning the unorthodox and shuddering at the eccentric – after all, it was an amateur who invented that weird oddity, the googly. Although the character was based on W. S. Gilbert's butler, an ex-actor called Warmi-

27 'MacLaren lorded it over the Lancashire ranks . . .'

low, P. G. Wodehouse named his dignified valet after the professional fast bowler, Percy Jeeves of Warwickshire, who was killed in the First World War.

The dualism was copied round the arena, with the class from which the amateurs were drawn sitting in the pavilion or the stands, and the *confrères* of the professionals assembled on the terraces or, more likely, on the grass. Here were the mis-named 'free' seats, which were unreserved but not always seats as such, and which, in terms of entrance money, were about as free as the public schools were public. The public house had its saloon and public bars; the theatre had its gallery and stalls or circle; the church had its free and its hired pews; the seaside resort had its 'select' and its 'common' ends, and so on.

It was all a part of that structured and carefully observed provision of recreation that characterized the period. From about the 1870s, and enduring until roughly the 1950s, Britain enjoyed its golden age of collective leisure. The place of large and regular paying assemblies has been a relatively short-lived phenomenon in this sporting life, and it is an extremely important element in the story of county cricket that, throughout its own critical period, it ran in harness with this tendency. The idea of 'going out', of being, like Max Miller's notoriously bow-legged dairy-maid (she could not, his fans will recall, keep her calves together) 'out on pleasure bent' was all the rage.

More than at any time before or since, and with the 1851 Great Exhibition at Joseph Paxton's Crystal Palace performing an opening ceremony, new manifestations of leisure were enjoyed *en masse*. It was the leisure equivalent of 'congregation'. Public transport itself – 300 million passenger journeys were annually undertaken in Greater London by the 1880s – was the key, as people crowded into the multiples such as Liptons or Boots or department stores such as the Universal Provider or Harrods for their shopping; as they ate out at Joseph Lyons or the Aerated Bread Company (ABC); as they swarmed into the theatres, the music-halls, the vast public parks, Madame Tussauds, the London Zoo (especially after reptile and monkey houses had been added),

28 'The young Jack Hobbs . . .' Pictured here (nearer the camera) with Tom Hayward, opening the innings for Surrey.

the museums and galleries, and, of course, the seaside resorts. Blackpool, like Manchester United and Lancashire County Cricket Club, is a Victorian invention.

Now all of these various leisure facilities had much in common, in that they obliged their devotees to depart from their homes and attend in a crowd. The parts of the populace thus attracted were normally peaceful in mood and of sober outlook, the social divisions loosely sustained, as has been remarked, by discreet price structuring. Self-improvement or 'rational recreation' was a key trait. The whole style and presentation of county cricket was ready and waiting for this audience which responded dutifully in heartening profusion.

First Worcestershire, in 1899, and then

Northamptonshire, in 1905, lengthened the list of first-class counties still further, as county cricket engaged in its most rapturous era. Nationally, it was regarded with affection and indeed reverence by those in high as well as in low places, enjoying a sporting pre-eminence which it was never again to achieve. Cricket's eventual decline was due partly to the post-war rise in the popularity of other sports, and partly to the fact that county cricket did truly strike its richest seam at this time.

It is rare that the social milieu for a game and its style of execution agree perfectly – as did the late Victorian and Edwardian world with the play of Ranji and his colleagues.

Of the counties it was metropolitan Surrey which actually set the pace in terms of outright performance, and it is a little ironic that, in a period when the debonair amateur drew the crowds, the Surrey club relied extensively on the pragmatic virtue of solid professional expertise.

29 & 30 'The pragmatic virtue of solid professional expertise . . .'
Surrey's G. A. Lohmann (left) and W. H. Lockwood

Luckily, the best of these stalwarts were full of grace as well as of virtue, and the likes of Tom Hayward, Bobby Abel, Tom Richardson, W. H. Lockwood, G. A. Lohmann, to say nothing of Jack Hobbs, offered hours of pleasure to those who thronged the Oval. From 1887 Surrey won the title nine times, once shared, before the end of the old century, and they won it in 1914 as war closed around cricket at the height of that sad season.

Yorkshire, having been champions three times in the 1890s, then proceeded, by courtesy of Wilfred Rhodes and George Hirst, to win the title six more times in the opening years of the new century, a characteristic show of power, foreshadowing their near monopoly of the County Championship between the wars. After lengthy years of seeming trial and error, Kent proved to be about the most consistent side of the pre-war seasons, taking no less than four titles, their first ever, between 1906 and 1913. Colin Blythe and Frank Woolley were their principal inspirations.

Middlesex, Lancashire and Nottinghamshire won the occasional title, but the piquant surprise was provided by Warwickshire who grasped the pennant in 1911, the first of the non-originals to do so. Truth to tell, Warwickshire had been by no means disgraced since their arrival on the first-class list, but their triumph carried a certain air of the unexpected. No one contributed more keenly than their young captain, the precocious all-rounder, Frank Foster, and the pocket-sized maestro, W. G. Quaife, that compiler of many tall scores.

These delights were abruptly ended by the First World War. However romantically, many fought that war to preserve the Edwardian way of life, and the literature, sermons and political rhetoric of the war were redolent of a pastoral calm worth fighting for, with the Grantchester church clock, in Rupert Brooke's eye, perpetually at ten to three. Cricket was a part of this attempted act of conservation, and it was to be preserved in almost total sanctity.

Two points were uppermost as cricket went to war. On the one hand, no one alive had a memory of a continental military menace. The martial arts

had been practised of late in faraway imperial settings, and the proximity of war concentrated the British mind sharply. On the other hand, cricket had become more than a metaphor for life; it had, dangerously, come to be regarded as the authentic business of life. It was now that cricket's closeness to Anglican religiosity and jingoistic patriotism was at its most heated. Cricketers reversed the scriptural injunction and beat the ploughshares of their bats into weapons, the amateurs as officers, and often the professionals as sergeants.

Most effectively of all, W. G. Grace, in his only excursion into political affairs, called for a halt to cricket, 'for it is not fitting', he wrote, 'at a time like this that able-bodied men should be playing cricket day by day and pleasure-seekers look on'. It was cricket's equivalent of 'Kitchener wants you'; the season was brought to a precipitate close; and cricketers flocked to the colours. Yorkshire were much applauded when they made their players' enlistment 'a strict condition of their continued engagement'.

Thus county cricket stuttered to a halt, and attention was turned to those 'who played their game in the field of France'. Until the latter months of the war, there was no substantial cricket, and none at first-class level. MCC continued its schools' fixture-list – wryly enough, for the public schools were the joint nurseries of both amateur cricket and the officer class. The wartime *Wisdens* mournfully record the deaths of 3000 young cricketers, almost all amateurs, some of them already established as county hopefuls or university Blues, but many more the heroes of their school XIs.

The cancellation of county cricket demonstrated that, for its devotees, one could not combine business with business. Cricket was the rehearsal for the battle of life: the 'show' (that apt soldier's euphemism) was now all too realistically staged, with nearly a million of the British Empire troops killed. County cricket was abandoned, not because it was too trivial, but because it was too important. The consequence of this was that county cricket was preserved in aspic, and has not, in any fundamental way, looked forward since.

31 'A characteristic show of power . . .' Yorkshire pose proudly before the highest total ever scored in the County Championship – 887 against Warwickshire in 1896. *Standing*: R. Barlow (umpire), Hirst, Wainwright, Denton, Hunter; *seated*: Tunnicliffe, F. S. Jackson, Lord Hawke, Moorhouse; *on ground*: Brown, Peel, F. W. Milligan.

FIVE

The Pastoral Myth

Cricket thus became atrophied at the end of the Edwardian era, and its English setting – the county pattern – was once more guaranteed, for it was an essential part of the sacred rite. Cricket characterizes all that was good and most of what was bad about that confident, bounding era. County cricket, in particular, has since been played and watched, so to speak, from memory. Especially between the two world wars and into the 1950s, generation after generation of talented cricketers helped catch and catch again the mood and process of this Victorian cult.

County cricket, as the war years passed and Australia, not Germany, once more provided the opposition, was the centre-piece of this cultural exercise in romantic conservation. This preservation of mood, this petrifying of a beautiful sport, meant that manners as well as skills were maintained. This explains the seeming obscurantism of the game's administrators and supporters. A game which had journeyed through countless upheavals and alterations was, quite suddenly, judged to be well-nigh perfect. Tinkerings with tiny points of the law or marginal changes in the method of awarding County Championship points became the only genre of reform permitted – and, even then, there were often ructions. No more was heard, for instance, of the radical plans canvassed prior to the First World War to adopt a divisional format, with promotion and relegation.

A pleasing instance of petrified behaviour occurs in the laws. In the Victorian tradition, there are no sanctions or penalties. There are mechanistic provisions, such as the no-ball or the wide, as there are in other sports, but there are no regulations against the equivalent of foul play. For example, there are no extra four runs or a free hit if a fielder impedes a batsman. More recently, sustained and dangerous short-pitched bowling has suggested that the problem may arise, but, at base, it is impossible to continue a cricket match without the participants accepting the general format as prescribed both by cricket's laws and its conventions.

Many now forget that the rules of most sports were framed in Victorian times without resort to enforcement by penalty. When, for example, the laws of the football codes were drawn up, it was presumed by the legislators that infringements would happen only as the result of accident. Sanctions were unnecessary. A player tripping or handling would retreat and forego possession to his opponent. Disputes, if they arose, were resolved by the captains; and it was the FA Cup which saw the arrival, cricket style, of an umpire for each half, and a referee, without a whistle until 1878, as their arbiter. It was 1895 before the referee was granted full powers, with the umpires demoted to linesmen, and, alongside cautions and dismissals, the penalty-kick was introduced no earlier than 1891.

To this heartening degree, cricket has retained a little of its innocence. This is no dewy-eyed account. Cricketers, then as now, have had a penchant for aggressive disagreement with umpires and for a variety of brands of 'sledging' and other forms of psychological warfare. The point is that the ideal which, in varying fashion, they espouse is redolent of Victorianism.

The County Championship is an illustration. In 1921, Glamorgan were able to attract a sufficiency of fixtures with existing first-class counties, and they were invited to join the Championship. Since then there has been little hint of change in the county structure, neither in terms of a new entrant nor of an old departure. With that one exception of the South Wales county, there has been no alteration in the format of the County Championship from before the First World War until the inclusion of Durham in 1992.

This continuity, of course, owed much to the sustained and deep-rooted enthusiasm of the

32 'The doyen of the cricketing
corps diplomatique . . .' Sir Pelham Warner
of Middlesex and England.

amateur. The standard of public school and university cricket remained high during the period between the wars, and, indeed, for some time afterwards. The county captaincies were largely held by amateurs, many of them Oxbridge Blues, and, beyond that, each echelon of amateur talent succeeded to cricket's senior administrative posts, so that the tradition was protected and maintained. The career of Sir Pelham Warner, for example, illustrates this, as he progressed through Rugby School, Oxford University, the Gentlemen, Middlesex and England to become the doyen of the cricketing *corps diplomatique.*

The determination of gilded youth to pursue its schoolboy sports into adult life was blamed, by some on the other side of the Channel, on the insularity of the island race, and, more especially, the introverted seclusion of its boarding education. This fixation with boyhood was peculiar, and, from Gordon of Khartoum to Lawrence of Arabia, there were famous men of that epoch deemed by their contemporaries or biographers to be psychologically or sexually immature. F. Anstey's novel *Vice Versa*, with its magical exchange of the Bultitudes, father and son, amusingly satirized this tendency in 1882, while the two creeds of not growing up – J. M. Barrie's *Peter Pan* and Baden-Powell's *Scouting for Boys* – were published in 1904 and 1908 respectively. Most strikingly, his contemporaries often referred to the junior school mentality of W. G. Grace. Three such assessments were: 'a big grown-up boy'; 'just a great big schoolboy in everything he did'; 'a great big baby'. Whether the Peter Pan syndrome permeated the body politic of cricket (after all, Barrie was both fanatical about cricket and obsessed by childhood) is arguable. What is certain is that men returned from the savagery of the First World War to inhabit the Never-Never Land of Hove, Canterbury and Lord's.

Thus cricket began its nostalgic playback of summers gone. It is true that, with first Hobbs and then later the imperious Hammond, the amateur was not allowed to dominate to the same extent, and the conditions of professionals of their ilk improved. With men such as Herbert Sutcliffe setting high standards, cricket, as a paid occupation, moved from a trade towards a profession. In playing terms, the race went to the professionally strong, and strength was synonymous with Yorkshire. Between the wars, they won the Championship twelve out of twenty-one times, and their poorest showing was fifth. No one, not even Nottinghamshire in the 1880s or Surrey in the 1950s, has been so dominant for so long.

Yorkshire revealed in abundance the pattern of the county design in this period: a full company of canny professionals led by a no-nonsense amateur, in the persons especially of F. E. Greenwood and A. B. Sellers. Leonard Green of Lancashire, B. H. Lyon of Gloucestershire, A. W. Carr of Nottinghamshire and F. T. Mann of Middlesex are other examples. There is no doubt that, in a numerical sense, the balance had passed to the professional, but the amateur captain remained more or less inviolate. Sometimes bringing, as

Percy Fender did to Surrey's cricket, an optimistic and unorthodox bloom, this notion of the 'officer' captain was left intact. It is doubtful whether the professionals were as bothered by this as latter-

34 'The imperious Hammond . . .'

33 'A full company of canny professionals . . .' The Yorkshire masters, Schofield Haigh, George Hirst and Wilfred Rhodes.

35 'Lancashire, playing probably the most consistent cricket in their history . . .' The 1926
champions, with their 'no-nonsense amateur' captain, Leonard Green, seated third from left.
Standing: Eddie Paynter, George Duckworth, Frank Sibbles, Jack Iddon, F. Webster, M. L. Taylor;
seated: Charlie Hallows; P. T. Eckersley, Leonard Green, Ernest Tyldesley, Frank Watson and Richard Tyldesley.

day liberals might surmise. There were some advantages in a leader who, if often lacking in skills of the highest order, was removed in class and manner of livelihood from them. At least, there was smaller chance of envy and acrimony. Just before and just after the Second World War, one or two crossed the floor of the house, Walter Hammond and Bill Edrich being the most notable examples.

The north dominated the County Championship in these years. Lancashire, playing probably the most consistent cricket in their history, won five titles, Derbyshire and Nottinghamshire one each, with the other two successes registered by

Middlesex. This was the Middlesex, first of Hendren and Hearne, and then of Compton and Edrich. They were also second in 1924, having won the Championship in two consecutive years, 1920 and 1921, and, after a more dismal spell in the early 1930s, they were third or second every season from 1935 to 1939.

The achievement of Middlesex reminds us that there was nothing distinctive about this hegemony of the north. What is surer is that, where resources were concentrated in the greater conurbations, reasonably-paid squads of players were recruited. The broader truth is that the County Championship was conducted, for better or for worse, as a two-tone pattern. It was as if a higher and a lower division existed covertly within the same table: a robust group, principally composed of the older counties, and a weaker set, chiefly the newer brethren. Hobbs, until his retirement, Sandham, Ducat, Jardine and Fishlock guaranteed that Surrey always assembled a talented batting combine. Between the wars they were in the top four places on eight occasions, and their lowest position was eleventh, a consistent attainment that, once more, indicated the strength of the well-supported club. Kent, although continuing to field many more amateurs than the leading sides, still had the majesty of Woolley and the wizardry of Freeman to keep them in contention. In these twenty-one seasons, they were nine times in the first four and only once out of the first ten. Nottinghamshire, with Larwood, Voce and Hardstaff, were another highly effective outfit, never dropping out of the first ten until the 'bodyline' row disturbed their equilibrium, and finding themselves in the first four on no less than ten occasions. Between 1927, when they appeared to gather pace, and 1939, Derbyshire were always in the top ten.

Conversely, some counties scarcely survived and suffered appalling records. Northamptonshire were in the bottom three fifteen times, including eight wooden spoons; Worcestershire, who were unable to compete in 1919, did little better, ending fifteen times in the last four; newly-elevated Glamorgan struggled piteously and were in the last three in twelve of their first nineteen seasons; Somerset were only six times in the leading nine as opposed to eight times in the bottom four.

This unremitting nature of the contest, while overshadowed by Yorkshire's predominance, was the enduring tendency. If (as, of course, they sometimes did) Somerset or Northamptonshire defeated Yorkshire or Middlesex, it evinced the surprise noted in Caesar's *The Conquest of Gaul* if the natives routed the invincible Romans. When it occurred, some of the excuses and explanations proffered were similar – ill-starred or inclement conditions, for example, or depletions because of other requirements (for recall to Rome to stem

36 Patsy Hendren of Middlesex in his prime.

insurgency, read Test calls). A glance at England's Test XIs over this period does, in fact, underpin the story, for the unfashionable counties provided very few internationals. In illustration there were five Yorkshiremen in the Oval Test of 1938 when Hutton scored his record 364.

At the same time, the lesser counties aped their

37 Frank Woolley at the beginning
of his long and illustrious career.

shire, as Geary and Astill had done so frequently to salvage their cricketing fortunes. The going was hard: when Northamptonshire won a game in May 1939, it was their first win since May 1935, while Glamorgan won only five times in their first three seasons. The fact that these junior teams fielded more amateurs than their more formidable colleagues was, for the most part, a matter of finance. What is clear is that no other solution was sought nor fresh strategy considered, such as, perhaps, the semi-professional approach or even the merging of counties. It all followed the pre-ordained fashion.

Much of this was determined by the three-day norm for the duration of play. There had been some campaigning for reform as the First World War ended. These included what have been termed the 'patent follies' of shorter boundaries and penalties for maiden overs or slow scoring. Basically, the traditionalists were hardly challenged, and the sole capitulation to the revisionists was a decision to restrict the county fixtures of 1919 to two days. The proposal was Lancashire's, and it was as much an attempt to regroup, economically as well as sportingly, after the long break as any fundamental quarrel with the old convention. It was soon regarded as a failure, producing an intolerable number of inconclusive draws. *Wisden* regarded it all as 'a sad blunder' and would have preferred a blank season. A main difficulty was time. The hours were extended to 7.30 p.m., and both spectators, anxious to return home, and players, faced with long train journeys, found this arduous. However, probably the chief reason why the experiment failed was because the players, more especially the captains, had neither the wit nor the motivation to alter the conduct and process of the game so as to exploit the reduced time available. For the most part, they continued to play exactly as if there were three days available. The experiment was swiftly abandoned.

In observing the changeless attitudes of the inter-war years, it is sometimes forgotten that the period between the wars was frighteningly brief, so much so that many were unlucky enough to be caught up in both conflicts. A short set of Cham-

seniors in approach, endeavouring to find the charismatic or disciplinarian leader, backed by a stolid group of professional tradesmen. Their problems were, of course, financial, and they simply could not buy their way out of trouble. Sir Lindsay Everard and Sir Julien Cahn, for instance, had to come to the financial rescue of Leicester-

pionships separated the invasion of Belgium from the invasion of Poland. Cricketers available and fit to begin their careers in 1919 might have expected to have played in the 1940 season, had there been one. Frank Woolley first played for England in 1909 and was already well established in the Kent side; he finally retired, aged 51, in 1938. Put another way, had, lamentably, a Third World War broken out, as Jeremiahs prophesied, at the same interval, then it would have been the season of 1966, when Yorkshire were yet again champions, that would have preceded Armageddon. We would have seen little or nothing of the abolition of separate status for professionals and amateurs, one-day cricket, sponsorship and overseas mercenaries.

On this perspective, the summers between the wars were something like the foreshortened dream of a long-drawn-out past, and, on that assessment, it is less surprising that there had been no moves to re-jig the structure of county cricket. At the same time, it had to be recognized that cricket had years ago given first place to football in the hearts and minds of Englishmen. Although the Test matches and some important county matches still drew the crowds, the majority of three-day games were, by 1939, not proving too popular, especially on the third day. Soccer, on the other hand, as well as one or two other sports, were enjoying something of a heyday. The Findlay Commission of 1937, formed to examine the structure of the game, had roundly condemned the two-day solution, claiming that money could not be saved by the curtailment of the third day. They favoured reducing the first-class county membership to fifteen and intro-

38 'To come to the financial rescue . . .' Sir Julien Cahn (*centre*),
most notable of cricketing backers, with members of his 1938–39 team to New Zealand.

ducing more representative fixtures, along the lines of the still-distinguished Gentlemen versus Players match.

Although, needless to say, such suggestions were ignored, they do indicate that some in authority were recognizing where cricket stood in its relation to national circumstances. The depression at the turn of the 1930s brought what George Orwell called 'frightful doom' to many decent working people. In 1932 there were nearly 4 million, and their dependents, living on the dole; and, when war broke out, there were still 2 million unemployed. The expanding and aspiring suburban estates did better, but the mood was, where not despairing, introspective and defensive. The politicians, compared with the verve of their Victorian predecessors, were staid and unheroic, the avuncular 'safety first' appeal of Stanley Baldwin catching the flavour accurately. It was an era which the historian, David Thomson, has shrewdly labelled one of 'incorrigible *immobilisme*'.

It is little wonder that county cricket stayed the same. Along, *inter alia*, with the wireless – 9 million sets by 1939 – the cinema – 20 million tickets a week – and the youth hostels, it offered a cosy escape. If (as literature has often portrayed the ostrich-like Britain of those two decades) the island home could be compared to a boarding school, such as Alan Bennett's *Albion House*, then the seventeen counties were engaged in an endless series of house matches through those lazy summers.

And yet it was a jittery age of eccentric exploits and agitated dances. It is odd that we shallowly view the Victorians as unimaginative and restricted, and later times as brash and liberated. Unlike the bolder Victorian age, the 1920s and 1930s lacked the assurance to tackle the major decisions, placating itself with fussy, minor alterations.

There was certainly considerable tinkering with county cricket, but there was no wholesale revision. The leading illustration of this was the methods employed for deciding the Championship. Prior to 1914, and remembering that the constitution of its membership was undergoing

change, there had not been too many variations. Until 1886, fewest lost matches was the mode, and thereafter single points were allocated for wins, sometimes with losses counting as some form of minus quantity, and with draws either ignored or given a half point. In 1910 the result was determined by the percentage of wins to matches played, and from 1911 the table was decided by the greatest proportion of points received against points possible. First-innings points were also introduced at this stage.

What can hardly be disclaimed is that the degree of complication increased precipitously after the First World War. It would be unnecessarily tedious to catalogue the fiddling alterations that were made. In those twenty-one seasons no less than eight formulae were deployed. There was much concern with first-innings points and with differing permutations of points, and also with varying types of proportions or percentages of points. More sensibly, there were occasional efforts to ensure that each side played the same number of matches. It was a restless time, with county cricket somehow refusing to settle what was, after all, a very straightforward question. Often the changes did not appear to affect the outcome, and the Championship would probably have gone to the rightful team whatever the method.

Otherwise, it all seems to have been overly fidgety. There were problems. The drawn game, an honourable result in cricket, was one of these, particularly as weather plays such a daunting hand in cricket matters, and it was this that led to the interest in first-innings points. Some of the schemes had, over the years, become slightly counter-productive, as there was too much concentration on the booty available from a first-innings lead, or, at one time, when no result on the first innings was more profitable than both first innings being played out. In 1929, for example, Nottinghamshire batted for over seven hours against Yorkshire, scoring 190 for 4, as they succeeded in negotiating the three days without the opening innings being completed.

A more basic problem was the number of matches played and the shape of the fixture-list.

The former had sometimes confused the Victorian Championships, for the range of fixtures had in some years been wide. Efforts had since been made to establish either a qualifying or a regulated number of matches. Twenty-four or twenty-eight were popular in the 1920s and the 1930s. But in those years when counties were deemed, and rightly so, as strong or weak, success could depend on a careful selection of opponents. This was balanced by the desire of members and, in all honesty, players for their team to face interesting opposition, but it was an awkward issue. In effect, the Championship was too large, for, with touring teams, universities and so on, to cater for, it had become impossible for the seventeen counties to play one another, home and away. That, quite evidently, would have been the fairest solution, but it has never really been attempted in the County Championship as such.

All in all, there were only four summers between the wars – 1929 to 1932 – when the counties all played the same number of games, that is, twenty-eight, albeit with widely varying points structures. As a brief excursion into cricketing arithmetic, it is intriguing to ponder on the application of the current Football League regulo of three points for a win and one point for a draw. Were the 1931 Championship to have been calculated on that basis, there would have been few changes from the published table, despite its sophistications. Fourth Sussex and fifth Nottinghamshire must perforce swap places, as must seventh Derbyshire and eighth Surrey, but with only one point separating each of those pairs. Somerset would be equal twelfth and not thirteenth, and Leicestershire equal fifteenth instead of sixteenth. These tiny alterations apart, the shape of the 1931 table would be unchanged, further testimony for those who campaign on behalf of the virtue of simplicity.

Whatever the analysis, however, the fundamental truth remains that the County Championship soldiered on, and, although football was now definitely in the ascendant as the nation's most popular game, and although county treasurers were obliged to look beseechingly at opulent local big-wigs, county cricket never underwent any genuine crisis at heart.

The 1919–39 period is probably the one during which the notion of a county 'character' appeared, or, at least, became accepted. These might have been, as they remain, a trifle specious, but they helped the sense of identity: gritty Yorkshire or hospitable Worcestershire; these became the tokens of cricketing converse and writing. The literature of cricket emphasized how established, indeed how immovable, was the county and the Championship. In style and manner, it aspired to be literature in the classical sense, and, during these years, reached a rich maturity. In particular, the flawless prose of Neville Cardus graced this era, and his memorable vignettes of county cricketers gave an aesthetic bent to the county game. In terms of the way this helped people to value county cricket, it really does not matter very much whether Neville Cardus, as astringent critics have urged, went beyond the bounds of literal fact in his search for artistic truth. The approach and the effect was

39 The notion of a county ''character'' . . .' Portrayed by Hampshire's Lord Tennyson and Phil Mead.

much the same as that employed by his beloved Dickens in the broader field of social existence.

This maturity of cricket journalism, with the wireless also beginning to play its important role in the communication of cricketing affairs, was reflected in other media, such as, for instance, children's comics. The weeklies of older boys – *Hotspur, Champion, Adventure, Skipper, Rover, Wizard* – usually featured a cricketing yarn. Each had its own minor public school in the grand tradition of Frank Richards and Greyfriars – Red Circle in the *Hotspur* being the most famed – and a potent reminder of the point made earlier about the embattled and secluded nature of English life at this time. Sometimes these schools were the sites for exciting cricket tourneys, and, out there

on the North-West Frontier there was an Afghan warrior in one comic who used 'clicky ba' as his indomitable weapon. But often these so-called comics, in which pictures were few and writing was plentiful and articulate, had their own fictional county team. There was always a Loamshire or a Greenshire to follow, and, sitting in retired dotage on many a county pavilion balcony, there must be older members who recall how Rob Higson, of the *Rover*'s 'It's Runs That Count', helped to fix county cricket in their minds and souls for ever.

And then, with appalling malevolence, came the 1939–45 war, and first-class cricket was stopped for only the second time in its long history.

SIX

Much Ado but Little Change

The four years' abstention from cricket during the First World War – the first gap in the enjoyment of first-class and county cricket since the very idea had been mooted – instilled into the cricketing mind a sacred sense of the inviolate nature of their sport, their credo. Nothing would now ever change it, and those who thought radical thoughts about it were regarded almost as traitors. The swirling alterations that had bravely marked the path of cricket's historic journey over the previous century and more were forgotten, as county cricket embarked on a lengthy phase of commemoration.

By curious paradox, the Second World War – the second and longest phase without first-class play in England – proved to be more critical in terms of change. However, this change occurred – hence the paradox – because the cricket authorities failed to distinguish that the war's end *was* a time for reform, and thus later found themselves faced with a critical necessity for unavoidable revision. This arose, then, from the folly of a missed opportunity.

The character and mood of the Second World War was quite different from that of the First World War. The concentration in the 1914–18 war on the horrors of the Western Front was replaced by a more general menace, often with the civilian populations under more threat than military personnel. It was a war fought on many fronts, and it was an aerial war, so that, for example, W. J. Edrich might fly in strafing raids over the enemy coast (winning a DFC into the bargain) and then hack up to Hendon by plane to report to Lord's for cricket. It was a war of longueurs and sudden alarms: there was the 'bore' war from September 1939 to May 1940; and there was the lull before the storm of the Normandy invasion. For much of the time the United Kingdom was an island citadel, either standing alone against German onslaught, or, later, a kind of

terrestrial aircraft carrier for the war in Europe. Thus the division between death in the trenches and delight on the sward which, probably rightly, cricketers had found 'unseemly' in 1914–18 was not repeated.

As for mood, people took a more sophisticated view of the psychology of warfare, and the need to boost morale and to consider the value of leisure was acknowledged. Cricket was given a high priority, and there was also the benefit that accrued to war charities from many games. There was, therefore, much extremely good cricket, with the Lord's programme of one-day matches most crucial and often drawing big crowds. These culminated in the three-day Victory Tests of 1945 and the famous England and Dominions game of the same year, described by Sir Pelham Warner as 'cricket *in excelsis*'. Throughout the country many attempts were contrived to keep the game alive, notably in the north-west, where a series of high-class fixtures was arranged, and in the leagues, in particular the Bradford League which, in 1942, recruited thirty-nine county players, including thirteen internationals.

Nonetheless, county cricket collapsed well-nigh completely. Initially, Lancashire proposed a regional competition, but most counties felt unable to sustain that level of commitment, and Lancashire themselves played few actual county matches, although many of their players featured in local games. It was apparent that some counties had special problems related to the exigencies of war – Hampshire, for instance, with its base at the war-torn port of Southampton – but the exception that disproved the rule was Nottinghamshire, who, under the energetic lead of their secretary, H. A. Brown, year in year out organized a splendid schedule of one-day matches. Other counties made different kinds of contribution, but did, at least, demonstrate that cricket did not need to come to a standstill on all county grounds. It is

40 'The palmy climes of the 1920s and 1930s . . .'
A fine crowd at Lord's in 1926, marshalled by somewhat unsophisticated public address mechanics.

clear that, with a little more verve, the counties might well have kept going with their identities intact, perhaps on a regional basis, and with one-day games.

Other formats developed in their stead. The London Counties XI, of professional vintage, and the British Empire XI, based on the ideal of bringing together English and overseas players, became the war's Players and Gentlemen, while the services, including the civil defence, fielded strong, sometimes Test-level sides. On the face of it, cricket had a good war, providing happy relaxation for war-weary citizens and the military. But against the wider perspective of recrea-

tion, that credit dims in lustre, for other leisure pursuits bloomed where cricket began to wither. Association football organized popular competitions, while many claim that the post-war audience for theatre, serious music and ballet was created by wartime efforts. The cinema, the pubs and the wireless – the BBC's staff rose from 4000 to 115,000 during the war – all prospered, as full employment, higher wages, despite rationing and shortages, ensured that expenditure on leisure increased by an astonishing 120%.

Cricket, especially county cricket, took few such initiatives. Microscopically, this reflected the ambivalence of war aims. Some were fighting for the freedom to return to the palmy climes of the 1920s and 1930s, some for the freedom to escape their drudgery and squalor. Innately conservative, the cricketing powers-that-were dreamed of a time when Perks would be bowling to Bradman at Worcester in the shadow of the cathedral. County cricket held the fortress; but it rarely went on the offensive.

The Second World War became a war of opportunities, with social and technical reforms and inventions. The favoured concept of the era was Reconstruction. In social terms, it found its apotheosis in the National Health Service, but county cricket did not utilize the war either to improve its immediate position or to plan imaginatively for the future.

Two instances of missed chances may be quoted. The severe wartime restriction on the production of sports goods and equipment led the government to devise a scheme whereby the priorities among cricket clubs for materials would be determined by the county clubs, both first- and second-class. This leverage was exactly what was required to construct what Rowland Bowen has called 'a central cricket organization', but this chance to build a thoroughgoing network throughout the cricketing fraternity, based on the county pattern, was jettisoned.

Even more colourful an illustration was the continuance of schools' cricket, as in the first war, so that MCC, true to its creed, ensured that about thirty fixtures with the leading public schools were annually negotiated. At a time when the schooling and sporting life of many children was disrupted by bombing, evacuation and the conscription of sports teachers and coaches, the cricket establishment might have spared a thought for the ordinary schoolboy and found some way of imbuing a love of cricket in him. A general impression is that, from about the 1950s, cricket ceased to enjoy its seasonal grip on boys as a knock-up street, park or meadow game, with football increasingly in the ascendant, formally as well as informally. Looking back in nostalgia to its public school antecedents, the wartime cricketing authorities forgot that, in a more democratic future, there was a need to capture the hearts and minds of the younger population as a whole.

The privileged blessing of hindsight would be less honourably deployed had not cricket undergone a theoretical course of Reconstruction, and then abandoned much of what had been profitably learned from the exercise. As early as 1940 and 1941 there were musings over the future, and, by 1942, both *Wisden* and *The Cricketer* were happy to argue the merits of the two-day game for the County Championship, in spite of the sad memories of the 1919 experiment. There was also talk of building in a regional competition.

The Lord's establishment was forcefully opposed to such heresy, warning of 'the danger of

41 'A plethora of fluent and rapid runs from Denis Compton and Bill Edrich . . .'
Walking out to the wicket in 1947.

tinkering with the game'. The Findlay Commission of 1937, which had condemned two-day cricket on grounds both of likely results and income, was used selectively in evidence. Sir Pelham Warner asserted: 'I can see nothing wrong with modern cricket.' These influential arguments won the day, and, by July 1943, the decision to retain three-day play had been taken, and a Select Committee requested to facilitate 'a speedy resumption' of such first-class cricket. This published its report in March 1944, expressing the hope that cricket would remain 'an essential feature of the post-war social structure of the nation'. But the mood was entirely conservationist. Cricket plumped for the status quo as its contribution to the new world. There was some tidying up, with an insistence on every county playing exactly twenty-six matches, including one against every county, and some general exhortations about adding vim to the old formula.

All else was negative or neutral. Elimination or amalgamation of counties, two divisions, Sunday cricket or cricket limited by time or overs or scoring rate – all these options were rejected. Above all, the 'slapstick turn' of one-day cricket, which had served so well during the war, could never compete with the 'three-act play' of the first-class game, and was barely countenanced. Discussion maundered on about a knock-out competition, until, in November 1946, it was 'decided to defer further consideration'. What now seems most peculiar about this debate is the outright refusal to contemplate anything other than a three-day cup competition, with all the attendant difficulties of draws and the like.

In short, cricket saw what the war had wrought – 'time after time a thrilling finish was seen'; 'the public want to see stars not results' – but failed to read the lesson. Nottinghamshire attracted 27,000 spectators (members apart) to eleven days' cricket in 1945, as compared to 1939, when only twice were the gates much above 2000. There were some thirty days' cricket in the season at Lord's and over 400,000 attended – over 12,000 a day on average – as against the 330,000 of a full 1939 season. The gates had to be closed four times. In the accurate belief that the public

were anxious to watch cricket, few observed what kind of cricket they wanted to watch.

In 1946, give or take a relaxation towards special registration, so that discarded players might the more easily find a berth, the scene was a replica of 1939. In chief, this applied to the players. Although many debuts were made,

42 'Tragic losses . . .' Ken Farnes, the Essex and England fast bowler, killed in the RAF during the Second World War.

43 'Tom Graveney, whose genius towered over his immediate contemporaries . . .'

first crack to the many cricketers who had willingly and bravely flocked to the colours, and that chimed in with the general rule that de-mobilized servicemen should be quickly resettled in their old roles. There is also little doubt that, in those first post-war years, crowds packed many grounds, delighting in a last chance to watch their favourites of the 1930s, relieved to find them-selves free of the strain of war and able to bask in the pastoral niceties of the glorious game. On the other hand – the negative – the main cricketing casualties of war were the generation approach-ing maturity in 1939. Of course, there were tragic losses, such as Hedley Verity, Kenneth Farnes and Maurice Turnbull, but they had not occurred in the same awful profusion as in the 1914–18 war; of course, such cricketers as Len Hutton and Walter Hammond and Denis Compton had lost six years of their prime. But the most telling effect on the county game was in the loss of young players of the mid-1920s vintage. In the worst quinquennium, 1924 to 1928, only sixty-five English regular county players were born, com-pared to more like 140 in most five-year periods. They gave rise to only sixteen Test players with a beggarly haul of only 151 caps, of which no less than seventy-nine were acquired by Tom Graveney, whose genius towered above his im-mediate contemporaries. The morale-boosting cricket of the war had been attractively sustained by pre-war stars; there again, the collapse of a county structure had perhaps contributed to this inadequacy in the induction of young players.

At first, all seemed well. In the sunlit splendour of 1947 Middlesex won the title with a plethora of fluent and rapid runs from Denis Compton and Bill Edrich, with sturdy support from the opening pair of Robertson and Brown. It has been said that this was the only Championship to be won on the strength of batting alone, that is, with only a modicum of bowling talent. Lancashire's 1904 triumph, when the express batting of MacLaren, John Tyldesley and Spooner constantly gave journeyman bowlers time to dismiss the opposi-tion, is probably the nearest parallel. In 1948, with the giant Australians storming across the land, there was again much to catch the interest,

almost all of these faded away, and the playing staffs were very much the same as in pre-war days. To complete this air of *déjà vu*, Yorkshire carried off the Championship in 1946 as they had done in 1939, and with much the same team including Sellers, Leyland, Hutton and Bowes.

Much of this was predictable and welcome. On the one hand – the positive – it was right to give

44 'At first all seemed well . . .' Great crowds at Lord's in 1948.

45 'In the sun-lit splendour of 1947 Middlesex won the Championship . . .'
Middlesex in 1947. *Back row*: P. I. Bedford, A. W. Thompson, L. H. Gray, Leslie Compton,
J. D. Robertson, S. M. Brown and J. A. Young; *front*: W. J. Edrich, F. G. Mann, R. W. V. Robins,
J. M. Sims and Denis Compton.

not least the engaging achievement of Wilf Wooller's Glamorgan in winning their first Championship, and only the third to be gained by a club outside the senior eight. The 139 wickets of Len Muncer, the ex-Middlesex off-spinner, was, in that decidedly damp summer, a crucial feature. Middlesex and Yorkshire shared the Championship in 1949, and there was another joint title in 1950, when Surrey, flexing muscles in preparation for their monopoly of the 1950s, and Lancashire, with Roy Tattersall the lord high executioner with 171 victims, shared the lead. In 1951 it was the turn of Warwickshire. This was their second Championship win, and it was significant in being the first modern title obtained by a team with, in the solid and astute form of Tom Dollery, a professional captain.

Yet the five years after the end of the Second World War has been called correctly 'a period of delusion'. After what might be considered a kind of second honeymoon, county cricket fell apart. Some of this collapse was financial. County memberships had remained high after the war, and subscriptions, pulling in what seemed to be a goodly sum, were barely increased, while ground attendances had been very reasonable. As in other aspects of national life, the insidious disease of inflation was not noticed or was ignored until it had taken a damaging grip of epidemic proportions. Sir Home Gordon's calculation that the annual cost of running the average county club would be £10,000 now looked quite awry. By the end of the 1950s it was nearer five or six times that amount, and rising fast. All this found many county clubs gasping for economic breath.

An aspect of the conservationist process in-

46 The first modern title won by a team with . . . a professional captain . . .'
Warwickshire, the 1951 county champions. *Standing*: G. Austin (scorer), D. Taylor, R. T. Weeks, A. V. Wolton, F. C. Gardner, C. Belam, A. Townsend, R. T. Spooner, E. J. Smith (coach); *seated*: C. W. Grove, W. E. Hollies, H. E. Dollery (captain), J. S. Ord, T. L. Pritchard; *inset*: R. E. Hitchcock.

cluded retaining wages at pre-war norms, but times had changed. For the whole of the lengthy era of County Championship cricket prior to 1939, the county cricket professional had earned more than the ordinary manual worker in the ratio, more often than not, of two to one. Now changing job patterns and improved wage rates, a legacy of wartime policies, many of them the responsibility of Ernest Bevin, made for increased competition from other occupations. Another boon wrought by the war was full employment. Inevitably, there was a decline in the calibre of cricket's recruits.

This was matched to some extent in the amateur ranks. Country house cricket and the famous touring XIs were, in general, finished. The premier universities, very properly, began to make sterner academic assessments about their intakes, and the gifted public schoolboy batsman, with little Latin and less Greek, was less likely to obtain a place than in the 1920s and 1930s. Oxbridge did produce a stunning, tiny troupe of maestros through the 1950s, among them Peter May, Colin Cowdrey, David Sheppard, Hubert Doggart, Donald Carr, John Dewes and Ted Dexter. Thereafter the well ran dry.

47 'A stunning, tiny troupe of maestros . . .' Including Colin Cowdrey of Kent and England, now a much-respected cricket administrator, knighted in the 1992 honours list.

Leisure patterns began to alter. Motor-car travel liberated thousands; family-based recreation grew; other pastimes flourished. Television became the art-form of the nation. With the car, it exemplified that miniaturization of society, which still continues. The cinema and the concert hall are now to be found in the sitting-room, and the golden age of collective leisure was ending. The more serious mood of wartime, which did wonders for classical music and made the 'Brains Trust' a winning radio series, waned: it was that very vein, sober and middlebrow, that cricket had failed to cap, and now it was vanishing. Schools, too, rightfully conscious of their broader obligations, were justifiably offering their charges a much wider choice of recreational and sporting pursuits.

Some commentators spoke gloomily of the decease of county cricket, but that was premature: it was resilient enough after its fashion. Surrey dominated the 1950s, their powerful bowling and rather unimpressive batting (the quality of Peter May apart) making them a mirror image of their Middlesex rivals. Especially on favourable Oval pitches, the all-round quality of Alec Bedser, Peter Loader, Tony Lock and Jim Laker made this one of the most deadly county attacks ever. Intrepid close catching, with W. S. Surridge, the energetic captain, always the example, was another feature.

The shared Championship with Lancashire in 1950 was, remarkably, only the second success that Surrey had achieved this century. As if anxious to compensate for such laxity, they now proceeded to head the table in seven consecutive seasons, from 1952 to 1958. It was the Yorkshire of J. R. Burnet, Trueman, Close, Wilson and Illingworth which wrested back the crown, winning the title in 1959, 1960, 1962 and 1963. In 1961 it was finally the popular turn of Hampshire, who won their first ever Championship under the cavalier leadership of Colin Ingleby-Mackenzie, with gifted support from such as Derek Shackleton and the West Indian star, Roy Marshall.

Nevertheless, by the early 1960s, county cricket was obliged by the inexorable calls of economics to reconstruct its being on an alarming scale. The

48 'The all-round quality of Alec Bedser . . .'
The mainstay of Surrey and England in the 1950s.

end of the professional-amateur divide, an invasion of overseas stars, wholesale sponsorship beside a bewildering array of other fund-raising schemes and the introduction of, eventually, three one-day competitions – here was a four-point agenda for change of huge proportions.

The reforms came quickly, perhaps hastily. First, the amateur and professional distinction, declared 'surely humbug' during the official wartime discussions, lasted nearly twenty years more. It was in 1963, amid a welter of other alterations, that the divisive business of separate travel, accommodation and dressing-rooms and the curious labelling of the scorecards (initials fore or aft according to status) finally was brought to rest.

Second, one-day cricket had also been shelved as an issue since the war, and then it was suddenly introduced. Indeed, the idea had been formally abandoned by the Advisory County Cricket Committee in the November of 1957. However, in the December of 1961, the Committee decided, by a narrow margin of votes, to inaugurate the Gillette Cup competition, and this was first played in 1963. The John Player League, the 40-over Sunday competition, was established in 1969, and the Benson and Hedges Cup, a mix of regional mini-leagues and sudden death play-offs, was first competed for in 1972. This was 55 overs a side, as opposed to the 60 overs (65 in the early years) of the Gillette tournament. Thus, after a hundred years without any alteration of a fundamental kind, three new competitions were added in ten.

Third, in 1968 the counties were permitted to register an unqualified player, that is, one not qualified to play for England, and they were forbidden to sign such another for three years, during which time the original signing could not play for another county. This fast lane witnessed the arrival of, for example, Gary Sobers to Nottinghamshire, Barry Richards to Hampshire, Rohan Kanhai to Warwickshire, Mike Procter to Gloucestershire, F. M. Engineer to Lancashire, Asif Iqbal to Kent and Majid Khan to Glamorgan. These were the standard-bearers for an illustrious parade of global talent over the ensuing years. Eventually, the authorities felt it necessary to restrict this development, and in 1982 they were limited to one specially registered player a match, and in 1991 to but one actual registration of this kind.

However, of the four chief features that so tardily transformed the face of county cricket, sponsorship was by far the most original and possibly the most far reaching. The Players and Gentlemen divide, although immensely significant in the history of the game, had always been blurred by the liberal use of expenses and testimonials, and by the provision of 'cod' jobs (assistant secretary was a well-tried one) for purported

amateurs. Many counties had already turned – as had the national side – to professional captaincy without civilization, as Lord Hawke knew it, crumbling.

Overseas players also had a long history. Ranji was scarcely the genuine child of Brighton, Hastings or Eastbourne. Australia's first captain, Billy Murdoch, had also skippered Sussex, while several of his fellow-countrymen – Albert Trott and Frank Tarrant for Middlesex; J. J. Ferris for Gloucestershire; E. A. McDonald for Lancashire – had contributed magnificently to the County Championship. After the Second World War others followed, and qualification rules had been relaxed. It was the even spread of high-class and attractive non-indigenous stars which was, if anything, now the novelty.

The third aspect – limited-overs cricket – was a function of, and related to, sponsorship. It is important to appreciate that one-day cricket was introduced as sponsored cricket. The commercial backing for the County Championship, first by Schweppes and then by Britannic Assurance, was a much later manifestation, while, conversely, there has been no serious non-sponsored limited-overs cricket. We have come a long way from the Gillette Cup of 1963, involving the division of £6500 among the counties, to the Foster's Oval or Bass Headingley of today and the indirect sponsorship of the counties through the broadcasting of Test cricket and limited-overs cricket (but rarely three-day county cricket) and the localized commercial subsidies sought by the counties.

The point may best be illustrated by reference to one county, Lancashire, the author's own heroes. In 1962, just prior to the build-up of sponsorship and one-day play, their turnover was £67,000 – £39,000 taken at the gate or in subscriptions, and only £8000 in Test and broadcasting receipts. In the summer of 1990 Lancashire's income was over £2 million, of which just over half a million came from subscriptions and match receipts, and a million and a half from Tests, one-day internationals, broadcasting, sponsorship, advertising and year-round catering. County cricket is now a huge business, generating close on £20 million of income annually, but, apart

49 'Barry Richards to Hampshire . . .' One of many overseas stars to play county cricket
during the last twenty-five years. (Another import, F. M. Engineer, of Lancashire and India, is behind the
wicket.)

from a reasonable maintenance of membership levels, exerting little popular appeal.

In real terms, one should consider that two million people, apart from subscribing members, paid at the turnstiles to watch county cricket in 1950. By 1966 this had dropped to 500,000, and it is now, for Championship county cricket, about 170,000. Today, a county would count itself lucky to muster 10,000 paying customers at its dozen or so three- or four-day games. In 1947, 12,000 paid to watch the first day of the university match. Spectators, and their income, are scarcely part of the formula any more: in 1990 only 8% of county income was from gate-money, and 17% from subscriptions, with 70% from commercial and TCCB sources.

Many critics would argue that the crisis occurred because the cricket declined, and the statistical evidence – over rates, batting and bowling performances – from the somewhat prosaic and dour 1950s do justify this argument. Nor, after a quarter century of changed conditions, would many urge that matters have much improved or that the quality of first-class cricket is consistently as high as the 1900s or the 1930s.

This wholesale revision bore all the signs of hasty action. Forced, at the brink of collapse, to reform, the resultant attempts were spatchcock. They were over-elaborate in one direction – in what Marxists would call the superstructure – and negligible as regards the structure itself. Where the Victorians, whom we tend to brand as antediluvian, had acknowledged the fluid state of cricket and encouraged it to grow organically, the New Elizabethans, like their predecessors in the 1920s and 1930s, gazed tremulously on the possibility of basic reform.

The dilemma, as in 1943–45, as throughout the game's history, was between cricket as 'the holy game' and as entertainment. The one amounted to a backward-looking statement about a high-minded and aesthetic ideal; the other pointed to a get-rich-quick whirligig of one-day whizz-bangery. The upshot of enforced change was mistakes on both horns of that dilemma. The 'structure' of the county establishment was left untouched, and the unshakable convention of

the immutable seventeen was reinforced: on the other hand, county cricket went berserk with one-day competitions which menaced the very fabric of the first-class game.

It is truly astonishing that no county has left or joined the sacred ranks since 1921. Buckinghamshire were invited to join in 1921, but declined because of inadequate facilities; Devon were refused in 1948, and (Durham apart) there have been nothing but vain flirtations since. There has been no routeway for the lesser breeds to improve status, whereas the Football League, apart from relegation and promotion, rather belatedly discovered a way of encouraging rising non-league teams.

However, just before the Christmas of 1990, the Test and County Cricket Board unanimously agreed – despite some subdued murmurings from southern counties facing extended travel – that Durham should become the eighteenth first-class county, and should join the main competitions in 1992. Durham's careful and businesslike preparations and presentations rightly won the hearts and minds of their new peers, but, if ever an exception proved a rule, this was it. The excitement – 'we have scaled Everest' cried one delirious Durham protagonist – spoke volumes about the sheer rigidity of the barricades erected by English first-class cricket. It had taken three generations and sixty-five Championships for the Bastille to be stormed: there are few more difficult tasks in sport than effecting entry into cricket's hierarchy – or, for that matter, departing from it. There was another point to note. Durham proposed to establish itself as a limited company, more after the fashion of a Football League club. All the other first-class counties began, of course, as members' clubs, and, while now in the form of commercial businesses, remain wedded to the importance of membership. It does seem somehow appropriate that the only county promoted after the gross commercialization of cricket should opt for this type of constitution.

This rare success apart, the first-class county rarely plays a minor county now over three days, and, although the two cup competitions allow for some involvement of minor county and university cricket, this is something of a hollow ritual. Their predictable lack of success demonstrates, for the last-ditchers, the genuine gap between first- and second-class cricket – but a 60-over contest, one day each June, is hardly sufficient incentive to prepare for the big time.

What had been required was a smoother gradient for senior cricket. The chasm between first-class and other cricket is a matter for bitter criticism, not complacent acceptance. Gentler steps might give young cricketers the chance to approach their careers more carefully, as opposed to risking the high jump into the first-class game. As it is, the Test team needs the County Championship to blood its recruits, and the counties require the Test team to provide them with financial succour. Thus we have the curious situation of the counties, each playing twenty-two fixtures in the tomb-like silence of eerily empty arenas, in order to find a Test team whose exploits will subsidize the defiantly unpopular County Championship.

It might be interesting to formulate a possible structure, entirely based on suggestions made during the Reconstruction debate toward the end of the Second World War, or, indeed, on ways the game was played during the war.

The first-class counties and twenty minor counties might form three divisions of twelve or so teams. This might, in fact, be reduced by amalgamations and mergers; Norfolk and Suffolk, for example, or Northumberland and Cumberland teaming up with Durham. Nor should it be forgotten that other combines might qualify. Wales is already classified as a 'Minor County', and Scotland, the Combined Universities, an XI from one or more of the Leagues, or even a powerful club might be accepted.

Let us thus assume three divisions of ten, promotion and relegation by twos, and an eighteen-week season. That would allow for a home-and-away weekend competition, with two-day games in the lower two divisions, and three-day games, including Friday, for the top echelon. All league programmes would simplify their scoring to four points for a win, two for a tie and one for a draw.

Bank Holidays and Wednesdays might be used for a 60-overs NatWest-style cup contest, with all teams involved, without any seeding as at the moment. As now, that would end with the final in early September. In brief, there would be one league and one cup competition for the counties.

The counties have begun to play some of their matches over four days, a conscious recognition that their role is to tutor those very few who will play for England. There is even a laughable suggestion that the county programme should be cut to sixteen four-day games. It really is preposterous that this sledge-hammer should be grasped to crack the nut of finding and training eleven or so Test players, when there is so little popular interest in the actual day-by-day play. It also demonstrates the blinkered view that only county cricket is viable.

There is a case to be made for four-day cricket – but it does not have to be county cricket. The Gentlemen and Players match; in ancient times, the North versus the South; and, until the post-war era, most Test matches except the Australian series, used to provide the stepping-stone between county cricket and higher things. There is, then, a case for regional cricket, which could be played, avoiding, of course, the cup and Test matches, from Monday through Thursday on this suggested schedule. Should the war have ended suddenly, a regional division for the counties had been devised in 1944. The sub-groups were the North – Derbyshire, Lancashire, Yorkshire and Nottinghamshire; the Midlands – Leicestershire, Northamptonshire, Warwickshire and Worcestershire; the South-west – Glamorgan, Gloucestershire, Hampshire and Somerset; and the South-east – Middlesex, Kent, Sussex, Surrey and Essex.

Presumably, teams based on regions would be made up of players eligible for England, and this would mean that an Overseas XI, culled from county registrations, might also take the field. The appropriate tourists could be added: that would make more sense than them playing, as now, against weakened county teams. Thus a six-strong mini-league could be formed. Were the Championship to be widened to three divisions, obviously other counties would be part of those sub-groups, and it would be attractive to use some non-Test venues – Hove, Worcester, Canterbury and so on – for this higher grade of cricket. Incidentally, the regional recommendation could be introduced independently of any other reforms; and, like all the other suggestions, is open to helpful sponsorship. Finally, during the regional tourney, senior counties could play encouraging friendlies against junior counties, as used to be the case, and bring on their own tyros as a bonus.

This might-have-been scenario is offered as one example of how, with a little lateral thinking, a new mode of top-class cricket could have been fostered, earlier and in more relaxed fashion. It certainly pleads the case for county cricket being part of the entertainments business, rather than, in its mystical connotation, Art. But that does not mean that entertainment should be spurious and superficial, with synthetic spills and thrills, such as those that have accompanied some of the one-day lotteries. What drew crowds to Lord's and elsewhere during the Second World War, and in such summers as 1947, was possibly the notion of a firm result; but it was perhaps more to do with cricketers, led by sporting but shrewd captains, producing exciting and stylish cricket, without undue contrivance. If the game is not played in that spirit, then, frankly, the case is hopeless.

The entertainment value of county cricket is about the theatre of dramatic plot, with actors playing out classical parts with style. The population retains its pleasure in the valiant clash and rich skills of such theatre at Test and one-day level. It is the mournful ritual of the County Championship that has been the sufferer.

SEVEN

The Continuing County

So acrimonious an assault on the well-fortified and unworried bastion of the county establishment should not, naturally enough, be taken as an indication that no good came from county cricket in its modern era, that is, from about the early 1960s. It is true that the star performers on the county circuit have tended to be of overseas origin, but such great players as Clive Lloyd, Barry Richards, Viv Richards and Richard Hadlee, whatever their native habitat, are now as much a part of the story of the counties as Wilfred Rhodes or Patsy Hendren. During the 1950s it was often said that county cricket, now somewhat bereft of the cavalier flair of the genuine amateur, had become a rigid and dour business, over-professionalized and over-coached. Assuredly, that rather staid and puritanical image shrouded the county game and contributed to its shortcomings at that time. But whatever else, the importation of splendid performers from abroad, and the freer flow of cash into the game, did galvanize the counties into more animated action.

Curiously, the 1940s grumble about one-day cricket – that it would be the death of the all-rounder – was proved totally incorrect as a prophecy. If anything, the counties came to rely too much on sometimes mediocre all-rounders, 'bits and pieces' players, as they were rather revealingly described. It was also argued that the combination of overseas players and limited overs made it difficult for the young and promising English batsman to develop his skills. It was, however, apparent that several West Indians managed to make the transfer from the shorter to the longer game without problems.

A contributory factor hereabouts may have been the decision to abandon the struggle for first-innings lead. From 1968 bonus points were awarded for batting and bowling through the first 85 and, later, 100 overs of each first innings. This gave ample encouragement to both attack and defence to stir themselves, but it was claimed by some that it led to middle-order batsmen being forced to bat one-day style, as they were enjoined to force the pace and catch the next bonus point. This pattern settled down to a bowling point after three, five, seven and nine wickets had been taken; and a batting point after 150, 200, 250 and 300 runs had been scored.

Gloom was expressed as to the future of spin bowling, as teams appeared to depend more and more on respectable medium pace. Strangely, the slow bowler, when accommodated, frequently did exceedingly well, but his shortcomings became something of a myth. The left-handed slow bowler, once an indispensable asset in every county side, was seen but patchily, while the leg-spinner was, tragically, a doomed species, his exoticism leading to his near extinction in that pragmatic age.

There may well have been problems caused by the vast changes in the superstructure of the county game, but there were at least two distinct gains. One was in the running between the wickets, for the dawdling lethargy of what used sometimes to be called 'the county single' had little place in the madcap world of one-day tournaments. Scampering leg-byes and short singles was the new order of the day, and many cricketers did grow more expert in this exciting aspect of cricket. The other profit was in the matter of fielding, for, until well after the Second World War, many county teams carried a passenger or two. There was no room at all for such as these in the brave new world of instant cricket. Chasing, diving, stopping, throwing, now every county team aspired to be a world-class fielding outfit. The impact of modern cricket on fielding has perhaps been more profound than in any other feature of the game. Nonetheless, the overall conclusion must remain that, since 1950, the general quality of English first-class play has declined considerably.

From 1963 the county scene became more and more kaleidoscopic, defying succinct summary, as two league and two cup competitions were established, and a fifth – the Refuge Assurance Cup – had its place for four years.

In the County Championship the forceful Yorkshire team first continued to uphold tradition. Their winning ways were maintained in 1966, 1967 and 1968, and they were fifth in 1964 and fourth in 1965. This was the side that witnessed Trueman's final and valued seasons and the early burgeoning of the young Boycott. It focussed on the ripe skills of Brian Close, Ray Illingworth, Phil Sharpe and Don Wilson, alongside the calm regularity of J. G. Binks, who kept wicket in no less than 412 consecutive County Championship matches. These successes took Yorkshire's tally of titles, including two shared ones, to thirty-three, Surrey coming next with twenty. At this point, just over a hundred years since the first Championship listed by *Wisden*, Yorkshire had won no less than a third of the ninety-five available titles. Over twenty years have now passed, and, apart from being runners-up to Leicestershire, led by the exiled Illingworth, in 1975, Yorkshire have made no thrust for the leadership. It is, obviously, their most fallow period since late Victorian times.

It was Worcestershire who took the eye and the crown in 1964 and 1965, and then again in 1974. Their leading lights were Don Kenyon, Tom Graveney, Jack Flavell, the West Indian Ron Headley, and Basil D'Oliveira. As with Leicestershire in 1975, these were the first times that Worcestershire had climbed to the top.

The 1970s exhibited a baffling variety. After Glamorgan had found their second and latest success under the tutelage of Tony Lewis in 1969, Kent, Surrey, Warwickshire and Hampshire arrived home first in the annual chase. Then Mike Brearley's revitalized Middlesex and the Kent of Derek Underwood and Asif Iqbal became formidable combines, the former taking the title in 1976 and the latter in 1978, with that of 1977 shared. Middlesex continued to be a mighty force, winning the title in 1980, 1982 and 1985.

50 'Leicestershire, led by the exiled Illingworth . . .' Ray Illingworth, once of Yorkshire, captained Leicestershire in their Championship year of 1975.

51 'Glamorgan, under the tutelage of Tony Lewis . . .'
Lewis led the Welsh county to
their 1969 Championship win.

Between 1976 and 1985 Middlesex were only
once pushed out of the top four. After collapsing
somewhat in the later 1980s, they were strengthened by the West Indian opening bat, D. L.
Haynes, and won again powerfully in 1990.
About this time, along with Gatting, Edmonds,
Emburey, Fraser and others, Middlesex often
fielded a near-international side. It was not before
time. Nearly thirty long summers – since 1949, to
be exact – separated them from their last title.

Now Essex, mindful perhaps of the touching
music-hall ditty, 'Why am I always the brides-
maid, and never the blushing bride?', finally
walked down the aisle. It had taken them over
eighty years since their first Championship
engagement in 1895 to approach the altar of
cricketing eminence. It was 1979, and Keith
Fletcher, Graham Gooch and John Lever were the
chief contributors. Shifting the metaphor quickly,
they soon showed it was no flash in the pan, for
these cricketing prospectors discovered gold
thrice more in the mid-1980s – in 1983, 1984 and
1986. Then, having been third and second twice
in consecutive seasons, 'Essex Man' thundered to
the fore again in 1991.

Nottinghamshire, bolstered by the substantial
talent of the South African, Clive Rice, and the
New Zealander, Richard Hadlee, collected the
pennant in 1981 and 1987, while the prodigious
run-making of Graeme Hick effectively guaranteed Worcestershire's success in 1988 and 1989.

Sussex, still without a Championship title, tried
to make amends by emerging as the first one-day
specialists. They won the Gillette Cup in its
opening two years, 1963 and 1964. Warwickshire, twice, and Kent were also early winners,
while Yorkshire, inspired by an uncharacteristically rapid Boycott century, trounced Surrey in
1965.

A fiercely combative Lancashire XI, with Clive
Lloyd providing pyrotechnic batting displays and
with unsurpassed fielding, dominated the early
1970s. They won four times and were beaten
finalists twice, Kent and Northamptonshire
managing to defeat them. Gloucestershire won in
1973; Sussex lifted the cup again in 1978, and
Somerset, at last enjoying some good times, were

52 'Middlesex continued to be a mighty force . . .' Middlesex in 1980.
Standing: W. W. Daniel, K. D. James, V. A. P. van der Bijl, J. E. Emburey, W. N. Slack, G. D. Barlow,
R. O. Butcher; *sitting*: M. W. Gatting, C. D. Radley, J. M. Brearley, P. H. Edmonds, M. W. W. Selvey and
I. J. Gould.

also worthy winners. The powerful Middlesex team were successful twice, in 1977 and 1980.

The Gillette Cup was transformed into the NatWest Trophy in 1981, when Derbyshire won one of their only two titles of the modern era. It was reported that the label Gillette had grown too familiar, that no one associated it with the shaving product the competition advertised, and even that some believed the cup was named after a renowned cricketer, maybe a Dr W. G. Gillette!

The first NatWest decade has been marked by a satisfying spread of success. Only Middlesex, continuing their winning habits, grabbed the Trophy twice, whilst there were happy autumnal Saturdays for Surrey, Somerset, Essex, Sussex,

Nottinghamshire, Warwickshire, Lancashire and Hampshire. This was a tribute to the wholesome breadth of ability across the counties and a commendation of this type of cup cricket. The 60-over contest is as near the ideal as one may find for instant cricket, and, over the years, it has offered an admirable mix of entertainment and artistry.

There have been fourteen cup-holders, while Glamorgan and Worcestershire have been defeated finalists, leaving only Leicestershire still to make a Lord's appearance in this particular tourney. That is an excellent and healthy record, and it would be wrong not to mention, in conclusion, the eight times that minor counties have confounded their senior brethren in the preliminary rounds.

The Benson and Hedges Cup has been fought over since 1972, when Leicestershire were the first winners. Curiously, Leicestershire, so unlucky in the older version, have carried off the Benson's Cup three times. Kent have also won this trophy on three occasions, and Middlesex, Lancashire and Somerset, in the summers of their high attainment, have won it twice each. These apart, the distribution has again been remarkably wide. Surrey, Nottinghamshire, Gloucestershire, Essex, Northamptonshire, Yorkshire and Hampshire have also been successful. Worcestershire won in 1991, their seventh appearance and first success in Lord's finals.

There have been thirteen different Benson and Hedges Cup winners, and now only Glamorgan have failed to place one cup or the other on their committee-room sideboard. There have been fourteen wins in the qualifying stages for the lesser breeds, eight for the university sides, four for the Minor Counties XI, and two for Scotland.

Lancashire set off like an express train in the Sunday League, sponsored by John Player. They won in 1969 and 1970, on the threshold of their derring-do in the Gillette Cup. Kent, exceedingly strong in the mid-1970s, won three times, and Hampshire, with three victories, have always proved a tough handful. As Essex came to prominence in the 1980s, they, too, were three times the leaders, but, latterly, Worcestershire, already the title-holders for 1971, were powerfully reinforced and swept to glory in both 1987 and 1988. Lancashire won in 1989, while Derbyshire were the victors in 1990, winning only their third trophy ever, and Nottinghamshire in 1991. From 1987 to 1991 the League was sponsored by Refuge Assurance, and, in the second year of their regime, the top four clubs played out a tiny knock-out contest for the Refuge Assurance Cup, Lancashire being the first winners. Essex, Middlesex and Worcestershire took what some regard as an inconsequential title in 1989, 1990 and 1991 respectively.

The Sunday thrash of 40 overs a side has not produced as many winners as the two cup com-

53 ' "Essex Man" thundered to the fore . . .'
Graham Gooch striking forcefully.

petitions; perhaps a level of consistency, even for so brief a sally, reaps a reward against the sudden and irrevocable finality of the knock-out mode. Even so, there have been twelve different winners: in addition to those mentioned above, Leicestershire (twice), Somerset, Warwickshire, Sussex and Yorkshire have carried off the title.

It is of some academic interest to assemble a county table based on the general success of the teams between 1963, when, for the first time, there was more than one title for which to play, and 1991. Over that phase there have been 106 such opportunities, including Kent and Middlesex as joint champions in 1977. The roster reads as follows:

1	Middlesex	13
2=	Kent	11
2=	Lancashire	11
2=	Essex	11
5	Worcestershire	10
6	Yorkshire	8
7=	Leicestershire	6
7=	Hampshire	6
9=	Somerset	5
9=	Sussex	5
9=	Warwickshire	5
9=	Nottinghamshire	5
13	Surrey	3
14=	Gloucestershire	2
14=	Derbyshire	2
14=	Northamptonshire	2
17	Glamorgan	1

The home counties, with the disappointing exception of Surrey, figure prominently, with Kent having made rather more of an impact than memory prompts, for much of the news appears to have been concerned with the triumphs of Essex and Middlesex. Yorkshire, with most of their titles culled in the earlier portion of this era, before controversy and carnage intervened, and Lancashire, dependent on their one-day bonanzas, keep up the north's wilting pecker. Worcestershire, with a late run, enter the frame, and, after a fairly unprepossessing history, Leicestershire's achievement is meritorious. Then the counties slip away to the sorry plight of Glamor-

gan. Northamptonshire are perhaps the prime case of a county which has huffed and puffed, but which has relatively little to show for many creditable campaigns. Like Damon Runyon's nice guys, Northamptonshire come second. Nottinghamshire, Yorkshire, Essex and Kent are the only four to have won all four main titles, and, of the leading sides, Middlesex have never won the Sunday League.

This phase in the history of county cricket has been a long one. Over a quarter of a century has passed since, with the abolition of the amateur and professional divide and the establishment of the 'cricketer' status, the modern era began. It is a fifth of the history of the County Championship, not by any means small beer; longer, for example, than the period between the two great wars. It is not an aberration, and the theme of seventeen, soon eighteen, counties locked in combat over four major competitions looks, for the immediate future, settled.

What have been the major characteristics of this era? First, and most important, a flattening evenness has spread itself over the seventeen counties. In the hundred years before 1963, five counties had dominated the Championship. Another six counties had managed, infrequently, to squeeze in: Gloucestershire four times in the age of Grace; Kent three times in the years just prior to the first war; Warwickshire twice, and Derbyshire, Glamorgan and Hampshire once each. That was a mere twelve titles in some ninety summers of endeavour – and six other counties had not even risen to that peak of achievement. Now the Championship is shared more equitably, and, although there are still a doleful trio awaiting that accolade, everyone has won something in the last twenty-nine seasons. To raid the scriptures, where once it had been a matter of 'Many are called, but few are chosen', now it is a case of 'In my father's house are many mansions'.

This is a consequence of vastly increased external funding, much easier transfer of players under relaxed registration procedures, and the effect of non-indigenous talent, as well as the realistic efforts of all counties to be more ruthlessly efficient and businesslike in their methods.

54

55

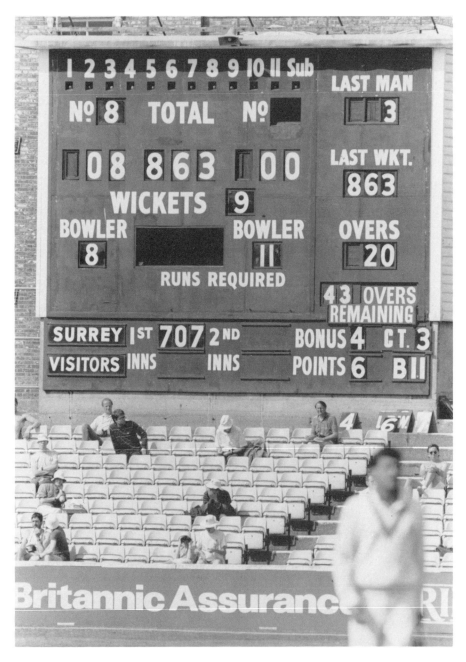

54 & 55 & 56 'Vastly increased external funding . . .' Essex versus Hampshire at Chelmsford in 1987 (top, previous page) – a sparse crowd but the boundary boards and the local radio van are evidence of advertising revenue and support throughout the county; plenty of media coverage as Essex win the 1983 County Championship (bottom, previous page); the Oval, 1990, with just a few people to see Lancashire making the highest county score this century – but with a pertinent reminder that it is the Britannic Assurance Championship (above).

There are strengths in this position, and significant ones. No one any more is a whipping-boy or a pushover. Every game in every competition begins, more or less, on equal terms – certainly compared with the 1920s or 1930s, when, for example, for Somerset to beat Yorkshire was tantamount to Halifax Town knocking Liverpool out of the FA Cup in the 1980s, or Poland overrunning the Soviet Union in the 1940s. It is a sign of health that all counties compete and aspire much more optimistically than they used to do, and that is good for the well-being of the county game. Such goodness may seem to put the lie to the assertion, urged in the previous chapter, that the county table itself needed dramatic reform. It must, superficially, appear contradictory to argue thus at one juncture, and then hail the apparent rejuvenation of the counties at another. It is, therefore, necessary to place this seeming egalitarianism in perspective.

Against the wider canvas of cricket, it is not more democratic, but, if anything, more oligarchic. First-class county cricket has indeed been restored and saved, but it has been the equivalent of the aristocracy obliterating its gradations, its dukedoms, its earldoms and so on, in favour of a uniform peerage. The County Championship remains an élite, admittedly a more regularized and close-knit élite, but nonetheless an élite. Moreover, transfusions of resources and personnel have been pumped so artificially into all the counties, especially into the ailing ones, that this élite is harder-shelled and more distanced from the pack than in the past. The retrospective argument for post-war reform was that, by adopting a more natural approach to revision, more organic and less synthetic changes could have been introduced in a more relaxed manner. To employ the language of social categories, English cricket now has a 'caste' system, when it might have benefited the more from a 'class' system, in the sense that the former is rigidly pre-ordained and the latter does admit of a certain elasticity.

Second, the very sameness of the counties may be, from one angle, disadvantageous. The niceties of residential qualification, always an uncomfortable topic, have been replaced with a much more

open contractual process, so that, even excepting overseas mercenaries, teams seem to be formed and re-formed, summer by summer, like seaside resort repertory companies recruiting a motley collection of actors for the season. In this the county scene begins to resemble the Football League landscape, which seasonally changes texture as colourfully as the English countryside.

It is true that, with trenchant exceptions such as Yorkshire, birth within a county has never been an overriding principle, and with, at first, only eight and, later, only seventeen counties involved, it would have been manifestly unfair if it had, for it would have been adversely restrictive of many aspirants. Residential qualification had been, in any event, a Victorian attempt to moderate the hyperactive mobility of some professionals, a search for some assurance that they would have to adhere to one place for some little while. Even Yorkshire have permitted nearly thirty aliens to sully their escutcheon, chiefly amateurs of the olden days, but also including, as perhaps the sweetest of his practical jokes, that clown prince of county cricket, Durham-born Cecil Parkin. Counties are now, however, even more cosmopolitan than in the past. In the trenches in 1914–18, legend has it that the private soldier whistled when he found a piece of meat in his stew, as warranty to its scarcity value. One might, for several counties, adopt a similar signalling system apropos of their representatives born within the county boundaries.

It is important, conversely, to refer to the rigidity of Yorkshire in this respect, as a stern warning to the conservative who prefers no change at all. Apart from tumbling from the dizzy and rarefied heights of permanent success, Yorkshire have found themselves locked in introverted and fratricidal dispute, with fine cricketers such as Wardle, Illingworth, Close and, most notably, Boycott overtly involved. In a long-running demonstration that the Yorkshireman's reputation for dour verbal restraint is falsely based, the club has pursued endless and incestuous wrangles which too closely resemble in tone the psychology associated with any closed system. These serve as a reminder that most human organizations find external influence and contribution warming and stimulating.

There is really no absolute virtue in parochial chauvinism and purity. At last Yorkshire realized that their inward-looking attitudes were stultifying and obtuse. After accepting Yorkshire breeding as well as birth in 1990, there came the astonishing announcement in 1991 that Yorkshire would fall in line with the other counties with regard to qualification. The Australian bowler, C. J. McDermott, became their first overseas signing. Somewhere between the past inelasticity of Yorkshire and the county with no players from the vicinity, one must seek some balance of local identification and entertainment value. Probably the most pragmatic definition would be that members and supporters want, first, an entertaining and successful team, and, second, if that team is larded with domestic talent, then so much the better.

Moving on, the county boundaries themselves require some exposition. Under the terms of the 1972 Local Government Act, implemented in 1974, the ancient county map was obliterated. The research of the Redcliffe-Maud Commission, which presaged that soulless reform, suggested that people can identify constructively and comprehendingly only with a relatively small locale, possibly no more than a few streets, the shape, that is, of a village or a small-sized township. Determinedly ignoring that wise counsel, the government opted for a major geo-political arrangement. The nation-state was divided into often large and often uncomfortable portions, to which the population still finds it difficult to relate.

At this point the conservatism of the cricket establishment stood it in good stead, and, very sensibly, it was resolved to cock a snook at this bureaucratic diktat and to stick to the grand old design; otherwise, it would have been goodbye Yorkshire and Gloucestershire, and hello West Yorkshire and Avon cricket clubs. The middlingly successful precedent of the London County cricket club, under the supervision of W. G. Grace, at the turn of the century, provided ambivalent evidence, but that of Middlesex, a club which had stayed in business since the demise of the county *per se* in 1888, was very positive.

The fact remains that over half the county teams no longer have their headquarters or principal ground in the county of their formation, and, what is more, several of those counties no longer exist. Yorkshire, Lancashire, Middlesex, Surrey, Gloucestershire, Glamorgan, Warwickshire, Worcestershire (now allied with Herefordshire) and Sussex (now split in twain) fall into this category. This is, in major part, a function of that connection of conurbation and county club emphasized earlier, for it was such heavily populated areas which found themselves detailed off for some of the severest changes. What, in effect, was being underscored was that the county banners were and are frequently no more than flags of convenience, something without much purchase or leverage in the political commonwealth.

The cricket authorities may have made the right decision about the new local government regime, since subjected to rearrangement by the Thatcher administration in the 1980s, but they may have done so for the wrong reason. They may have felt that change was unnecessary and that the county pattern was ideal. The reason why the parvenu network of municipal activity was wrong was not because it was unnecessary, but because it was the wrong sort of change. And it was the wrong sort of change chiefly because it was non-organic and had no linkage with any natural or logical processes of human existence in the United Kingdom – a lesson the controllers of county cricket might have applied to their own affairs.

That is, perhaps, only incidental to the main plot, whereby the counties grow more cosmopolitan and less easy to distinguish the one from the other. The levelling down of the playing methodology and, a tiny but picturesque illustration, the floppy sun hats and Flash Gordon helmets instead of county caps, add to the anonymity. Worried by poor Test results, the authorities attempt to preserve the nursery for first-class cricket, but, somehow, the entertainment quotient is partially lost. It is not only the actual play, but how the players present themselves in and around the game. That is not a matter of looking back in blimpish anger to a Corinthian myth, nor an anxiety about what players decide to do in their homes or hotel rooms. It is a plea for the spectator, rather than for those intimately caught up in the running of county cricket. For the normal watcher, the hallmark of cricket is theatre. When a player performs badly or behaves badly or is turned out badly, that sense of the stage lapses.

As well as the mundane uniformity of county standards, there is an internal variation, and that is the comparative collapse of cricket in the north of England. Although Derbyshire has contributed only one Championship title, the region, through what was once called 'the Northern Triumvirate' of Yorkshire, Lancashire and Nottinghamshire, has won sixty-five Championship titles, outright or jointly. But only two of them date since 1970. From the late 1930s, Nottinghamshire slumped badly and were bottom of the table a number of times, albeit rallying briskly in the last decade. Lancashire's thrilling run of one-day successes has been a trifle illusory, for the county has gone forty years without even a shared Championship title, while there is no further need to recite Yorkshire's grief.

The axis has altered. It is also true that the south-western clubs have not been dominant, while the midland counties have remained reasonably sound. A regional table for the last twenty-nine years since the 'hinge' year of 1963 shows this pattern. It draws on thirty Championship titles (one shared), the conventional touchstone of all-round consistency, over that period.

South-east	(Surrey, Kent, Middlesex, Sussex and Essex)	15
Midlands	(Leicestershire, Warwickshire, Northamptonshire and Worcestershire)	7
North	(Lancashire, Yorkshire, Derbyshire and Nottinghamshire	6
South-west	(Glamorgan, Somerset, Gloucestershire and Hampshire)	2

Of course, one explanation must lie in the general flattening of standards, so that the once strong northern combines are now as ordinary mortals. One must also take into account humdrum explanations such as poor man-management, internal squabbles and other instances of human failure, although it is a moot point sometimes whether these are the cause or the effect of impoverished results. All that said and agreed, however, the changed balance still requires some additional explanation.

Because of the way in which sport is a social and cultural manifestation of society as a whole, it would be surprising were not some aspects of the increasing North/South divide played out in professional games and other recreations. To begin with, there is the sordid matter of money. The rich industrial counties could at one time recruit and command players with ease. In the current climate, and although, for example, Lancashire has the largest county membership, that kind of monetary dominance no longer automatically prevails, and, if anything, the economic boot is on the other foot. For example, Essex, nearly bankrupt at the start of this modern era, is now perhaps the best-balanced club financially, and it draws more of its income from subscriptions and gate-money than the other counties.

The decline and stagnation of northern industry, unlike the hothouse infusion of the London regional economy, leaves its dual mark on the fall and rise of cricket in those areas. Cricket is not alone. The robotic efficacy of Liverpool and the occasional vivid flourishes of Everton and Manchester United (like Lancashire, a cup-winning side of late, with no League Championship between 1967–91) has masked the collapse of association football in the north. Now there are, in 1991–92, only eight northern teams in the proud élite of a twenty-two-strong first division; while nine might be broadly defined as hailing from the south-eastern quadrant, including no less than seven from London itself, an unheard of capital largesse. Conversely, fourteen of the twenty-three fourth division clubs are from the north, and, languishing there and in the other two divisions, are northern teams of past eminence, household names such as Blackpool, Burnley, Bolton Wanderers, Preston North End, Sunderland, Blackburn Rovers, Newcastle United, Stoke City, Derby County and Middlesbrough – all of whom would, not many years ago, have blanched at the thought not only of their deposition but of the elevation of such clubs as Norwich City and Wimbledon to the first division.

So there is something of a pattern; not so much trade following the flag as the cultural flag of sport – and other forms of art and entertainment – in pursuit of trade, especially as business sponsorship persists in influencing the action so tellingly. The collapse of manufacturing industry, only partially ameliorated by diversification into light industry and the rather twee erection of a heritage-led tourist trade, continues. It leaves grave scars, both human and physical, on the landscape of the north. The other peripheries suffer likewise. This may also help to account for Gloucestershire's floundering and the serious trouble in which Glamorgan finds itself.

The Channel Tunnel, the consolidation of European linkages in 1992, and, in general, the construction of a massive bureaucracy and commercial entity in north-west Europe, mean that the cauldron of the south-east will continue to bubble and boil. Through British history, until the Industrial Revolution, the area south of a line from the Wash to Bristol was paramount: the administration; the trade; the very language and culture – including cricket – emanated therefrom. The restructure of manufacture and transportation in the late 18th and 19th centuries altered the focus, making international centres of Liverpool, Manchester, Leeds and Birmingham, just at the point county cricket was coming to the fore. Now the nation reverts to type, and the south-east reassumes what seems to be its natural hegemony in the post-industrial era. Perhaps in a thousand years historians will view the Industrial Revolution, with its associations with the north, as an aberration, no more than a minor dislocation of the normal order.

It is not a total explanation. Few historical statements are. York was not unknown and uninfluential in medieval times, while Derbyshire

won the Refuge Assurance League in 1990. These are organic matters, and, therefore, concerned with relativities, not absolutes. Still, this analysis offers the most realistic interpretation of the modern shape of county cricket: an unrelieved sameness, modified by a slight swing towards the south-east and away from the north.

Some saw the giddy run-riot of 1990 as a signal of basic change. The 428 centuries scored surpassed the previous best of 414 in 1928, while twenty-nine were scores of 200 or more, with three triple centuries. Reflection might suggest that what we enjoyed was no more than an exchange of mediocrity. There was a dry summer, a much less blatantly seamed ball, and pitches, with clubs facing punitive losses of points for shortcomings, more durable than the M1. Such conditions presented batsmen with easy pickings, where, in previous seasons, ordinary bowlers had performed similar miracles in opposite circumstances. The season of 1991 was more normal, with a well-fought County Championship, still split between three and four-day games. But the tempo continued to seem dull over the opening days, with bogus declarations establishing a species of one-day cricket aimed at a result on the final day.

There is still no rational balance, let alone a noticeable measure of improvement. Perhaps the cricket establishment should begin with the premise that, in an evenly matched three-day game, one might hope to see, on average, 110 or 120 overs bowled, some 400 runs scored, and 12 or 13 wickets fall. Natural, uncovered wickets, hailing the return of many more spin bowlers, might help do the trick. As it is, the county clubs soldier on, that sense of uniformity dominant.

The cricket establishment is fortunate that the current county structure is underpinned by large funds, even if most do not derive directly from county cricket. It relieves them from pressure, and, however rigid and inward-looking they might be, there is little likelihood of major change. Had the counties to rely on subscriptions and gate-money, none would survive at their present rate of expenditure. It has a decided element of the illogical, even of the absurd, about it, but it is undeniably solid.

Thus the continuity is preserved. A group of county clubs controls the fulcrum of the English first-class game. Now they provide the silent classrooms for those chosen for the ceaseless round of international cricket. Once again, the county system has found some reason and some resource for survival.

One cannot ignore the historical character of the counties, which has been stored up simply by their long survival. The counter-argument to reform is the peril of throwing out the baby of continuing county cricket with the bath water of its present inelastic context. The sheer symbolism of the county names and badges, and the profound allegiance paid them, is not easily dismissed: that is why the alternative programme, diffidently proposed in the preceding chapter, stopped short of brass-faced rationality, and tried to work with the grain of the county system.

The affection for a particular county has often, in the past, been linked with a sense of that county's 'character', a thumb-print or identikit of these seventeen great clubs. The cricket press and literature contributed to this harmless and frequently mythical gallery of portraits, which probably had much to do with winning and being branded as 'dour', or losing and being labelled as 'sporting'.

Whatever the truth of this hypothesis in the past, the ironing out of the major economic and allied discrepancies among counties has all but put paid to any lingering vestiges of distinctive character. In any event, the ubiquitous culture of the motorway and the television and the supermarket has destroyed much of the fragmentation, charming and otherwise, of British society. It is evident that this 'nationalization' of British life has wiped out almost all of that which, were it genuine or fictional, passed for local and regional habits and manners. In so doing, it has contributed to the apparent sameness, even the anonymity, of county cricket.

That said, each of the seventeen counties does have its separate history, and each has exulted or wept over its separate ups and downs, and has produced its crop, greater or smaller, of famous players. Nonetheless, as we turn, in Part Two, to

57 'A more authentic pressure . . .' Pressure must have been placed on a talented wicket-keeper such as Herbert Strudwick, of Surrey and England, struggling to make ends meet on paltry wages, compared with the large sums earned by some of today's players.

an individual appraisal of each of the counties, the parallels will be as telling as the differences.

And there is one ever-present similarity across the counties and across the ages, probably as true in the fledgeling days of county cricket as in these troubled, selfish and neurotic times. When all the complaints have been laid at the door of county cricket, the abiding and compensating truth remains – it is impossible to find a saner or more relaxing diversion from the rigours of life than an hour or two at a county cricket match.

That cheery note perhaps needs some elaboration. Cricket cannot avoid the influences of the culture in which it is played and offered to the public. The 1980s was the age of – in Orwellian Newspeak – 'the enterprise culture', an euphemism for the relentless pursuit of individual materialist gain, and devil take the hindmost. As the glittering prizes grow for cricketers, so, we are told, do the pressures – although one might have

felt that a more authentic pressure was that on Herbert Strudwick, keeping wicket with broken fingers in order to gather a few shillings for his modest subsistence. Raucous argument, dissent, discourtesy, dangerous bowling and crowd incidents, some of a racial nature, have been an aspect of this more intense ambience.

These have been dark years, with the classic right-wing paradox rampant: harsh central controls and severe unfreedoms to guarantee brutal and egoistical scope for undiluted market forces. It is true that county cricket has frequently been identified with conservatism, and no one would pretend that it is a bastion of radical progressivism. However, the Victorian epoch, which ushered in the county cricket structure we have

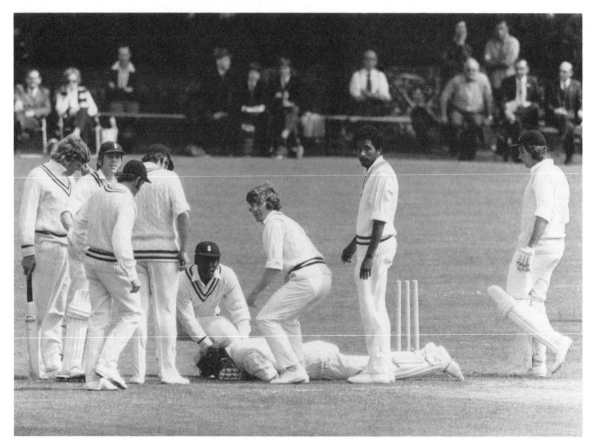

58 'This more intense ambience . . .' Colin Cowdrey struck by Andy Roberts, of Hampshire and West Indies, during the Hampshire v. Kent match at Basingstoke, 1974.

59 'Durham joining the fray . . .' in 1992, under the direction of Geoff Cook,
who for several years had captained Northamptonshire.

inherited, was an age which, at least, sought balance. Paternalist and patronizing it may have been, but there was an attempt to harmonize civic duty and responsibility with the commercial motif, and it was upon that platform that a fairer and more democratic Britain was gradually being erected.

Sadly, there is no permanence in human affairs: ground has been lost and the moral values of the nation are afflicted both politically and socially. Cricket frays a little at the edges as a result. But surely it will endure. The hope must be that soon more rational and compassionate views will prevail, and that first-class cricket will re-discover all of its wholesome unpretentiousness.

Of course, county cricket is but a small aspect on a mighty landscape, more affected by than affecting. But all things are part of the whole pattern, and cricket is no bad symbol – as it has been in previous sloughs of woe – of decent and simple pleasure in collectivity.

That is why county cricket is worth a visit: it speaks to us of past sensibilities; it is a bolt-hole during a cruel present; and it is a tiny part of the dream of a brighter future. Perhaps Durham joining the fray and Yorkshire's acceptance of the norm are apt and happy notes on which to end this 200-year survey.

60 'A bolt-hole during a cruel present . . .'

PART TWO

The Counties

ONE

Derbyshire

Nothing illustrates better the murky dimness of county cricket's early history than Derbyshire's formative years. At least it is agreed that the county club was formed in 1870. A number of useful club sides already existed, among them Ilkeston, Brimington, Staveley, a Chatsworth estate side, and – perhaps the most influential – the South Derbyshire club, based at Chaddesden. It was an old club cricketer, Walter Boden, who convened a meeting in the November of 1870, following some years of desultory agitation throughout the Peak county about the desirability of emulating its larger neighbours in this regard. It was resolved 'that a cricket club be formed representing the whole strength of the county, to be called the Derbyshire County Club', and the ground, recently opened at Derby racecourse, was available as a venue.

The county began in spectacular manner, hustling out Lancashire for 25 – still that county's lowest-ever score – in its début match in the summer of 1871, and winning comfortably by an innings. It is after that that the outlines of the plot grow misty, for it is difficult to conclude what exact status Derbyshire enjoyed. Older authorities are a trifle dismissive or, at best, vague. 'They do not seem', wrote H. S. Altham, doyen of the old school of cricket historians, 'to have reached first-class status for good until 1894.' A sympathetic chronicler in Ranjitsinhji's famous *Jubilee Book* mentioned 'the deposition of the county from first-class rank' and spoke of 1894, 'the official recognition that year of the county being promoted to first-class rank invested the matches with keen interest'. W. G. Grace, in his equally celebrated volume, *Cricket*, declines to include Derbyshire at all in the reckoning.

The alternative view is that Derbyshire were as large as life among the top company in their initial years, making the conventional 'octarchy' something of a 'nonarchy'. The most optimistic case, presented by Roy Webber in his invaluable and detailed *County Cricket Championship*, proposes not only that Derbyshire took part from 1873, the first year in which the rules of qualification applied, but that they were champions in 1874. 'It has been decided officially for many years,' he claims, 'that Derbyshire were champions.' He also quotes them as second in 1877. *Wisden* offers the 1874 honour to Gloucestershire, but it does include Derbyshire for these years in its summary of match results. But then *Wisden* also includes Hampshire for over a score of seasons around this era – and no one appears to allocate a placement to that county in any of the Championship tables.

It is most confusing. Apart from the variations over deciding the title, the complicating factor was what was meant by a first-class county match. It seems to have been the case that a first-class county match was not necessarily included by everyone in the calculations for the Championship; and in those years Derbyshire did have a very thin set of fixtures.

What is beyond argument is that, by the mid-1880s, Derbyshire, having lost key players, had collapsed woefully. In seasons 1880 to 1887, they lost forty-nine matches out of sixty-three played, including all ten fixtures in 1884 and all six in 1887. With only a handful of counties willing to continue fixtures and with the press fussing noisily about this decline, Derbyshire dropped out of the running.

Stalwart friends rallied to save the club from the insolvency that menaced as support fell; and, as Derby County football club was formed and played close by, with consequent ground improvements, the county were well prepared for first-class status in 1894, along with other new boys.

In that last quarter of a century, Derbyshire were well served by a native-born quick bowler, William Mycroft, a wholesome and destructive

61 William Mycroft, the Derbyshire bowler
of late Victorian times.

also fired for intemperate behaviour – were the tempestuous attackers, and quite successful they were too; but, unluckily, the batting was weaker than in the past. The West Indian, C. A. Ollivierre, was the most colourful of the batsmen, though far from consistent. These three starred in an epic contest, when, faced with an Essex total of 597 at Chesterfield in 1904, Ollivierre's dashing 229 and then 92 not out, following Warren and Bestwick's routing of Essex in their second innings for 97, led to a 9-wickets win.

Derbyshire exemplify the non-rural factor in county cricket. It is a hybrid county. The rugged attractions and agrarian activity of its northern sector vie with the industrial south and east, with

62 William Bestwick,
the Derbyshire fast bowler before and
after the First World War

attacker; the fine all-rounder, George Davidson; and wicket-keeper-batsman William Storer. During the interregnum, the demon Spofforth, the deadly Australian fast bowler, who married a local girl, played some eighteen games for Derbyshire, and helped to revitalize their ailing ways.

Although Derbyshire started off well enough for a couple of seasons, they lapsed later, and for many years, until the late 1920s, they languished too near the bottom of the table. William Bestwick – sacked for bawling at team-mates, yet reinstated ten years on – and Arnold Warren –

coal mining the primary employer then, and the source of bowlers such as Mycroft and Bestwick. Although the pastoralist might have expected to discover the cricket among the dales and rivulets of the north, in fact, it was Derby, to the south, and the attendant mining communities, that supported the development of the county club.

Thus Derbyshire turned their sturdy face not so much to the hills and rivers of Yorkshire, but to the coal-fields of Nottinghamshire. They relied, in their beginnings, not on the expansive textile trades of Yorkshire and Lancashire, but on the harder graft of the pits; more D. H. Lawrence, that is, than J. B. Priestley. While the outlying grounds of Chesterfield or Buxton are prepossessing, the Derby headquarters did not belie this rugged nature. It was not and is not a pretty ground. It is workmanlike, a little bleak and sometimes wind-swept. Horse-racing is no longer available, and, since the early days, the playing area has been shifted northwards. The ground was modelled after the fashion of urban utility, with Derby providing the necessary rail link from London.

The least well supported of all the counties, in terms of membership, Derbyshire loyalists would say that their heroes have to be doubly heroic to claim the selectorial attention lavished on the stars of more fashionable clubs. In *Beyond the Fringe*, Alan Bennett and Jonathan Miller exchanged gloomy comparisons about the disbenefits of being working-class or Jewish. Then they imagined the burden of those both working-class *and* Jewish. 'There is always', they dolefully concluded, 'someone worse off than yourself'. Derbyshire found themselves in that slough of despond: both impoverished *and* northern – there could, in the eyes of Test selectors, be no one worse off. In part, it was to do with what Bestwick and Warren illustrated, that is, a mien which erred on the side of uncouth robustness. In part, it was the old story of the difficulty of shining in an anxious and struggling team.

Certainly, the county's achievements have been humble and earnest, not exhilarating, and yet, in the dozen or so summers prior to the Second World War, when northern cricket was generally resurgent, Derbyshire were carried along on that tide of excellence. In those years when Yorkshire dominance was well-nigh absolute and Lancashire reached their zenith, Derbyshire, too, demonstrating that same brand of no-nonsense severity, accomplished much for so small a club. From 1927 Derbyshire were never out of the top ten, and they fought their way into the top six in seven of those seasons, being second in 1935 and third in 1937.

Those brave years sandwiched 1936 when Derbyshire assumed the mantle for, thus far, the only time. They did so with a display of highly competent cricket which was most creditable, not only in itself, but because it represented only the second time, if *Wisden*'s authority be accepted, that any outsider had usurped the sanctum of the holy octet.

The character of the team, and the style of its victory, were not those normally associated with the vivid hues of revolutionary fervour. If it was an historic occasion, it was one wrought by dint of solemn toil. And yet, in another sense, the perpetrators of this outrage on the cricketing aristocracy stood, in nature, four-square with their native habitat and that of their club. Moreover, their success was a rightful index of what passed for cricketing attainment in that watchful age.

To that end, the team was very similar in construction to those of its successful northern neighbours at Old Trafford and Headingley. It was a side of proficient and experienced professionals, with just one amateur, Arthur Richardson, to offer a middle-class lead. Derbyshire have been as proligate with the captaincy as their medium-fast bowlers have been miserly with loose deliveries. Over thirty have shared this presumably unenviable duty, but A. W. Richardson did inherit a reasonably settled situation from G. R. Jackson, then the county's longest-serving skipper, and then he himself held the office for six seasons, delivering the title in his final year.

As one often finds with winning teams, this one remained more or less unchanged. Apart from George Pope, it was fairly free from injury, and the temptation to placate amateurs with occasional inclusion was resisted. The batting was

63 Derbyshire – the 1936 champions. Arthur Richardson, the captain,
is seated in pads with Tommy Mitchell to his left. Bill Copson is standing behind,
third from the left in the picture.

stout and gritty, with Denis Smith, Derbyshire's only batsman to pass 20,000 runs in aggregate, T. S. Worthington and A. E. Alderman preparing the ground. Along with the gifted all-rounder, Leslie Townsend, these were the ones to score above the statutory mark of 1000 runs. They were loaned assistance by Charlie Elliott, near the beginning, and by Harry Storer, in the autumn, of their respective careers.

Yet it was batting of solidarity rather than brilliance, and much depended on the bowling. From the coal-fields came Bill Copson, mighty of heart, to take 153 wickets at an average of 12 or so, while the bespectacled Tommy Mitchell, that volatile leg-spinner, took 121 wickets and Alf Pope weighed in, lucklessly, with 99. Townsend and Worthington also took wickets. With Harry

Elliott the safest of wicket-keepers (he abstemiously permitted not one bye in twenty-five completed innings in 1936) and with the collective fielding sound and hostile, opponents were quickly dismissed. All this was accomplished despite the fact that George Pope, potentially their leading all-rounder, did not play, because of cartilage damage, beyond May.

This haste of dismissal was vital in a rainy summer. Derbyshire won thirteen matches and drew eleven, while Yorkshire won ten and drew eighteen. It was a singular performance.

After the war Derbyshire sustained this same tradition, if not quite the same success, at least with some consistency. They remained in the top half of the table, save for a handful of years, until the early 1960s, sustained in that upper echelon by a remarkable heritage of strong pace bowling. Copson and George Pope continued, to be replaced, in turn, by Cliff Gladwin and then Leslie Jackson, sons of the pits and Derbyshire's chief wicket-takers. Charlie Elliott, in company with the Yorkshireman, Arnold Hamer, and A. C. Revill, were the leading batsmen, while the wicket-keeper, G. O. Dawkes, played in 283 consecutive matches, a formidable record. Dusty Rhodes was the post-war leg-spinner, and then his son, Harold Rhodes, although beset by problems with his action, maintained Derbyshire's reputation for penetrating fast bowling. During the 1950s the captaincy was dashingly undertaken by two university skippers and alumni of Repton, Derbyshire's nearest equivalent to an Etonian nursery, G. L. Willatt, the Cambridge left-hander, and Donald Carr, the stylish Oxonian, nonpareil close fielder and destined to be a famous cricket administrator.

Since then, and for some twenty-five years, Derbyshire have languished a little, a place in the top six three times representing their nearest acquaintance with the swells. At times the saga of captaincy resembled a Byzantine political maze, although latterly, with Kim Barnett, there has been some resolution of the situation. Veteran importations – John Hampshire and Phil Sharpe from Yorkshire, J. B. Bolus also from Yorkshire but arriving via Nottinghamshire, Barry Wood from Lancashire, and David Steele from Northamptonshire – have come and gone, while overseas succour, from the likes of the South African, Eddie Barlow, and the world-class fast bowler, Michael Holding, has been sought. Sometimes these shared in the lottery of the captaincy. The New Zealand opener, John Wright, gave faithful service, with 1000 runs in each of six seasons, and so did South Africa's P. N. Kirsten.

Of the homespun products, D. C. Morgan, with nearly 18,000 runs for the county, P. J. K. Gibbs (now a playwright), Alan Hill and John Morris have been prominent in the batting, while Morgan, with most catches (563) and with over 1200 wickets, is, on figures alone, Derbyshire's leading all-rounder. The three bowlers who caught the eye over these years were Mike

Hendrick, who won thirty England caps, the pacy Alan Ward, and Geoff Miller, with his thoughtful off-spin (an unusual Derbyshire element).

However, it is the wicket-keeper, Bob Taylor, who must take pride of place in the modern era. With 1304 victims for the county, and 1649 in all first-class cricket, he has been Derbyshire's most sterling wicket-keeper and possibly their most talented player ever. Miller's thirty-four caps fall a poor second to Taylor's fifty-seven Test appearances, easily a Derbyshire record; even so, he was unfortunate to have contemporaries who were judged, not always accurately, to be his superior as a batsman. Technically, he was near enough immaculate, and a faultless exponent of that intensely concentrated art-form. Personally, his patience and good cheer complemented that expertise with a sportsmanship beyond reproach.

Despite these offerings, Derbyshire have never adapted to the whirligig of two, three and then four competitions, and, administratively and professionally, they have given off an air of unease and restlessness. They have just once won the Sunday League, and that was in 1990, when their West Indian fast bowler, Ian Bishop, also topped the first-class averages. His partner was Devon Malcolm, the England bowler of West Indian origin.

They have never won the Benson and Hedges Cup, being comfortably beaten in 1978 by Kent and in 1988 by Hampshire. Yorkshire defeated them in the Gillette Cup in 1969 by the wide margin of 69 runs, but, in 1981, when the sun shone late and brightly after a damp early summer, Derbyshire finally landed a pot.

They won the first NatWest Trophy final, the successor to the Gillette prize. Having beaten Essex in the semi-final at Derby by a narrow squeak off the ultimate ball, Derbyshire now demonstrated this Pearl White technique at Lord's against Northamptonshire. Derbyshire's opponents made a promising start, their captain, Geoff Cook, scoring a century, but good out-cricket throttled back the midland challenge to 235, no mean score, but less than had seemed likely. Derbyshire's response was sure, but slow, and they found themselves requiring 38 runs in

4.4 overs. After breathtaking alarums and excursions, they needed one run off the last ball to tie, and, on the basis of fewest wickets lost, win. Rather as Cliff Gladwin did with his famous legbye off the last ball of the Durban Test in 1949, Tunnicliffe made contact with his pad. In a scramble not unlike the pellmell antics of some Regency cricket, Miller dived to make good his ground, as fielders converged and the wicket was broken: Miller survived and Derbyshire had won.

One Championship: two one-day titles. It is not an epic record. In fact, it is, by that criterion, almost the worst of all the counties. Still, Derbyshire has its tale to tell, and perhaps the most abiding convention has been that worthy lineage of fast or medium-fast bowlers, resolute, conscientious and wryly enduring. As with the similar Nottinghamshire breed, several came, with a literary trait bordering on cliché, from or around the collieries. Whether they temperamentally espoused the masculine virtue of the coal industry, or whether their character was moulded by that tough apprenticeship, is a moot point.

Under Kim Barnett, a sparkling bat and fielder, Derbyshire have seemed more determined and settled of late. Sixty years on, they must feel it is high time for another sequence of strong and improved results such as pleased their supporters, and others, in the years before the Second World War. In 1991 they were third, their batting elegantly strengthened by India's captain, Mohammed Azharuddin.

The self-indulgence of selecting a county's best-ever XI does have the analytical advantage of offering a chance to compare and contrast its gallery of notables. One must proceed with caution. Founded simply on appearances for Derby-

64 Bob Taylor

65 Kim Barnett

shire, the bowling would be opened by Spofforth and Holding, with the sleekly gifted Indian, Venkataraghavan, to share the changes with Eddie Barlow. This is more of an assessment of those whose first and lasting home was in the Peak county, and, even then, one pauses over Wright and Kirsten, who, while hailing from alien climes, played a substantial amount of their cricket with Derbyshire, and are the only two batsmen to have an average of over 40 in matches for the county.

The batting would have to be shaped around the efficiency of the 1930s, around the talented left-hander, Denis Smith, with his thirty centuries for the club. His contemporary, A. E. Alderman, would probably join him. From a later era, Alan Hill and Arnold Hamer might be in contention, for they both played with straightforward consistency, being two of only a few – Smith, Storer and Barnett are others – to achieve an average of 30 or more.

What Derbyshire, true to their tradition of humble economy, have in profusion is durable all-rounders. George Davidson achieved the double in 1895, the third player after W. G. Grace and Wilfred Flowers of Nottinghamshire to do so. L. F. Townsend accomplished the feat four times, and, with over 17,000 runs and nearly 1000 wickets, must join the contest. However, the tall, balding George Pope, who did the double twice and played for England once, is often regarded as Derbyshire's premier all-rounder, despite his loss of six war-time seasons at the peak of his career. We have already noted D. C. Morgan, a southern exile in Derbyshire's line-up, as an all-rounder of considerable merit, while Stan Worthington, 17,000 runs and a host of wickets, bears consideration.

From a plethora of naggingly accurate fast bowlers, the sheer figures of Les Jackson (1670 wickets for the county) and Cliff Gladwin (1536) urge their dual case, with Bestwick and the ginger-headed Copson not far behind. Edwin Smith, a doughty contributor over twenty post-war seasons, and Geoff Miller are the only off-spinners of note, and, compared with the other northern counties, the absence of left-hand slow bowlers is astounding. Leg-spinners are more abundant, with Tommy Mitchell (one of cricket's funsters, if reputed to be temperamentally suspect – a _canard_ aimed at many of his kind – at the highest level) the pick of the bunch. Another ex-miner, Mitchell's leg-breaks and googlies brought him, and Derbyshire, 1417 wickets at an average of 20, a fruitful harvest for a wrist-spinner.

Bob Taylor, who has taken more wickets behind the stumps (1473 caught, 176 stumped) than anyone else ever in first-class cricket, obviously must keep wicket, Dawkes and Elliott notwithstanding. D. B. Carr, against stern competition from Guy Willatt and A. W. Richardson, should be captain, his flair as a leader combining well with his cavalier prowess as a cricketer.

Thus a solid-looking side emerges of Denis Smith, A. E. Alderman, Stan Worthington, Donald Carr, Leslie Townsend, George Pope, Geoff Miller, Cliff Gladwin, Les Jackson, Bob Taylor and Tommy Mitchell. With a wide range of bowling and some steady batting, it is a side which, for all Derbyshire's past disappointments, might surprise some more exalted teams.

TWO

Essex

The negative elements in the early history of county cricket are clearly demonstrated by the efforts of Essex to establish a first-class club. Although cricketing activity was for many years rife in the county, it lacked a major conurbation – a Birmingham or a Manchester, even a Taunton or a Canterbury – around which the shire could be rallied. This continued to be a perennial problem, and Essex have never been as closely identified with one ground as, say, Gloucestershire or Worcestershire have. There are benefits: Essex have been keen, or at least have found it desirable, to spread their favours around the several townships of the county. By the mid-19th century, a railway line did straggle out of London into Essex, petering out near the Suffolk border, and, as sometimes happened with country towns fearful of the fiery horse, tending to near-miss the leading settlements.

Lack of urbanization and communication bedevilled Essex, although *Wisden* claims for them the earliest organization of the seventeen first-class clubs, and they are the only survivor from the 18th-century. This is a trifle specious. As elsewhere, there was some confusion with the clubs, with, for instance, the Hornchurch club sometimes described as Essex in the press. The amateur aspect was strong, and, along with other shires, it was the Gentlemen of Essex who were occasionally convened to do battle. In the mid-1860s the Colchester club ambitiously obtained a lease on 'a large and nearby level field' with the purpose of creating a county club, but this venture was short-lived.

Ten years later, in 1876, a meeting was called at the Shire Hall, Chelmsford 'to consider the desirability of forming a county club', and a ground was rented from the Countess of Tasker at Brentwood, a town part way between Romford and Chelmsford. That summer the first county game – a win over Suffolk – took place. The chief protagonist was James Round, lawyer, parliamentarian and perhaps the most capable amateur wicket-keeper of his day. Professional bowlers – notably Henry Pickett and Frank Silcock – were imported, and Essex did passing well.

However, support was patchy, and the Brentwood ground, while picturesque, was difficult of access. A move was planned to Leyton in 1886, where the Lyttelton ground was purchased for £12,000. Matches in Leyton, with its monumental pavilion, had proved more popular than those at Brentwood, for, of course, it was basically a part of east London, close to the well-populated district of Stratford, and with the Midland Road station soon to be opened on the London to Southend line as an improvement to existing rail links. It was, in essence, an attempt to procure for the east of the capital what the Oval provided for the south. Backs were turned on the bleaker, emptier reaches of Essex, and, according to O. R. Borradaile, secretary for thirty years from 1891, 'County cricket may be said to have started from that date'.

The major presence in these important developments was C. E. Green of Uppingham, Cambridge and Middlesex, a zestful all-round sportsman and hunter. Born in Walthamstow, and returning to the county of his birth in 1882, he captained Essex from 1883 to 1888 and remained a forceful and occasionally explosive eminence for many years. It was he who drove Essex inward to seek crowds and increased members at Leyton, and who then worked hard to achieve first-class status for Essex. With the stylish A. P. Lucas; that expert professional bowler, Walter Mead; and Charles Kortright (said by some assessors, by no means naïve judges, to be the fastest bowler ever) in the Essex ranks, this was a rational aim. In 1894, with Derbyshire, Leicestershire and Warwickshire, the county was granted first-class status – and lost its opening

66 Charles Kortright in the 1880s

first-class game to Leicestershire by 68 runs. Indeed, 1894 proved a poor summer, and, in 1895, when MCC eventually agreed to arrange the Championship for the now fourteen counties, Essex were hard pressed to negotiate the necessary sixteen fixtures. Nonetheless, they did reasonably well, and finished ninth.

During this time, the events on the field were less chequered than those in the counting-house. Like many counties, Essex suffered grievously in financial terms, with debts rising and with the membership ever insufficient. Wealthy patrons, including C. E. Green and C. M. Tebbutt, both old boys of Middlesex, were constantly dipping into their own wallets to effect temporary respite, and, in 1894, the club came perilously close to being wound up, when the bank refused to advance more money.

Thus the tale continued, the exploits of Essex as likely to be recorded in the financial as in the sporting prints. A creditable third in 1897, under the steadying lead of Hugh Owen, proved to be Essex's best performance until 1978, for, over that lengthy phase, the county reached the top five on only half a dozen other occasions. It was not spellbinding stuff, although, in fairness, Essex only touched the bottom rungs of the ladder in a dozen seasons. For the rest, they persisted in the relative and decent anonymity of mid-table.

An intriguing example of this interplay of fiscal and sporting instability occurred in the years before the First World War. The father of J. W. H. T. Douglas had dedicated his son to cricket in much the same way that the Earl of Chatham had pledged the Younger Pitt to politics. It is reputed that he offered to haul Essex out of one of its monetary scrapes in exchange for the captaincy for his son. This loftier version of the child taking his bat in if given out lbw did not (as, alas, is often the real-life case) end in tears after the fashion of a moral parable. Johnny Douglas, for some years an ordinary all-rounder, blossomed as captain, and, holding the post until 1928, served longer than all but the legendary generals such as W. G. Grace and Lord Hawke. He also captained England on many occasions.

Uncompromising, bullishly fit, as dogged in

67 J. W. H. T. Douglas

defence as he was invigorating in pacy attack, J. W. H. T. Douglas held the county together before and after the First World War. The Leyton pitch had developed an immaculate placidity; the Essex bowling, apart from Douglas, and, on occasion, George Louden, was fragile; and the fielding, even by the lower criterion that existed then, was over-friendly. On the other hand, the batting was invariably strong. F. L. Fane, who captained England as a deputy on the 1907–08 tour of Australia, was an attractive batsman in the Edwardian years, and, over this middle period of Essex history, the amateur, C. P. McGahey, and the professionals, H. A. Carpenter and C. A. G. Russell, were chief contributors. The most distinctive influence, however, was that of Percy Perrin, a heavy but creative front-foot bat, for years holder of the Essex record aggregate of runs and whose highest score – an expansive, undefeated 343 against Derbyshire – included the highest number of boundaries ever hit in an innings, a veritable avalanche of sixty-eight. Strangely for so venturesome and destructive an attacker, his fielding was pitiful and cumbersome, a barrier to international honours; he was thus the personification of Essex's strength and weakness.

As often seems to happen with a long incumbency, Johnny Douglas parted company with Essex on a sour, disgruntled note, and, sadly, his father and he were drowned at sea in 1930. Just as Douglas had bestrode the first war, Tom Pearce, a wise and unruffled skipper, took charge for much of the 1930s and in the first seasons after the second war. Like Green and Douglas before him, he was an administrator-captain, hugely involved in all the affairs of the county.

The immediate pre-war summers were the happiest in the county's story, until, that is, the triumphs of the last ten years or so, and they were fourth in both 1933 and 1939. At last the bowling enjoyed parity with the ever-dependable batting, with Jack O'Connor in handsome trim. Sixteen times to 1000 runs in a season, including four times beyond the 2000 mark, he stands third, behind Percy Perrin and Keith Fletcher, in Essex's personal aggregates. His seventy-one centuries constitute an Essex record. The quick bowling

68 Percy Perrin

evoked memories of Kortright. H. D. Read and J. W. A. Stephenson, albeit in dramatically brief careers, were very fast, while the tall and lithe Ken Farnes emerged as England's attacking spearhead in the late 1930s, his fruitful career tragically ending during RAF service in the Second World War. He took 367 wickets in only seventy-nine county matches. The cricketing mantle of Johnny Douglas fell on Maurice Nichols, and with some effect. A determined and conscientious fast-medium bowler and left-handed bat of substantial utility, he proved to be one of the most capable all-rounders produced by county cricket. He achieved the double eight times in eleven years, and he also won fourteen England caps. With Tom Wade the long-serving wicket-keeper, Essex hereabouts were as good as most.

However, money pressures did not lessen, and, because of these stresses, the Leyton ground was abandoned in 1933, and Essex, like the Anglo-Saxon monarchs who had once ruled over that shire, began a nomadic existence, shifting camp from place to place, hopeful of finding succour and hospitality in each. Southend and Colchester had hosted cricket weeks from before the First World War, while Clacton and Chelmsford, where the county set up an office, had been more recently added. There was now a return to Brentwood, and Ilford and Westcliff joined the whistle-stop touring itinerary. Despite the self-evident disbenefits *vis-à-vis* practice and organizational facilities, this circus approach did carry first-class cricket to different parts of the county, and a little more support was engendered.

Initially, Essex's post-war record was not so promising, although the Smith cousins, Ray and Peter, continued that all-round vein that has been so much a part of Essex cricket, while Dodds and Avery settled into useful roles high in the order. The captaincy passed, first, to Douglas Insole, a tenacious, productive bat and splendid leader; and, second, to Trevor Bailey.

Trevor Bailey had already inherited the secretaryship and the stock role of Essex all-rounder. He developed from what had been termed 'a rather brittle' fast bowler into a seam bowler of immense control and thoughtfulness. To this he added a watchful defensiveness which brought a touch of folk-lore to his batting. Like Insole, he was an athletic fielder, and, in all these tasks, he was as hungrily required by his country as by his county. His sixty-one caps were a county record, but recently overtaken by Gooch. He bids fair to being judged the greatest English amateur all-rounder, apart from W. G. Grace, although his last handful of seasons followed the demise of the old division of players and gentlemen. He completed the double in eight seasons, all first-class play considered, and, apart from Grace, he is the only amateur to figure in that extremely short and hallowed roster of the nine cricketers to have taken more than 2000 wickets and scored more than 20,000 runs.

Through these years there were signs of hope, as Essex moved into the higher half of the table, but the 1960s were, on the whole, less pleasing in terms of results. Good players were around – another fine all-rounder in Barry Knight; the gifted leg-spinner, Robin Hobbs; a most competent wicket-keeper, Brian Taylor; Gordon Barker, a free-scoring batsman with over 20,000 runs for the county – but, thus far, the mixture had not gelled. Brian Taylor captained a largely untried, young side for a number of seasons, insisting on eager fielding, if with an unsophisticated stance on tactics, and then Keith Fletcher assumed the reins. Ultimately, the players who had been introduced in the late 1960s and early 1970s evolved into a distinguished combine. Several times they came near to success in both championship and one-day cricket, and commentators mused that they lacked, after a hundred years of comparative failure, the necessary assurance. Suddenly, in 1979, two trophies were won, and, over the following years, nine more were added, made up of five Championships (1979, 1983, 1984, 1986 and 1991), three Sunday League titles (1981, 1984 and 1985) and three Cups (1979, 1985 and 1989).

Over this intense phase, and in a combative atmosphere, Essex showed themselves to be the most successful county team in the modern era. Eleven titles in thirteen years was astounding; an

69 A young Trevor Bailey

urgent, volcanic eruption of attainment after a slumbering century. Essex were assisted by the basic changes in the game's frame of reference: the increased financial stability that accompanied sponsorship; the recruitment of overseas players; and the relative ascendancy of the south-east in national economic terms. Nevertheless, social factors only create channels of opportunity in sport, and Essex responded shrewdly, deploying never affluent resources with astuteness and selecting talent from abroad more wisely than some of their colleagues, who shortsightedly opted for bright but fading stars. Moreover, they accomplished this astonishing measure of success in a pleasant and none too solemn a manner. This brought entertainment to all cricket-lovers, as well as relished excitement to their devoted followers.

Keith Fletcher, himself no stranger to fortune's buffets at international level, led the side with something akin to cunning, his instinctive grasp of the game's intricacies being his perpetual asset. He was, of course, a valued cricketer in his own right, as his fifty-nine caps and his captaincy of England remind us. No Essex player has surpassed his score of seasons with 1000 first-class runs, many completed in seasons with less first-class play than in the past; and, with over 37,000 runs, he is far and away their leading run-maker in all cricket. A utilitarian but forceful batsman, eschewing frippery and concentrating intently, he also, like the best of the moderns, ran pertly between the wickets. Throughout his quarter-century career, his endearingly elfin appearance and shuffling gait made him immediately recognizable in an era devoid, by and large, of character.

The batting was formidable. As well as Fletcher, there was Graham Gooch and Ken McEwan. Military of stature, serious of moustached aspect, Gooch recalls the grandeur that was Edwardian batting. Effortless of dispatch, especially square of the wicket, he reflects something of that combination of discipline and swagger which renders trooping the colour so enjoyable. He followed Fletcher as captain (although Fletcher took over again in 1988) and gained the early reward of the

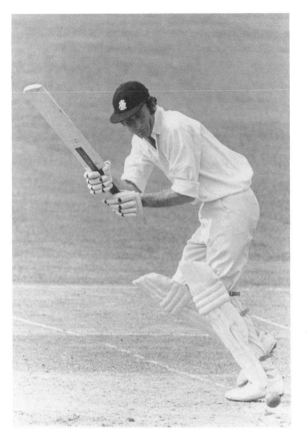

70 Keith Fletcher

Championship in 1986. Graham Gooch is, currently, one of England's tiny band of world-class players and he dominated both the Test and county scenes in 1990 and 1991. He was, for several years, supported in the Essex ranks by another, the South African, Ken McEwan, who, in a dozen seasons, scored 18,000 prolific and enjoyable runs. No cleverer overseas signing has been made among the counties: his abundance of runs betokened class as well as value, but, eventually, the hopelessness of ever finding admission to the Test arena drove him from the game. Alan Border, the Australian captain, replaced him in 1986, bringing his estimable quality to bear on the proceedings.

There were others. Brian Hardie and Keith Pont batted well, and a brace of wicket-keepers, Neil Smith and David East, had 400 victims apiece to join the best half dozen of Essex keepers. Keith Boyce and Norbert Phillip were two telling West Indian assets, and Stuart Turner was a dedicated and hard-working all-rounder. The bowling was always well balanced. The off-spin of David Acfield and the left-hand spin of the good-humoured Ray East blended with the pace attack, focussed on John Lever, winner of twenty-one England caps and, that rarity, a fast, accurate and enduring left-arm bowler. In later years, the bulky all-rounder, Derek Pringle, and the quick bowler, Neil Foster, slim of build and precise of action, bolstered Essex cricket and won England places. Then younger players such as J. P. Stephenson and Nasser Hussain and the imports, Mark Waugh and Salim Malik, gave Essex extra strength.

Admirable as the batting was, and as penetrative the bowling, what must have brought most joy to older Essex fans was the fielding. Slowly, over the years of Insole and Bailey, and then to fruition in the years of Taylor and Fletcher, the outcricket became enthrallingly keen. When fielding had, in general, been ordinary in the first-class game, that of Essex had been woeful: when, overall, it was excellent, that of Essex was outstanding and thrilling. It was the hallmark of collective action, and inspired well deserved tribute. Aptly, proudly, Keith Fletcher, with 517 first-class catches for Essex, and a further 119 in one-day tournaments, is the county's best-ever fielder.

There seems no reason why Essex should not remain in vigorous contention as a cricketing county. They have achieved rhythm and balance; they seem to have a flair for knitting newcomers, particularly from abroad, into their teams; their financial anxieties are less pressing than in the past; they shelter among the richest tracts of a divided nation; above all, they have the buoyancy which comes with success, that psychological lift, that sense of the likelihood, not the improbability, of doing well.

Running the rule over a hundred years of Essex players, in an attempt to tease out a representative XI, has two snags: a preponderance of captains and a profusion of all-rounders, with

71 Tom Pearce

Douglas and Bailey falling into both camps. Opening the batting and the bowling comes easier to resolution. Percy Perrin and Graham Gooch would make for a massive partnership in the grand tradition, as long as the former worthy could be hidden in the field, with Jack O'Connor, Keith Fletcher and, save perhaps for his South

African origins, Ken McEwan dancing attendance. Kortright and Farnes would provide lethal fire-power, fierce enough for anyone's blood, even unto the highest level. And both these pieces of selection would leave McGahey, Lucas, Mead, Russell, Barker, Lever and others waiting forlornly in the wings. Nor would there be much dispute over Brian Taylor's right to be wicketkeeper, for, with 1205 county scalps, he has not far off three times as many victims as the next on the list.

Spin bowling could be a headache, for, although Peter Smith's leg-breaks and googlies take him, with 1610 wickets, to the top of the Essex bowling honours, his *confrères* have been willing and able, but rarely devastating. One turns again to the plethora of all-rounders, with Douglas (roughly 18,000 runs and 1400 wickets, just for Essex), Nichols (16,000 runs and 1600 wickets) and Bailey (22,000 runs and 1600 wickets) difficult to separate. Alongside half a dozen long-serving captains, usually carrying a major responsibility in the club's organization, it is this virile tradition of all-round play, based on perceptive, never mechanistic seam bowling, and cussed batsmanship, that has ensured the survival of Essex through tempestuous times and finally witnessed the county's sudden and continuing reward.

Staying with the players who learned and played their cricket in and with Essex, one might do worse than hazard this trio, and, at least, there would be an appropriateness, given the thrust of all-rounders throughout the history of Essex. Contemplate, therefore, this talented XI: Graham Gooch, Percy Perrin, Jack O'Connor, Keith Fletcher, Trevor Bailey, Maurice Nichols, Johnny Douglas, Brian Taylor, Peter Smith, C. J. Kortright and Kenneth Farnes.

It has several interesting features. It includes five post-war players, and three whose careers were ended, prematurely in Farnes's case, by that war, and this probably indicates how Essex have developed lately as contenders. It also includes seven men who regularly captained Essex (Perrin led the side in the absence of Douglas in 1926). Indeed, with the addition of C. E. Green, A. P. Lucas, H. G. P. Owen, F. L. Fane, C. P. McGahey, T. N. Pearce and D. J. Insole, it would be much simpler to find a winning team of skippers from Essex than from practically any other county. Their captain has rarely been the pontificating passenger.

This neat conceit leaves a final poser: who would captain the side? The judicious selector, adopting Solomonite discretion, would sagely ask a group so awash with leadership potential to resolve the question among themselves. The likeliest outcome would be that J. W. H. T. Douglas would enjoy the honour, doubtless encouraged by the manipulative skills of his enterprising father.

THREE

Glamorgan

Brightest, but not best, of the sons of the morning: that might be the text for Glamorgan, brightest because the newest and, until the advent of Durham, the only post-Edwardian entrant to the county scene but sadly not among the most successful. It might even be argued that, a small number of pleasing occasions apart, their lack of success has been a hidden, an unspoken, case against other would-be intruders. Compared with other sports, the changes in county cricket assume the style of scriptural ageing. It is now over three score years and ten since Glamorgan, in 1921, became the baby of the County Championship.

Nor, by the nigh-on-geological dating necessary in cricket history, was it an ancient club, having been formed in 1888 – a proto-typical meeting at the Angel Hotel in Cardiff – and having played its opening match – losing to Warwickshire at Cardiff – in 1889. As with many counties, there had been attempts to develop representative sides since the 1860s. The South Wales Cricket Club had for some years played MCC and some English counties, a clear illustration that a club was usually the potent force. Although it is now suggested that the existence of the South Wales club 'delayed the formation' of the county organization, it might equally be argued that, until its demise, in 1887, it did no more and no less than many other club-cum-county combines in England.

It serves as a negative example. It might have evolved, from that base, into a more powerful force. It collapsed, and the way was open for officials of the leading Glamorgan clubs – in particular, J. P. Jones, the Cardiff captain, W. Bryant and J. T. D. Llewellyn, respectively secretary and president of the Swansea club – to establish the Glamorgan club. In one sense, the narrowness of 'Glamorgan' as opposed to the broader sweep of 'South Wales' may seem retro-grade, although the latter club had been somewhat socially exclusive. There are two sides to that. In that county cricket needed an urban locus, Glamorgan, as a geographic entity, had a near monopoly of such venues, notably at Cardiff and Swansea; and five of the XI that lost to Warwickshire in that opening game were from the Cardiff club. Conversely, Glamorgan have never stuck closely to Glamorgan cricketers, born and bred, nor, for that matter, to Welshmen.

The club has perhaps suffered from a kind of regional perplexity. The twin aspirations of Cardiff and Swansea have possibly never been reconciled, in the manner in which, by contrast, Manchester or Bristol each dominated its relevant area from the start. Contrariwise, Glamorgan, concentrating on its urbanized bases, has never quite struck the authentic chord of being the national team from Wales. Communication with the north and middle of the principality was and remains sparse, and it might be equally correct to surmise that the Welsh rugby XV is a product of the industrialized sector of South Wales, and little beyond.

It was and is a speedier journey from Cardiff to London than from Cardiff to Caernarvon, and that fact is a telling one. We are dealing with transport history rather than constitutional history. Observing the rather puny results of cricket in the celtic fringe, some have chosen to proclaim the integral Englishness of cricket, inferring that the wilder and less restrained temper of the Scots, the Welsh and the Irish have led to a rejection of the mannered ritual of cricket in their lands. The alliance of demographic intensity and rail, later road, links is the penny-plain explanation, and the twopenny-coloured one must be shelved. Glamorgan is both the proof and the exception to the rule: a non-English club with an industrialized populace and a fast railway. Its lateness of foundation and of first-class elevation has something to do with the relatively late arrival of large-scale mining and manufacturing and of the inevitable railway.

In 1897 Glamorgan entered the Minor Counties competition, and, over the years, did reasonably well, although never winning the competition. Their best years were 1907 and 1908, when they were beaten finalists in the play-off tourneys. After the First World War, the club tried to strengthen its ranks, and, while as low as sixth in the 1920 Minor Counties Championship, Glamorgan investigated the possibility of upgrading. They owed a profound debt to one of their players, T. A. L. Whittington, whose arduous job it was to persuade eight first-class counties to guarantee a double fixture, home and away. This was the minimum MCC would accept. He obtained agreements from Sussex and Gloucestershire of the older counties, and from Leicestershire, Worcestershire, Derbyshire, Hampshire, Northamptonshire and Somerset.

The cyclic odyssey for first-class status was, for ambitious counties, akin to the would-be theatrical's search for an Equity card: you have to perform to get one; you can't perform unless you have one. Counties keen on first-class grading had to persuade those whose company they sought to 'receive' them, after the fashion of the London social season. It should be added that Lancashire's support also had a bearing on Glamorgan's upward mobility.

In 1921 Glamorgan began sensationally. They beat Sussex at the Cardiff Arms Park to the delight of the excited audience. It was a false herald. The frenzied 1920s was a decade of nervous disappointment for Glamorgan, their unease seeming to reflect the social neurosis of those years of disillusion and near-hysteria. Only four matches were won in three seasons, and, although 1926 saw a fine opening to the summer and a final placement at eighth, that was Glamorgan's best display by a long chalk. In 1927 there was one victory, in the very last game of the season, and in 1929 they were last, having suffered the confusion and indignity of playing under seven captains. Professionally, administratively and financially, the club was on its uppers, and in considerable trouble.

The bowling was reasonable, with the offbreaks of J. C. Clay, the enduring medium-pace of Jack Mercer, late of Sussex, and, too infrequently, the left-arm spin of the unpredictable Frank Ryan, American-born and once of Hampshire. The batting, however, was brittle. Norman Riches had been a prodigious second-class run-getter, his 1000 runs and average of 92 in twelve innings of 1911 constituting an amazing Minor Counties record. Although he did well enough in the Championship, and scored his 1000 runs in Glamorgan's initial season, he had little support, and, talented as he was, his years soon told against him. Certainly it was his kind of form which, rightly, had warmed the hearts of doubters, and eased the passing of Glamorgan into the upper

72 J. C. Clay

bracket, but, as 1930 dawned, this promotion looked as if it had been ill-advised.

It was now, like some legendary Welsh prince appearing from a mountain fastness to save his realm, that Maurice Turnbull was appointed captain in 1930 and secretary in 1932. He was as young as one might legitimately expect of a legendary prince, being but twenty-three. A startling product of Downside and Cambridge, he made his début for Glamorgan at seventeen, and, after successfully captaining his university, he caught up the dual reins at Glamorgan. It has been said that he was the most effective captain-secretary in county history. He scored almost 18,000 runs; held over 300 catches, most of them

73 Maurice Turnbull, the greatest influence on Glamorgan cricket.

through his inspirational displays at short-leg; gained nine caps and was Glamorgan's first Test player; and for ten years proved to be an unruffled and rational leader. Complementary to this attainment, he was responsible for turning a near bankrupt organism into a solvent one by dint of myriad functions and activities, and his administrative endeavour was exemplary. In 1935, showing much verve, he organized the affiliation of Monmouthshire with Glamorgan, and thereby enabled a Minor Counties team to be run. It is precisely that kind of initiative that might have transformed the construction of the first- and second-class structure, and Turnbull's skills in that regard were as evident as in his all-round sportsmanship – for he also played rugby and hockey for Wales.

With the batting steadied by the captain, by the graft of Dai Davies, probably the first notable Welsh-born professional bat, and by the discovery, in Emrys Davies and Arnold Dyson, of a solid opening pair, matters improved, reaching their height in 1937 when Glamorgan finished seventh in the Championship. It was a calamitous day for Glamorgan cricket, in all its facets, when Maurice Turnbull, a courageous soldier, was slain by a sniper in Normandy soon after D-Day in 1944.

His legacy was a surprising and delicious one. After two mid-table outings in 1946 and 1947, Glamorgan, seizing the advantage of a moist summer and the distraction of household names with the visiting and invincible Australians, contrived to carry off the Championship. Wilf Wooller, already a rugby hero, was now captain, and also, in the Turnbull tradition, secretary. His mix of keenness and discipline was to serve Glamorgan well for many years. The bowling had been strengthened by the migration from Middlesex of Norman Hever, a young quick bowler who shared the new ball with Wooller, and Len Muncer, whose 139 wickets at sparse cost really sustained the Championship thrust. The veterans, John Clay and Arnold Dyson, brought timely succour to bear in the last part of the season, the former taking 9 for 79 in the crucial match at Bournemouth. There was a bevy of all-rounders – Allan Watkins, who earned fifteen England caps; Willie

Jones, a strangely ill-assured but talented left-hander; and the skipper himself. The batting was not forceful, but it was competent and thorough, with but a twitch of a tail. Younger hopefuls, such as Gilbert Parkhouse, soon to be a Test batsman, and Phil Clift blended with the experience of the cautious Emrys Davies, who scored 26,000 runs and took 885 wickets for the county. Haydn Davies, large and vocal, was the wicket-keeper, and Muncer and he were Wilf Wooller's tactical advisors. It would have pleased Plaid Cymru to record that the majority of the players used were Welshmen.

Sufficient batting and rational bowling were galvanized by as riveting an all-round and season-long display of fielding and catching as the Championship had witnessed. Wooller engaged in a strategy of leg-theory, albeit with a plethora of tactical variation, and, by example and through strict practice, he led a covey of on-side catchers, among whom Watkins and Clift were superbly impressive. For a team which, twenty years before, had been feeble in the field, it was especially gratifying, and the title was a just dessert for an amalgam of sheer, detailed endeavour and valiant catching. Thus Glamorgan won half their twenty-six fixtures, and nosed ahead of a strong field.

Twenty-one years were to pass before this act was bravely repeated. Under Wooller, Glamorgan were never again higher than fourth. Compared with Maurice Turnbull, there was a defensiveness about Wooller's approach, reflective of his own serious intent and of the narrower spirit of the age in which he played. There continued to be sound players, such as the off-spinner, Jim McConnon; the batsmen, Pressdee and Hedges; and the all-rounder, Peter Walker, a natural replacement for Watkins as a remarkable close catcher. O. S. Wheatley, who became a leading administrator, succeeded Wilf Wooller as captain, and enjoyed a couple of good seasons (second in 1963 and third in 1965) and then came a half dozen summers under the captaincy of Tony Lewis, who also, in 1972–73, against India, became the only Glamorgan player to lead England in a Test series.

The middle years of A. R. Lewis were crowned with distinction. A third place in 1968 and a second place in 1970 sandwiched a noble Championship victory in 1969. Glamorgan had to overhaul Gloucestershire and did so in the grand manner, comprehensively beating them twice, before moving consistently on to complete the summer with eleven wins and no losses.

It was a team largely modelled like its predecessors. As with the 1948 side, relatively few players were used, often a sign of men in form and

74 Allan Watkins

confident enough to shrug off slight injuries. Like the 1948 winners, they included several useful all-rounders: eight of the main XI took wickets, and runs came from Eifion Jones, the wicket-keeper. Peter Walker, Tony Cordle, Roger Davis and Malcolm Nash all succeeded in both departments. Tony Lewis and the ever dependable Alan Jones were continuously among the runs. Lewis scored 20,445 first-class runs, while, in twenty-six seasons of knowledgeable craftsmanship, Alan Jones assembled no less than 36,000 first-class runs, easily the highest aggregate for a Glamorgan player. Bryan Davis was a third batsman with 1000 runs, but vivid colour, now that overseas players were in abundance, was provided by Majid Khan. His 1500 runs lent glamour to their 1969 campaign.

Among the several bowlers, Malcolm Nash took 80 wickets and Don Shepherd 81. Shepherd had long since developed that reliance which is the hallmark of the British medium-pace bowler. Extraordinarily tidy and inexpensive, he plied his wholesome trade to great advantage, his 2218 first-class wickets making him Glamorgan's leading wicket-taker by a gulf-like margin. All the bowlers, as in 1948, were assisted by close fielding of devastating sharpness. This always maintained the county's surge for honours.

Since then, life with Glamorgan has been sombre. After the wise management of Norman Riches, John Clay, Maurice Turnbull, Wilf Wooller and Tony Lewis, there has been instability, with chopping of captains and changing of players. In almost every year until 1991 Glamorgan have found themselves, as music-hall artists were wont to say of the bottom of the bill, among the wines and spirits. They have failed abysmally in the three one-day competitions, winning none, their best attempt leaving them beaten finalists to Middlesex in the 1977 Gillette Cup, when, untypically, their fielding was below par.

The world-class Javed Miandad played for six seasons and scored over 6000 runs, while other players have looked the county part, such as Rodney Ontong from South Africa, R. J. Shastri from India, J. A. Hopkins, Matthew Maynard, Hugh Morris, A. R. Butcher late of Surrey, and, of course, the 1990 recruit, the great Viv Richards. Notwithstanding this, Glamorgan's record has been a dismal one, and, over the last twenty years, they must be regarded as the least successful first-class county. It may have been of poor encouragement to second-class counties that Glamorgan, newest of the recruits, have not fared better.

Glamorgan have spent their seventy first-class years like a man in a lifeboat, not sinking, but

75 Wilf Wooller

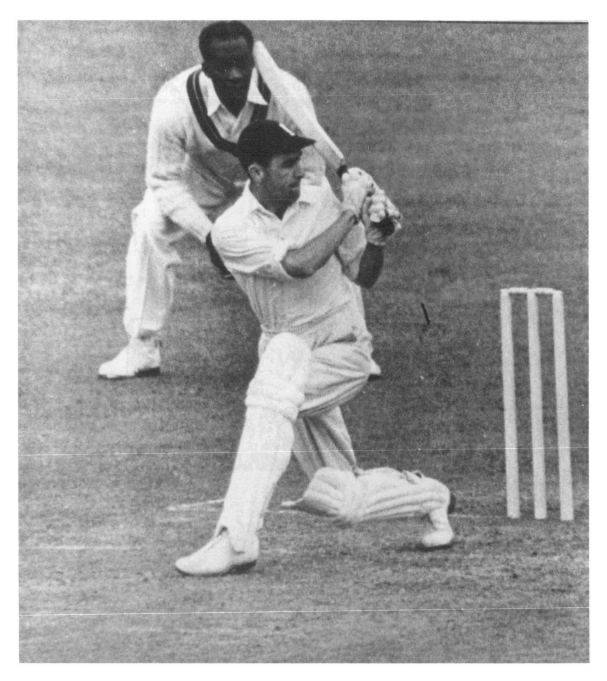

76 Gilbert Parkhouse

drifting, and with the firing of a bright flare on two occasions the only major essays in reminding others of their existence. In over sixty outings in the Championship, Glamorgan have struggled to a single figure placement on only eighteen occasions, an approximate measure of their normal languishing in the bottom half of the table.

The Welsh county has properly tried to carry first-class cricket to various parts of Wales. Although Cardiff (both the Arms Park and Sophia Gardens) and Swansea have been Glamorgan's chief grounds, with over three-quarters of home fixtures played in those two cities, crusading ventures have struck as far afield as Colwyn Bay on the north coast; while Pontypridd, Neath and Newport have also figured among a dozen or so venues over the years. As with other counties of similar stature, there is the benefit of spreading the faith and pleasing the widespread faithful, over against the issue of using primarily club grounds. Over the years it may have been that the uneven quality of some Glamorgan pitches has balanced out, hindering their batsmen in the bad years and helping their bowlers in the good.

All in all, and while Glamorgan have not been overwhelmed by golden fortune, their existence has or could have been influential, a guarantee of first-class cricket in the Principality and some surety, insufficiently heeded, that a club on short commons may make something of a showing. There has been ill-luck as well. For instance, Glamorgan's overseas players have brought dramatic flavour rather than sterling attainment, in the way that Richard Hadlee ensured success for Nottinghamshire. A final perspective might be to recall that, whereas such as Northamptonshire and Leicestershire remained for donkey's years in the first-class basement, Glamorgan have not been wholly failed protagonists, and, in sickness and health, have given pleasure to countless Welsh supporters.

Like Abou Ben Adhem, Maurice Turnbull must lead 'all the rest' when Glamorgan is assessed for its best-ever eleven. Although, and rightly, the wartime deaths of Ken Farnes and Hedley Verity were publicly mourned and English cricket, as a consequence, maimed, one might urge that Turn-bull's death in action was equally damaging to the game in Britain. As a batsman and fielder, as a captain and as a farsighted administrator, he was only in his early thirties when war was declared, and the effect that so genial a cricketer and so imaginative an organizer might have had thereafter may only be guessed at. In a game cluttered by over-wary players and backward-looking officials, he was and could have been a statesman of immense stature.

In assembling a team he certainly would have turned to a sturdy pair for what, in rugby circles, is known as the engine-room. His anchor batsman and stock bowler would certainly have been Alan Jones and Don Shepherd, respectively high in the world lists for runs scored and wickets taken, but with not a cap between them, save for the vaguely suspect one which the former acquired playing for England versus the Rest of the World in 1970, when the South African tour of that summer collapsed.

There will be many passionately ready to argue, and not only in the sing-song lilt of the valleys, that had either found himself in a more fashionable or successful club, international selection would have been automatic. They are the highest scorer and wicket-taker among uncapped players in first-class history.

To assist Alan Jones and the captain at the head of the innings, the elegant modesty of Gilbert Parkhouse, who amassed over 22,000 runs for Glamorgan, and the dogged orthodoxy of Emrys Davies, who collected over 26,000 runs, must suffice, pushing out such as the Yorkshireman, Arnold Dyson, the free-scoring Norman Riches, or, for all his handsome strokes, Tony Lewis.

All-rounders are plentiful. Wilf Wooller himself and Peter Walker, of South African extraction and high in the list of the world's catchers, would be in contention. The chunky effectiveness of Allan Watkins cannot be dismissed, while Jim Pressdee, with an average of nearly 30 and just on 400 wickets, must be considered. Perhaps Watkins and Walker, with over 36,000 runs and over 1600 wickets between them, must be chosen.

Nor is there any difficulty – except whom to omit – with off-spinners and their kin, with Len

Muncer, John Clay and Jim McConnon up for choice. Perhaps Clay's 1292 wickets in 358 matches should give him the place, and one should recall that Davies, included for his batting, did the double twice. Malcolm Nash, with 991 wickets for Glamorgan in the modern era at both fast and slow pace, must be counted unlucky to be excluded. An opening pair of bowlers would be harder to come by, although, latterly, Jeff Jones, until stricken with injury, and Greg Thomas enjoyed Test honours. Oddly, Jones shares with Watkins the distinction of being Glamorgan's leading international with only fifteen caps. Jack Mercer, who took 1460 wickets for Glamorgan at medium pace, must surely be included, along with one of those faster men. Glamorgan have always lacked a really hostile opening attack. Choice is also a little restricted as to wicket-keepers. The main trio are H. G. Davies, who played in Wooller's title-winning team; D. G. L. Evans, who played during the late 1950s and through the 1960s; and E. W. Jones, who overlapped with Evans and retired in 1983. On figures alone, Jones, with over 900 catchings and stumpings, must be preferred.

Two issues are certain. Despite lacking a world-rated wicket-keeper, the team would field with blistering potency, and practically all its members would, at request, bowl. Sceptics might add that, given batting of solidity rather than finesse, both these qualities would be in testing demand, for Alan Jones, Gilbert Parkhouse, Emrys Davies, Maurice Turnbull, Allan Watkins, Peter Walker, John Clay, E. W. Jones, Jack Mercer, Don Shepherd and Jeff Jones.

FOUR

Gloucestershire

One of the grand originals, and fuelled by the Grace family, Gloucestershire drove off like an express locomotive, winning or sharing the title four times in the 1870s, and then slowed to the pace of a cross-country provincial train, never winning the title since.

As usual, club cricket was the fulcrum. Dr H. M. Grace, father of the famous brothers, had instituted the Mangotsfield club in 1844, and, by amalgamation with Coalpit Heath, the West Gloucestershire club two years later. The All-England XI visited the Bristol area and played against teams whose core was West Gloucestershire, while, in the 1860s, H. M. Grace, again in pursuit of a trend to be observed elsewhere, organized fixtures for the Gentlemen of Gloucestershire. It was the standard evolution toward full county status.

Like Italy and the United States, Gloucestershire had and has a north-south problem, and, at this time, there were at least two attempts to create a county team in the Cheltenham area. These rivalries clearly illustrate the thesis that county teams did not rise spontaneously as patriotic entities: they were the expansion usually of one major club, often in some contest against another. The Cheltenham project contributes to some small argument as to whether, officially, Gloucestershire were constituted in 1870 or 1871; certainly by the end of the 1860s a county side was playing and usually beating other first-class sides.

The reasons why the south, contrary to the Italian and American parallels of the same period, vanquished the north are plainly descriptive of the 'industrial' theory of first-class cricket. Cheltenham and Gloucester, to the north, were agrarian centres and had been the focus for the declining wool trade. Bristol was, as it had been for centuries, a thriving port, and now it enjoyed its own brand of industrial revolution, with new manufactures bringing a new prosperity. The coal-field in the area of Bristol and south-west Gloucestershire was a contributory factor, while the advent of the railway, linking the city with London, was a crucial feature. When West Gloucestershire CC played its matches, there was, of course, a rural, even a pastoral air, but the townships the team visited were equally industrial bases. So Bristol became the headquarters of the county, although, very soon, Cheltenham began to stage its famous festival week.

So much for those who espouse economic determinism as the prime mobile. For those preferring the emphasis placed by Voltaire or Thomas Carlyle on 'great men', then it could be argued that, without W. G. Grace, Gloucestershire, for all the magic of the railway and the bounty of the Severn hinterland, might not have risen so rapidly in stature. An honest broker might agree that, without the city to support a first-class club and a rail link to convey its members to London and elsewhere, W. G. Grace might have been extremely restricted; and that, without W. G. Grace, Gloucestershire might have found difficulty in obtaining first-class status. Such are the circles of cause and effect.

There can be no doubt that 'the great cricketer' must be judged in such primary terms. He took the amiable pastime of the countryside and the somewhat jolly recreation of the large town and, fashioning it to his purpose, created, first, a national sport, and, next, an international one. Of course, the moment was opportune, for the determinants of transport, spectatorship, newspaper coverage and several other aspects were suddenly together in cumulative interaction. Nonetheless, the man had to be present as well as the occasion ripe. W. G. Grace, through the strength and authority and implacable consistency of his batting, changed the values, numerical and social, by which the game was assessed. In ten days that shook the world in the August of 1876, he scored 839 first-class runs, including the first and second triple centuries in history – and, before the end of that month, he had helped himself to 400 against XXII of Grimsby. His effect on the shape of cricket was as if, today, an athlete contrived to run a three-minute mile, or a golfer regularly turned in scores of less than 60. He became the first famed sportsman of the modern era, and the first internationally known sportsman of all time. Not only did he, in fact, create modern cricket, he was and remains its chief exponent.

Brevity might seem to do him less than justice, but, alternatively, to embark on a full analysis of the Grace story would distract from the county plot. His tale has larger dimensions, both of a national and world variety, but he assuredly set Gloucestershire off to a spectacular start. He scored 54,896 first-class runs and 45,238 in minor cricket, and, had his batting been frail, he would still have been famous for his 2876 wickets (and another 4578 in minor games). He scored nearly 23,000 of his runs for Gloucestershire, for whom he played from 1870 to 1899. His average touched 40, and fifty-one of his 126 centuries were scored for the county. He captained Gloucestershire from 1873 until his abrupt and ill-tempered departure in 1899 to organize the London County club at Crystal Palace, and this remains a record spell of county leadership.

Socially, he fell between the cracks. He was not a public school and university product, the son of a rich house; nor was he of the artisan classes, whence the professionals came. He struggled to qualify as a doctor, and practised with forthright competence for many years, while finding ways and means of procuring sufficient money from cricket to sustain his untiring passion for the game; he played at club level from the age of nine to the age of sixty-six. Indeed, until the arrival of the modern golfers and boxers, no one made as much money out of sport as W. G. Grace. His comprehensive mastery of cricket, allied to an awesome stamina, allowed him a singular control over the game to a degree that few sportsmen have ever attained. In character, he was a strange mix of courage and kindness, of cunning and downright deviousness, of petty rage and a form of adolescent immaturity.

Grace's preference for the upper crust he could not aspire to, and the feeble finances of the county, caused Gloucestershire to field a mainly amateur squad. One of the criticisms levelled at Grace's autocratic captaincy was that he seldom gave local club cricketers a chance, depending rather on public school and Oxbridge players. He was not entirely averse to professionals, but it was 1877 before Gloucester's first regular 'pro' was signed. This was William Midwinter, whose career reads like the answers to a specialist sports quiz – he was born in the Forest of Dean but brought up in Australia, and became the first trans-oceanic cricket commuter and the only man to play for England versus Australia and vice versa. Later W. A. Woof, a slow left-hander, and Jack Painter, an all-rounder, became trusty paid servants of the county.

These apart, Gloucestershire were a crack regiment of amateurs, or, at least, gentlemen, and, on that basis, probably the most successful amateur county team there has been. E. M. Grace, 'the Coroner' and W.G.'s elder brother, was the county secretary, and, although he was not over-keen on what he regarded as the formalism of the County Championship, his sometimes unorthodox contribution was most valuable. The younger Grace, Fred, was, until his untimely death in 1880, a stylish and dashing bat, and there was useful support from their cousin, W. R. Gilbert, 'the Colonel', who blotted his copybook by pilfering in the dressing-room, and, to avoid the scandal, was exiled to Canada.

Almost as titanic, bearded and impactful a figure as W. G. Grace was J. A. Bush, W.G.'s best man and stout friend, and perhaps the most efficient amateur wicket-keeper of his generation. Frank Townsend, a local headmaster, T. G. Matthews, an excellent bat, and R. Fenton Miles, a most able spin bowler, completed the principal cast.

Gloucestershire's initial achievement was phenomenal. In 1873, the first official year of the Championship, in so far as qualifications were

77 W. G. Grace captained the Gloucestershire champions of 1877. J. A. Bush, the wicket-keeper, and Grace's best man at his wedding, is at the far left of the picture.

insisted upon, they won four and enjoyed the best of two draws in their six outings, and were declared champions along with Nottinghamshire, who were similarly undefeated. In 1874 Gloucestershire were outright winners, losing only one of their half a dozen fixtures, and, after a disappointing 1875, they were once more champions in 1876, winning five, drawing three and losing none. Gloucestershire were again undefeated champions in 1877, winning seven out of eight games. In the four years of victory, they lost only one county match. Then they were considered to be second to Middlesex in 1878; tumbled a little in 1879; rallied marvellously in 1880; and, with just one defeat, were runners-up to Nottinghamshire.

In 1881, they came second again, this time to Lancashire.

After a quite sensational introductory decade, Gloucestershire then assumed a more sedate and moderate mood. They lost their sound amateur players, and it was only when W. G. Grace enjoyed one of his extraordinary summers – as in 1895 and 1898 – that Gloucestershire edged up the table. In the meanwhile, in 1889, the club had acquired its own headquarters at Ashley Down. The ground was sold to J. S. Fry and Son in 1915, with the club using it as one of the firm's tenants, and then it was re-purchased in 1933.

This temperate mood persisted until almost the 1930s, with Gloucestershire perched in mid-table, with occasional lapses into the depths. The club's finances were seldom rosy and often debilitated, so much so that, had the First World War not intervened, it is probable that Gloucestershire would not have competed in the 1915 season.

In spite of these misfortunes, Gloucestershire still included some fascinating individuals within their ranks, even if a unified and compact deployment proved beyond them. Jack Board kept wicket with valour and rustic wit for 430 games through the 1890s and up to the outbreak of war in 1914. His 1016 victims are still a runaway county record. Chubby Fred Roberts took many wickets with his pacy left-hand deliveries in the seasons around the turn of the century, but for many of these years the bowling relied wholly on George Dennett, the left-hand spin bowler. Unlucky to be a contemporary of Rhodes and Blythe, he succeeded to the mantle of Miles and Woof, and established an intriguing procession of Gloucestershire spinners. At a speed bordering on the dilatory and on a length cautiously chosen, he contrived to take over 2000 wickets. On occasion, C. L. Townsend, son of Frank Townsend, bowled his fierce wrist-spin at the other end. A precociously talented all-rounder, he found neither the opportunity nor perhaps the physical strength to follow a regular first-class career. From 1908 to 1932, Alf Dipper, with nearly 28,000 runs for the county, was the anchorman. He was peasant-like both in his painful shyness of manner and in his unsophisticated accumulativeness of method; almost a parody, in name, nature and practice, of the stubborn opening batsman.

Gloucestershire is a county of legends, and, as if linking the saga of Grace with the epic of Hammond, the melodrama of Jessop was staged. Gilbert Jessop – 'the Croucher' – is the yardstick by which huge hitters have since been assessed, with scarcely one reaching the required standard. By no means a large or a strong man – indeed, his health was not permanently robust – he assailed bowlers with an orthodoxy reinforced by explosive violence. Fearless, not foolhardy, he made some 19,000 runs for his county, many of them in bewilderingly short spans of time. He played in

78 Gilbert Jessop

eighteen Tests, captured plenty of wickets with his tearaway quick bowling, and captained Gloucestershire over thirteen seasons. Beyond that, he was affectionately regarded as a miracle-worker in the covers, and he was certainly the finest English cover-point prior to the First World

War. Just as a sparkling orator will bring members flocking back into the Commons, so did crowds watch with excited anticipation, and nearby property-owners with some apprehension, as Gilbert Jessop adopted the taut, keyed stance that earned him his soubriquet.

The county officials worked hard to sustain the club through the 1920s. They were chiefly dependent on Charlie Parker, successor to George Dennett. This irascible and outspoken bowler was aggressive in mode and temper. Although he was capped but once (and Dennett not at all) he took 3278 wickets, despite turning to spin late in his career. He was assisted by the bowling of Percy Mills and the able wicket-keeping of Harry Smith, but Gloucestershire lacked class and vigour in their batting.

Gradually, this fault was corrected. First, there was the brilliant stroke-play of Charlie Barnett, who, from 1927 to 1948, plundered over 25,000 first-class runs, and then came Wally Hammond. Tall, aloof and masterly, with exquisite style and unerring craftsmanship in united and productive array, Walter Hammond succeeded Jack Hobbs as England's premier batsman. Like Jessop, he was also a most valued bowler and world-class fielder, particularly noted as one of cricket's most agile slips. Like W. G. Grace's, his biography is international, not parochial, in scope. His 50,000 runs (nearly 34,000 for Gloucestershire) place him sixth, a little behind Grace, on the world list. His average of just on 56 is surpassed by those who have scored more than 25,000 runs only by Geoffrey Boycott, by a fraction, and, inevitably, by Don Bradman by rather a lot. The essential arithmetic, of course, tells little of the command and imperious authority of Walter Hammond, England's outstanding cricketer between the wars.

With B. H. Lyon as a smart and imaginative captain, Reg Sinfield as an off-side bowler of decent consequence, and the likes of Bill Neale in support, Gloucestershire's fortunes improved. As Charlie Parker overlapped with Dennett, now did Tom Goddard, strong and craggy in physique, raucous in appeal, supplement, then replace, Parker. His lengthy fingers snapped his off-spin

79 Charlie Barnett

fiercely and stingingly, and he progressed to a little short of 3000 wickets in his long career.

These fine cricketers formed Gloucestershire's second-best side to date, their shortage of some fast bowling barring them from genuine achievement. They were runners-up in 1930 and 1931, fourth in 1929, 1936 and 1937, and third in 1939. With Walter Hammond batting as if born to the purple diadem, and Tom Goddard and Charlie Barnett, his hardened tribunes, their contrasting

80 & 81 Tom Goddard (left) and Charlie Parker ,
two of Gloucestershire's most successful bowlers between the wars.

brands of destructiveness, Gloucestershire challenged the capable Yorkshire XI of that decade. The comparison with the years before the First World War could not have been greater: the 1915 season might have seen Gloucestershire dispatched to oblivion; in 1940 they might have been champions.

The second war impeded but did not halt the impetus, in spite of Hammond's disappearance after a splendid 1946 season. In the late 1930s George Emmett and Jack Crapp, utterly reliable in their skilled batting trade, and, at last, opening bowlers in Colin Scott and, more especially, George Lambert (he took over 900 wickets for the county) arrived. Sam Cook joined Gloucestershire after the war, a spin bowler of little flight and large deviation with a bag of 1782 first-class victims, and who, in the county's pleasantest rite of passage, first supported and then substituted for Tom Goddard. It is often forgotten that Gloucestershire gave Middlesex something of a run for their money in their splendid Championship year of 1947.

Thereafter Gloucestershire's years were uneasy. There were the good times: for instance, runners-up in 1959 and ten years later in 1969. There were the bad years: for instance, three times bottom in 1964, 1967 and 1970. There were pitch troubles and financial troubles, and something of a general malaise. As always, Gloucestershire preserved their pleasing convention of fielding attractive players. Abundant spin bowling was provided by Bomber Wells, David Allen (well over 1000 wickets in his career) and John Mortimore (just over 1800 in his, plus nearly 16,000 runs). Tony Brown, at medium pace, and with useful runs as well, was another valued contributor. The batting was steadfast: Martin Young, Ron Nicholls and Arthur Milton (the only one, apart from Hammond, to score more than the coveted 30,000 runs for Gloucestershire) must be honoured with a mention.

But for a dozen years from 1948 until he left for Worcestershire in 1960, Tom Graveney topped the bill, almost on cue to replace Hammond as the fourth of Gloucestershire's supreme batsmen. Elegant, strikingly built, fluent of movement and stroke-play, Tom Graveney followed his illustrious predecessor into the England as well as the county side, scoring nearly 20,000 runs for Gloucestershire and nearly 48,000 in his classic career. He stands ninth in the world aggregates; he scored 122 centuries; and he played seventy-nine times for England. A Northumbrian, born in 1927, he was practically the only world-class England cricketer to emerge from the doldrums of the mid-1920s.

There was a recharging of the county's batteries in the 1970s, and Gloucestershire were indeed fortunate in their selection of overseas assistance. Mike Procter, the South African, catapulting into violent action with the ball and aggressive venture with the bat, stands second only to W. G. Grace as a Gloucestershire all-rounder. Zaheer Abbas, a surgical clinician among batsmen, and Sadiq Mohammed proved enormously successful. They were abetted by sturdy county cricketers such as David Shepherd, Jack Davey, Andy Stovold, and, in the spinning mode, David Graveney and John Childs.

Procter demonstrated his match-winning

82 Mike Procter

prowess in 1973, when, a hundred years on from those titles draped in the mists of time, Gloucestershire won a trophy. It was the Gillette Cup, and Sussex were the opponents. After a faltering start by the early order, Mike Procter drove and thrashed a spectacular 94, which, with Tony Brown's highly competent 77 not out, left a total of 246, too tall for the Sussex batsmen.

In 1977 the Benson and Hedges Cup was carried off by Gloucestershire. This time the batting was solid from the start, with Stovold, Sadiq, Zaheer and Procter all progressing well, leaving Kent an unreachable sum of 237. During the earlier rounds, Procter had been something of a one-man-band, and Gloucestershire's flurry of triumphs in the mid-1970s were very much to his credit.

There were some healthy challenges for the Championship, with third placings in 1972, 1976 and, after an exceptionally tight end to the season, 1977. In 1986 Gloucestershire once more chased to the season's end, but had to be content with second place. In between times they declined alarmingly, and were bottom in 1970 and 1984. It was a snakes and ladders sort of team, and financial worries, so often Gloucestershire's bane, were pressing. They were relieved in 1974, when, with the club close to ruin, a deal was arranged with Phoenix Assurance which involved that company's purchase of what is now the Phoenix County Ground. But still the cricket lacked stability, and there were dissensions over the captaincy in the late 1980s . . . *plus ça change.* From Grace in 1899 to Tom Graveney in 1961, arguments over the captaincy had been disputatious and acrid. In 1990, the South African Eddie Barlow was appointed senior coach, only to announce his departure at the end of the 1991 season. However, on the credit side at least Gloucestershire enjoy the services of the current England wicket-keeper, Jack Russell.

Turning to the happier pastime of selecting an all-time Gloucestershire XI, one finds the first half self-selecting. At their peak, W. G. Grace and Wally Hammond were acknowledged lords of all they surveyed, while Gilbert Jessop and Tom Graveney could confidently lodge a similar claim. The assured belligerence of Charlie Barnett and the sheer productivity of either Alf Dipper or Arthur Milton would complete the batting. Jack Board, Gloucestershire's most flourishing wicket-keeper, was a handy batsman, and might marginally edge out Jack Russell in a Gloucestershire team of all time. Happily for a county (ignoring Procter's case from across the oceans) with little history of outright fast bowlers, Grace, Jessop and Hammond were all Test-level bowlers, and Barnett was a useful seam bowler.

George Lambert, the nearest to a home-spun fast bowler, might be summoned to join this talented band, and, with no need to seek for middle-order all-rounders, the luxury of three spin bowlers could be indulged. Out of Gloucestershire's many exponents one might draft George Dennett, Charlie Parker and Tom Goddard. It would be, incidentally, a side of great specialist fielders. On reflection, it is largely a pre-war side, with scarcely a member from the last forty years. And the captaincy on this other-worldly occasion would cause no ripple of disturbance on the celestial fields. No one would dare contest the candidature of W. G. Grace to act as overlord for Charlie Barnett (to open with Grace), Alf Dipper, Walter Hammond, Tom Graveney, Gilbert Jessop, Jack Board, George Lambert, George Dennett, Charlie Parker and Tom Goddard.

FIVE

Hampshire

The harlequinade of Hampshire has danced hither and thither for scores of years, with, for the romantically-inclined, its beginnings way back among the Hampshire hills, in the village of Hambledon. Those rolling meadows and lush valleys, and memories of Windmill Down and Broadhalfpenny Down, allow cricket-lovers to muse nostalgically, but the sterner call of realism must point to Southampton as the authentic locus of Hampshire cricket.

It is truly a county of mixed assortment, with Winchester and the New Forest redolent of a medieval past, and Basingstoke turning its more modern face to London. In the local government reorganization of the 1970s, Bournemouth and Christchurch were lost to Dorset, while the navy at Portsmouth and the army at Aldershot remain, as they have long done, ingredients in this polyglot mix. Like so many counties, the southern district took the lead, with its three large towns – the naval base of Portsmouth, the holiday resort of Bournemouth and the great port of Southampton – providing the impetus.

Hampshire is also like its fellow counties in its tale of vicissitudes. In 1842 Daniel Day, a Surrey professional, opened the Antelope Inn and ground in Southampton, under the patronage of local gentry. The cricket did not prosper, although a form of county organization is recorded for 1849. In 1863, with one of Day's sponsors, Thomas Chamberlayne, in the chair, a meeting was held at the Antelope, its purpose the formation of a county club. Still the cricket failed to flourish, nor did the intercession of Clement Booth, another gentlemanly enthusiast, in 1874 prove any more respectful. The current constitution of the club dates, in fact, from 1879, soon after which, at a meeting at the George Hotel, Winchester, a form of district representation was introduced.

Colonel Fellowes and Dr Russell Bencraft were joint secretaries in the early 1880s. It was mainly the former's energies which secured the county ground at Bannister's Park, Southampton. Since its formation in 1863, the club had played on the rather restricted Antelope ground, about half a mile away, but now the new field was leased from Sir Edward Hulse, and a pavilion erected. In 1893 the owner was paid £5400 for the freehold.

The following season, 1894, Hampshire's form was good, so much so that, in October, the county captains agreed to their admission to the Championship. Four other counties had been invited in May, so Hampshire's elevation was a late tribute to an outstanding season.

They began in middling fashion, but, from 1900, often sank to the deepest reaches of the table. Frail bowling, with the corpulent off-spinner, Harry Baldwin, the only salvation, and batting incommoded by service calls contributed to this disappointing start. R. M. Poore, E. G. Wynyard and J. G. Greig were soldiers three who were not regularly available. They were each adventurous batsmen, and another, Alec Johnson, was described by C. B. Fry as 'the best of the soldier-batsmen'. Fry himself, in command of the TS *Mercury* on the Hamble, also played for Hampshire. With the army plentifully garrisoned in or near Hampshire, the county enjoyed the mixed blessings of having talented soldiers irregularly on tap. The captains Quinton and Jameson were two others.

Fortune swung Hampshire's way only when the professional bowling improved, as it did with the advent of C. B. Llewellyn of Natal (said to be the first person to bowl the 'chinaman'), Jack Newman and Alec Kennedy. Newman, a lean, rather melancholy figure, took over 2000 wickets and never played in a Test match. With his sharp off-spin and resolute batting, he achieved the double five times. His partner, the Scot, Alec Kennedy, also enjoyed five doubles, and he took

83 Jack Newman

2874 first-class wickets with the robotic accuracy of his fast-medium attack.

George Brown, powerful and versatile in all branches of the game, and Alec Bowell, a neat and thoughtful bat, also figured prominently before the First World War, but the batting, for some thirty years, was practically in the gift of Philip Mead. Unhurried to the point of ritual, and with the build and gait of an able seaman, he scored a little over 55,000 first-class runs, an aggregate passed only by Hobbs, Woolley and Hendren. Each summer, monumentally, he piled up huge amounts of runs; he had 1000 runs in each of twenty-seven seasons; and no one has scored more for one team (48,892 runs) than he did for Hampshire. Left-handed and patient, he is fairly judged by John Arlott as 'among the major batsmen of history'. And he took 688 first-class catches, for he was the surest of slip fielders.

Hampshire were, by good luck and good management, able to sustain this thick core of professional excellence over a lengthy period. All but Bowell played into the 1930s, and they averaged some twenty-five years' service with the county, a remarkable record. After the first war, they were captained by Major the Hon. L. H. Tennyson. The third Lord Tennyson was more forceful and less dignified than the first. As a captain, he was erratic, but as a batsman he was exuberantly belligerent, Thor-like in his demolition of pace bowling. That cricket buff, P. G. Wodehouse, must have relished the fact that Walter Livsey, the adept if nervous wicket-keeper, was also Tennyson's manservant, always loyal to his master on and off the field. On one occasion Tennyson's appeal against the light had been disallowed by the umpire. Livsey was the next man in, and as he approached the wicket called out: 'Where are you, my lord? I can hear you but I cannot see you.' Tennyson's instructions to Livsey when packing his cricket bags were to put in enough bottles of champagne to celebrate victory or to drown defeat.

In these years, while never challenging for the Championship title, Hampshire were never easy meat, and, year in year out, they maintained a respectable position amidships in the table. Most

1. Champagne flows as Hampshire win the Benson & Hedges final, Lord's, 1988

2a. R. E. Foster
(*Worcestershire and England*)

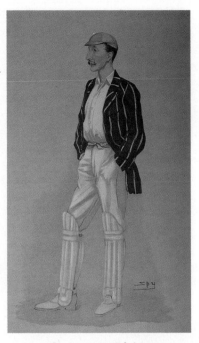

2b. L. C. H. Palairet
(*Somerset and England*)

2c. J. T. Tyldesley
(*Lancashire and England*)

2d. S. M. J. Woods
(*Somerset*)

3. Outer rim, starting top centre and reading clockwise: W. H. Lockwood (*Nottinghamshire, Surrey and England*) Emrys Davies (*Glamorgan*), C. P. McGahey (*Essex*), A. E. R. Gilligan (*Sussex and England*), A. W. Carr (*Nottinghamshire and England*), M. D. Lyon (*Somerset*), Jack Ikin (*Lancashire and England*), Maurice Leyland (*Yorkshire and England*), J. W. Hearne (*Middlesex and England*), Tommy Sidwell (*Leicestershire*), Jack Board (*Gloucestershire*), Bill Copson (*Derbyshire and England*); centre trio: Gordon Greenidge (Hampshire and West Indies), Allan Lamb (*Northamptonshire and England*), E. J. 'Tiger' Smith (*Warwickshire and England*); bottom pair: Leslie Ames (*Kent and England*), R. E. Foster (*Worcestershire and England*).

4a. Jack Simmons
(*Lancashire*)

4b. Peter Roebuck
(*Somerset*)

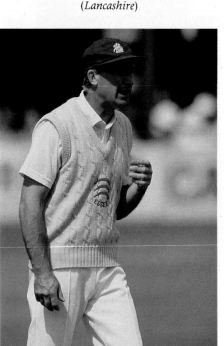

4c. Keith Fletcher
(*Essex and England*)

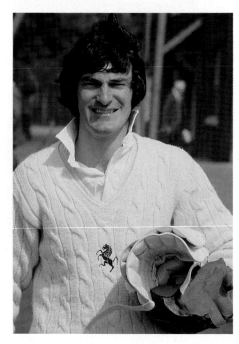

4d. Alan Knott
(*Kent and England*)

5a. Richard Hadlee (*Nottinghamshire and New Zealand*)

5b. Viv Richards
(*Somerset, Glamorgan and West Indies*)

5c. Bishen Bedi
(*Northamptonshire and India*)

6a. The County Ground, Worcester

6b. The last day of first-class cricket at
Sussex's historic ground at Hastings, 1989

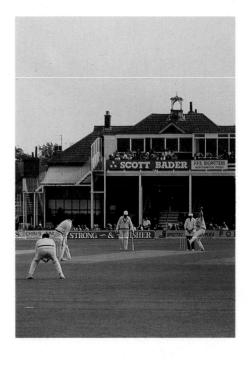

6c. The County Ground, Northampton

7a. The pavilion and Warner stand at Lord's,
packed to the rafters for the Benson and Hedges final, 1990

7b. A minimum of spectators at the Oval
reflects on Lancashire's huge total in a County Championship match, 1990

8a. The pavilion, Worcester and **8b.** Canterbury Week
capture the quintessential spirit of county cricket.

of these famed names were present during the amazing events of June 1922, when, after Warwickshire had scored 223, Hampshire were tumbled out for 15, including four extras, on an immaculate Edgbaston pitch. Invited both to follow on and to play golf once the second procession had ended, the noble and irate Tennyson took a hundred to one wager in tenners that Hampshire would win. Six wickets fell, and Hampshire were still 22 behind, but Brown, 172, and Livsey, 110, lifted them mountainously to 521. A perplexed Warwickshire were swept aside by Kennedy and Newman; Hampshire won by 155 runs; and champagne, courtesy of his Lordship, flowed in bubbling largesse.

During the years before the Second World War, apart from 1932 and 1936, Hampshire were always on the ladder's bottom rungs. A. E. Pothecary, Lofty Herman and John Arnold (also a noted footballer) were their mainstays around this time. With harsh bombing a depressing prelude to the ceaseless activity in the Southampton area before and after the invasion of Normandy, Hampshire had a rough war. With few players of note and none of sweet promise, the future was bleak indeed. However, E. D. R. Eagar was appointed secretary-captain after the war, and he proceeded to do for Hampshire something of what Maurice Turnbull had achieved for Glamorgan before the war.

Eagar led the side as astutely as such meagre commons permitted, and, in the damper summers of 1948 and 1951, Hampshire battled into the middle of the table. At other times, on sound wickets and in dry spells, their lack of class was evident. Desmond Eagar, however, was about the business of creating a nucleus for future glory. He was instrumental in switching Derek Shackleton from leg-spin to seam bowling, and, exactly and tirelessly, Shackleton developed into the leading stock bowler of his era. As spruce in appearance as he was immaculate in length, he was shaped in the Kennedy mould, and, happily, they share seventh and eighth places in the world roster of wicket-takers, Shackleton, on 2857, a handful of victims behind his model. Vic Cannings appeared to bowl his penetrative away swing, and, later, Butch White, in furious array, joined the attack. The spinners were C. J. Knott and Jim Bailey, and then Peter Sainsbury, a precise left-hander and brilliant field.

In the immediate post-war summers, Hampshire depended too heavily on the consistency of N. H. Rogers, while Neil McCorkell, already a resourceful wicket-keeper-batsman in the 1930s, continued his career with success. He was replaced by Leo Harrison, another who could keep wicket and bat with some ease. Gradually a coterie of valuable batsmen became established.

84 The scorecard of Hampshire's famous victory over Warwickshire in 1922.

85 Desmond Eagar   **86** Derek Shackleton

They included Jimmy Gray, a redoubtable opener, Henry Horton, squat and pugnacious at the wicket, and the Antiguan, Danny Livingstone. Outstanding among them was the bespectacled and, on occasion, temperamental West Indian, Roy Marshall. His cavalier assaults at the beginning of an innings not only entertained richly, but also gave the bowlers that much more time to rid themselves of the opposition.

In 1958 the flamboyant Colin Ingleby-Mackenzie became captain. The 1960s and the 1920s share an atmosphere of gaiety, bordering on the frenetic. Ingleby-Mackenzie, his man-about-town image firmly implanted in the public mind, emulated Lionel Tennyson's ebullience of the earlier decade, that similarity balanced by the aptness of each to his particular time. Ingleby-Mackenzie inculcated a cheerful brand of camaraderie among his men, and, in his first year as captain, Hampshire were second to Surrey, then completing their formidable run of successes. After two middling years, the new captain led Hampshire to their first title, holding off the challenge of the strong Yorkshire and Middlesex teams.

It was a surprising success, unpredicted by the cricketing gurus, and a triumph of teamwork without reliance on world stars. It is true that Shackleton and Marshall had bonny seasons, but the achievement was well earned by lively out-cricket and determined, often quickfire batting. It was at Dean Park, Bournemouth, that victory over Derbyshire brought the Championship to Hampshire, it being only the fifth time the pennant had escaped the greedy clutches of the plutocratic six or seven counties which had dominated the proceedings for a hundred years.

Moons wax, then wane. This team, much the result of Desmond Eagar's promptings and searchings, was not a young one, and half a dozen

87 Roy Marshall

lean years passed. Bob Cottam, one of Hampshire's few quick bowlers of first-class merit, had blossomed, and then moved on to Northamptonshire. Only Peter Sainsbury remained of the old guard, but other faces emerged, notably David Turner and Trevor Jesty, Tom Mottram and Bob Herman (son of Lofty Herman), with Bob Stephenson taking Harrison's place behind the stumps. Richard Gilliat was a forcing bat, and, in some judgements, Hampshire's cleverest skipper. However, the basic factor in the county's recovery was their gifted opening duo from overseas: Barry Richards, the imperious South African, and the West Indian, Gordon Greenidge, brought up in the south of England, and just then coming into his own as a world-class batsman. Richards, denied opportunities because of his country's scabrous political condition, occasionally lacked commitment, the county circuit sometimes proving too desultory for one of his majesty. Nonetheless, with Greenidge, he provided sufficient runs rapidly for Hampshire to prosper, and, with sensible bowling supported by excellent fielding, they won the Championship a second time in 1973.

Five out of seven matches were won at the start of the season, and then, after some midsummer doldrums, a late run of six wins from seven matches played decided the issue. A low-scoring game at Southampton saw Hampshire crucially defeat their close rivals, Northamptonshire, and, finally, the beating of Gloucestershire at Bournemouth clinched the title. Hampshire were second and third in the next two years, but have not since touched the heights of 1973. Their roller coaster story continued. They were bottom in 1980 and runners up to Middlesex in 1985.

Hampshire have always been fortunate in their choice of West Indians. After Roy Marshall, first Andy Roberts and then Malcolm Marshall, each at his peak the world's fiercest fast bowler, joined Greenidge, who, by the 1980s, touched superb stature as a comprehensively talented opening bat. Under the assured captaincy of Mark Nicholas, players such as Tim Tremlett, Chris Smith and Paul Terry did well and, by 1990, when Robin Smith had emerged as a leading England

batsman, Hampshire were third in the county table.

On balance, Hampshire's stronger sides have competed in the era of one-day cricket, and Hampshire have always been regarded as a likely proposition in these competitions. Richards, Greenidge, Roberts or Marshall could, after all, win a one-day contest out of hand in a few overs of individual magnificence. Surprisingly, Hampshire, despite some goodish runs, never even appeared in a Lord's cup final until 1988, when they won the Benson and Hedges Cup. It was a match billed as Derbyshire's bowlers versus Hampshire's batsmen, but Steve Jefferies made a mockery of newspaper prediction. Catching Derbyshire flat-footed in helpful early morning conditions, the South African took 5 for 13 (the best figures ever in a Benson's final) with his left-hand seam, and thus Hampshire were able to proceed with little discomfort to their first trophy. Three years later, in 1991, they won the NatWest Trophy at their first attempt, beating Surrey in the last over of an evenly contested final. After competent work in the field, they gradually overhauled the Surrey total, with Robin Smith the determined mainstay.

If Hampshire have sometimes disappointed with below-par performances in the knock-out competitions, their vigorous and enterprising batting over the last twenty years has served them well in the less intense and less immediate battles of the Sunday League. This Hampshire have won three times, and no one else has bettered this. They won in 1975, in the palmy days of Richards and Gilliat, and then again in 1978. Their last League title was in 1986. Despite two August losses, they concluded their programme in style, winning the last four games, and fending off the tough challenge of the holders, Essex. Tim Tremlett, with the ball, and Robin Smith, with the bat, made the most influential contributions.

Hampshire, like other counties, may point to jovial cards reflective of the shire's rumbustious character. We have noted the positively Wodehousian traits of some of their giants. The irascible Lord Tennyson could burst into aristocratic wrath like one of Bertie Wooster's uncles, or, indeed,

88 Robin Smith

aunts, while Colin Ingleby-Mackenzie's languid style was of a piece with the debonair Psmith or Piccadilly Jim. But are these more typical than, say, the conscientious Phil Mead or Derek Shackleton, the one accumulating runs with prudent care, the other wheeling away with geometric precision?

Perhaps there was never too defined a Hamp-shire character. Perhaps the cheerful sportsman-ship associated with their winning spells was the buoyancy which comes from playing well and winning. What is certain is that, in the cosmopoli-tan ethos of today's county cricket, whatever local character did exist must have disappeared. No team illustrates the assorted quarterings of present-day cricket more colourfully than Hampshire. Of the fourteen key players listed in *Wisden* as having represented the county in, for example, 1987, not one was born in Hampshire, and no less than seven were born abroad, with London, Chippenham, Cuckfield, Lambeth, Shaftesbury, Wellington and Somerset given as the birth-place of the others. Some of the seven 'foreigners' contrive to have licit England qualifications, but it does seem a little hollow when folk rhapsodize over Hampshire as the cradle of cricket.

It also makes the selection of an All-Hampshire team vaguely spurious, but, in the main, one would turn to the earlier phases of the county's story, and eschew the splendiferous overseas stars of recent years, even including Gordon Greenidge, who joined Hampshire as a colt. Roy Marshall — who qualified by residence — must open the batting, and his venturesome flair would need the backing of one of Hampshire's more cautious openers, such as Arnold, Rogers or Gray: on balance, the consistency of Johnny Arnold must tell. Philip Mead, of course, massively prolific, would be the other certain batting choice, with Robin Smith, the current star, and George Brown perhaps picking up two more places against substantial opposition.

Four captains might struggle over the sixth position: Tennyson, Eagar, Ingleby-Mackenzie and Gilliat, all handsome forcing bats. In spite of his erratic manners, Lord Tennyson, who did on occasion captain England, should possibly be permitted to lead the enterprise. Hampshire have had a worthy rather than a resplendent line of wicket-keepers, right through to Bobby Parks, inheritor of the famous Sussex lineage, and now Adrian Aymes. Sentiment might indicate that 'Lordship' — as Tennyson was customarily known — should be permitted his Jeeves in the person of Livsey.

The main bowling is straightforward. Newman, Kennedy and Shackleton would be as automatic in selection as Mead. That leaves scope for a spinner, maybe Charles Knott or Peter Sainsbury, or that rarity among home-bred Hampshire players, a genuine fast bowler, such as Butch White or Bob Cottam. Perhaps the die should be cast for the latter.

Thus it would be something of a curate's egg, this Hampshire team. It would have five capable of holding their heads high in any company; a couple of good-class performers; and the rest just a shade short of major recognition: Roy Marshall, Johnny Arnold, Philip Mead, Robin Smith, George Brown, Lionel Tennyson, Walter Livsey, Jack Newman, Alec Kennedy, Derek Shackleton and Bob Cottam.

SIX

Kent

No county is more redolent of the idyll of cricket than Kent. The senses are engaged. One easily visualizes the typical village green, with the brawny smith bowling fast long hops at the perturbed young clergyman. It is a timeless rapture, evoking the musty smell of linseed oil in cramped pavilions, and the eternal crack of leather on willow.

Kent has as early and as good a claim as any shire to epitomizing, in its origins, that rhapsodic picture. The great estates of the Garden of England resourced cricketers, and the lords of these estates were Kent's first patrons. In the pre-history of county cricket, Kent were the most notable. The Sackville family and Sir Horace Mann, Stephen Amherst, and Edwin Stead of Harrietsham were the leading benefactors, employing talented cricketers and organizing representative games, usually for a substantial stake. Throughout the Hanoverian period, 'Fierce Kent, ambitious of the first applause', were exceedingly strong, and certain grounds of note emerged, such as Horace Mann's Bishopsbourne Paddock, near Canterbury, or the Vine at Sevenoaks, belonging to the Sackvilles.

After a quiet time around the start of the 19th century, an exceptional side, representative of Kent, developed during the first two or three decades of Victoria's reign. It included the champion of England, 'kind and manly' Alfred Mynn; Fuller Pilch and Felix, both quick-scoring bats; Ned Wenman, wise captain and fearless wicketkeeper; and Hillyer, most accurate of medium-pace bowlers. In 1842, the famous Canterbury cricket week, with the theatricals of the Old Stagers a constituent part, was inaugurated, and, from 1847, its venue was the St Lawrence ground. In all these ways did Kent enjoy the impetus of a glorious start, and, in 1859, a preliminary attempt at a county structure was made. The acknowledged establishment of the Kent

club was, however, in 1870, when, with the redoubtable and autocratic Lord Harris taking the chair, a meeting was held at the Bull Inn, Rochester. It was resolved to amalgamate the Kent cricket club and the Beverley cricket club and thus form a county combine, with its headquarters at Canterbury, and it was proposed to form a committee equally representative of the east and west portions of the county.

This essay in merging the two halves of the county, and the two clubs that served them, is noteworthy. In the east lay Canterbury, the prestigious ecclesiastical base and an important staging-post on the road to the ports of Dover and Folkestone. In the west were the fine towns of Sevenoaks, Maidstone, Tonbridge and Tunbridge Wells. Maidstone had the biggest population, but none of them was large, and Sevenoaks was quite small. The administrative offices of the county came to reside in Maidstone, and, although these Kentish boroughs and ports were busy enough, none of them commanded massive authority. With Lord Harris an imposing presence, and captain from 1875 to 1889, there was no fear of coup nor rebellion, and, while Canterbury was unchallenged as the stronghold, the other towns had some share of the games, usually through the medium of a festival week.

Despite their tradition, Kent were, Sussex apart, the least successful of the princely eight-some, and spent over twenty years in the greyness of mid-table. Why was this record so unprepossessing? Part of the answer must lie in Kent's position as third in line of the immediate home counties, with Middlesex and Surrey reaping some reward in support, and, through the financial strength of that support, in players, from their central London locations. Kent cricket was just too far out of town to benefit from the metropolitan influence, and yet near enough to be possibly affected adversely. Even in the 18th century, the

Kentish bucks had often opted to stage their games in London itself, for there they found convivial society and interest. Lord Harris persuaded some of the likely amateurs to play county, and not country house, cricket, but they were rarely able to play with collective regularity, and there was scarcely a professional backbone to the side. Until he emigrated to be Bombay's governor, Lord Harris was a stout-hearted batsman, and E. F. S. Tylecote was one of the finest amateur wicket-keepers there have been; but a general consistency was lacking.

Slowly, that harmony arrived, and Kent broached their most satisfying phase in the seasons prior to the First World War. From 1890, when the Championship became absolutely 'official', Kent surpassed all with their habitual success. Save for 1895 and 1897, when they unaccountably fell headlong down the table, they were frequently strong contenders. They won the Championship for the first time in 1906, and repeated that feat in 1909, 1910 and 1913. They were also forceful runners-up in 1908 and 1911, and they were third in 1890, 1900, 1904, 1912 and 1914. They were, by some considerable margin, the most brilliant county team of the Edwardian era.

In the early days of the decade, Kent depended very much on Jack Mason, said to be the best-loved of Kent captains, and on the professionals, Alec Hearne and F. H. Huish. As the team approached its victorious run, there appeared K. L. Hutchings, a powerful driver, and Arthur Fielder, a genuine fast bowler, both of them amateurs. Gradually, however, Kent were bending to the inevitable, and, by the outbreak of war, they fielded, bar the captain (and an occasional visitant, such as the leg-break bowler, D. W. Carr), a full professional complement. H. T. W. Hardinge and James Seymour, two competent bats, and W. J. Service, the steadiest of stock bowlers, were among them. Hardinge, with over 32,000 runs, and Seymour, with nearly 27,000, stand respectively second and fourth in the county's list of run-getters. The scoring was zestful, and the fielding was akin to modern standards, while, in Colin Blythe, Kent had the

89 Colin Blythe

perfect match-winner, one of the classic left-handers of that or any other period. Of a highly taut and sensitive nature, he raised the science of spin bowling to the plane of artistry, his sharp turn on bad wickets and perplexing flight on plumb ones causing anxiety among the most confident batsman. He was killed in the First World War, having taken 2210 wickets for his native county.

Kent maintained their equilibrium between the wars. Although they never won the Championship, they were out of the top eight on only three occasions, and out of the top five in but five seasons, a most consistent record.

No single contributor was more influential than Frank Woolley, who played first in 1906 and was well established by the outbreak of war. He continued afterwards, and sustained his unrivalled all-round performance until 1938. Despite the loss of wartime seasons, the tall, almost balletic Woolley contrived to score just short of 59,000 runs, second in the world rankings behind Jack Hobbs; to take over 2000 wickets with left-hand spin, beautifully moulded on Blythe's pattern; and to take 1018 catches with sublime nonchalance in the slips: this was a world record, for no one else has caught 900, let alone 1000, victims.

It is something of a cliché for cricket commentators to complain that statistics are a banal way of describing such cricketing artists, but all are agreed that this is true of Frank Woolley, who must compete only with W. G. Grace, George Hirst and Wilfred Rhodes for the title of England's greatest all-rounder. What E. W. Swanton called his 'majestic indifference' of carriage lent Woolley a poise which watchers found alluring. The telescopic reach, which also benefited his slip catching, allowed him to make mock of the concept of the good length, and, with a lissom gracefulness, he deftly stroked the ball hither and yon. Yet, for all that effortless pliancy, there was also a grandeur of power, so that, in an encapsulation of sport, orthodoxy, potency and style were as one.

Kent were lucky to enjoy the services of a galaxy of bright amateur stars alongside the inimitable Woolley. A. P. F. Chapman, B. H.

90 A. P. F. Chapman

Valentine and F. G. H. Chalk, who all captained Kent, were among this lively troupe of scintillating batsmen. Eventually, the utility of a capable opening partnership developed in the hands of Arthur Fagg and Leslie Todd, while that most enterprising of wicket-keeper-batsmen, L. E. G. Ames, was already well established. There was something of Jekyll and Hyde about his cricket: on the one hand, the impeccable but unobtrusive wicket-keeper; on the other hand, the lethally explosive batsman. Few wicket-keepers have been his equal; none approach him in the all-round sense, for his 37,000 runs place him in the top thirty of world batsmen. He had over 1000 dismissals to his credit, and his 1929 total of 128 and his 1928 total of 122 victims are the first and second highest in a season.

Ames may have been fortunate in keeping wicket to Tich Freeman, who stands next only to Wilfred Rhodes as a captor of wickets. A. P. Freeman took 3776 first-class wickets from his début in 1914 to his retirement in 1936. For a leg-spin and googly merchant, he was extremely accurate, especially as he imparted acute deviation. Moreover, he had an inexplicable resource of stamina, and so this tiny, wizened figure could rock and roll through over after over, summer after summer, scarcely ever than with devastating consequences. He took 100 wickets seventeen times, including a record eight seasons when he passed 200; indeed, his 304 in 1928 and 298 in 1933 are the best trawls ever in a season. There was something goblinesque about Freeman, not only in configuration, but in the magical fashion he danced the overs away inexhaustibly, with mortal indiscretions contributing to his matchless tallies.

Overlapping slightly with him and then playing on until the late 1950s, the Second World War erasing what would have been his prime years, came D. V. P. Wright. Here was a leg-spinner of a different type. Marsupial-like in his bounding, springing run, he bowled leg-spinners at fizzing pace, with bounce and spin in correlated amounts. He took 2000 wickets in a career in which he strove mightily after the ideal, and during which, when that ideal was attained, he tormented batsmen of world class.

91 Leslie Ames

He was unlucky enough to find himself in Kent teams principally bereft of other high-class bowlers, and which, in post-war years, was not so rich, as Kent had usually been, in attacking batsmanship. The old hands kept the flag flying breezily for a couple of seasons, but, from 1948 to 1963, Kent managed a single figure placement just twice. Little went right, and, as so often happens in parlous times, there were captaincy troubles. Throughout these years, the standard-bearer of the ancient Kentish tradition was Godfrey Evans. Mercurial and exuberant in attitude behind the stumps, where Ames had been restful and quiescent, he brought an ebullient spirit as well as an energetic talent to the game. With a thousand dismissals to his name, he became one of England's most popular sportsmen and earned no less than ninety-one Test appearances.

From 1957 to 1971, Colin Cowdrey captained Kent, emulating the fifteen-year reign of Lord Harris. He had no designs on imitating his Lordship's dogmatic character, to the point where some believe his brooding introspection hindered and curtailed Cowdrey's noble genius. Freed from such agnostic doubtings, there was no one to equal the rich and composed gravity of his delicate technique, no batsman more exquisitely bred in the proprieties of unhurried method. His 114 caps and his captaincy of England on twenty-seven occasions testify to his weighty class, and, in first-class cricket, he scored over 42,000 runs. With 1000 runs in each of twenty-seven seasons (only Mead equalled and only Grace and Woolley, with twenty-eight seasons, surpassed this); with the aplomb of his virtuoso slip fielding; and with the chivalry of his leadership, Colin Cowdrey proved to be one of England's few post-war cricketers of outstanding merit. He was portly of build, like unto a friar, and his compound of contemplation and joviality also fitted that image.

Wright, Evans, Cowdrey: Kent continued to produce great names, but great teams were slow to materialize. Then, after being second consecutively in 1967 and 1968, Cowdrey's side won the Championship in 1970. Leslie Ames had continued to be an influence as cricket manager, and

92 Doug Wright

a well-balanced team carried off the trophy, scoring 282 in three hours to beat a strong Nottinghamshire side at Folkestone, trouncing Leicestershire on the same ground, and taking sufficient points off Surrey at the Oval to clinch the title.

Brian Luckhurst and Michael Denness, both of whom had international careers, the latter as England's captain, were as solid an opening pair as Fagg and Todd had been, and now, with overseas players available, Asif Iqbal, the exciting Pakistani batsman, and John Shepherd, the solid West Indian all-rounder, proved to be invaluable contributors. Alan Knott, of the callisthenics between deliveries and the innovatory batsmanship, became one of the world's great wicket-

93 'Tich' Freeman

keepers. With 1344 dismissals, he stands fourth in the world list, and his 269 international victims make him, on figures, England's most successful, with only R. W. Marsh, of Australia, and Jeffrey Dujon, of West Indies, his masters, numerically speaking, at that level.

His athletic wicket-keeping was a splendid foil for the destroyer, Derek Underwood. Only Freeman and Blythe have taken more wickets for Kent, and, in all first-class play, Underwood had 2465 confounded victims. He bowled his left-hand spin more quickly than Blythe, hustling batsmen with this liveliness of pace, accompanied by exactness of length and that bare sufficiency of movement which is often more destructive than wide-angled turn.

While lacking top-line fast bowlers, this was, effectively, the first Kent team that bore comparison with their Edwardian predecessors. Nor were Kent content with that solitary achievement. They won the title twice more in 1977 and 1978, under the captaincy of Asif Iqbal and A. G. E. Ealham respectively. Players such as Bob Woolmer, Graham Johnson, Chris Tavaré, who later moved to Somerset, and Norman Graham reinforced or replaced the 1970 originals, and the same vein of attacking bowling, diligent batting and colourful fielding was tapped.

Then leaner times returned. Kent were next to bottom in 1980, and looked unlikely competitors throughout the 1980s, although, under the leadership of Cowdrey's son, Chris, they assembled a conscious and united effort to be runners-up in 1988. Richard Ellison and, until departing to Worcestershire, Graham Dilley came to the fore in these later years.

Apart from a quarter century after the Second World War, therefore, Kent have been a team of excellent, if not superlative, achievement, and their style has been generally one that is relevant to one-day cricket — one may imagine what joy J. R. Mason's Edwardian heroes or the likes of Woolley, Ames or Valentine would have found and given in limited-over combat.

The flourishing Kent XI of the 1970s was at home in one-day as in three-day cricket. They beat Somerset by 32 runs to win the 1967 Gillette

94 Derek Underwood

Cup, and then, having been defeated, in spite of an exhilarating knock by Asif, by Lancashire in a splendid match in 1971, they next beat those same opponents by 4 wickets in a final sadly affected by rain in 1974. The Benson and Hedges Cup brought more successes. They beat Worcestershire twice by strangely similar margins – 39 and 43 runs – in 1973 and 1976, and they beat Derbyshire by a comfortable 6 wickets in 1978. They lost to Gloucestershire by 64 runs in 1977. That amounted to six final appearances during the 1970s. The 1980s brought three more such appearances, but less good fortune: Somerset and Middlesex carried off the NatWest Trophy in 1983 and 1984, while, in a pulsating finish, Middlesex robbed them of the Benson's Cup by a mere couple of runs in 1986.

Kent also won the John Player League three times in the 1970s, in 1972, 1973 and 1976. In Cup or League, they were always reckoned bonny battlers, as, over a twelve-year span, 1967 to 1978, they won eleven titles. Few counties can point to so intense a record of concentrated achievement, even if the last few years have been much less fruitful.

An embarrassment of riches confronts the selectors of a greatest-ever Kent XI, the unease compounded by the replication of some forms of largesse – wicket-keepers – and the absence of other examples – fast bowling.

Wicket-keeping is a rare poser. Fred Huish, Jack Hubble, Ames, W. H. V. Levett, Evans and Knott: it is an imposing lineage, with three competing (were one deaf to the strangled cries from the advocates of Strudwick, Duckworth and Taylor) for an All-England XI. The busy Evans, obdurate or invigorating as the occasion invited, and Alan Knott, carving weirdly, were valued middle-order batsmen, especially when on Test duty. However, Ames's hundred 100s give him the clear edge. Over against the elfin vim of Evans and the gnomic assiduity of Knott, Ames brought to wicket-keeping a faultlessness equally beyond mortal ken: it is said he missed only four chances in his forty-seven Tests.

The Kentish proclivity for quality wicket-keepers is scarcely explicable, save by delightful coincidence. One might, nonetheless, muse over their relation to Kent's heritage of spin bowling – Huish and Blythe, Ames and Freeman, Evans and Wright, Knott and Underwood – and see in these duos mutually endorsed arts.

If dismissed batsmen be labelled victims, then Freeman must be something of a mass murderer, and the leg-spin of his contemporary, C. S. Marriott, should not be forgotten. Doug Wright, when environmental conditions and personal balance co-existed, worried the greatest, whereas Freeman, some whispered, picked off the weaklings. Oddly, Kent have never had an off-spinner in the same category, yet, in Blythe and Underwood, whatever their contrasting methodologies, they have had a pair of left-handers of international renown. The judgement of Solomon might be to jettison convention and play all four maestros, arguing that Kent's quick bowlers over a hundred years would not warrant inclusion beyond any of this distinguished quartet. Only Arthur Fielder, with over 1000 wickets for Kent, or Dilley, on his dog days, might be considered, and no room could be found for those sturdy journeymen who have been

Kent's stock bowlers over the years, men such as Hearne, Ridgway, Martin, Dixon, Fairservice and Halfyard.

From Ashdown and Hardinge, Kent have usually found useful opening combines, and, on figures alone, Hardinge and Fagg would get the call. With Woolley, the complete all-rounder, and Cowdrey in the slips, next to Ames, the Kent fielding would be true to the county's proud yardstick, but the tail would be on the longish side, and it would be necessary to call up that steady run-maker, James Seymour. An alternative might have been Percy Chapman, who played for and captained England, for he was, between the wars, a swashbuckling bat and a blistering fielder.

Chapman, along with Lord Harris, Mason and Valentine might each have made a more dynamic skipper than Colin Cowdrey, but this would be a self-propelled side, in little need of an external spur: H. T. W. Hardinge, Arthur Fagg, Frank Woolley, Leslie Ames, Colin Cowdrey, James Seymour, Arthur Fielder, Doug Wright, Derek Underwood, Tich Freeman and Colin Blythe.

SEVEN

Lancashire

The tale of Lancashire describes what, in other circles, might be called a curve of normal distribution: beginning slowly, with little initial success; rising to taste the joys of Championship delight, with first A. N. Hornby and then Archie MacLaren in the lead; and next, halfway through their story, reaching the pinnacle of their notability in the late 1920s with a hat-trick of titles and a further one in 1930 – for this was Lancashire's greatest XI. Then, having peaked, they drifted slightly, picking up a title in 1934 and a share of the Championship in 1950, with a sturdy post-war team; and finally sliding downhill into oblivion for nearly forty years, saved only from bleak despair by the brilliant antics of their one-day performances in the 1970s and the nascent hope of their most recent summers.

For Lancashire, read Manchester. As the great north midland city, spurred on mainly by the cotton boom, increased in size and prosperity during the early 19th century, it sought to match its rivals culturally, with its orchestra, its newspaper, its parks, its public works, and so on. The first major industrial city, at once astonishing and frightening, its mercantile gentry sought respectability in a county cricket team, and one such was formed – at the Queen's Hotel in 1864, chiefly around the weighty membership of the Manchester Club, which had been in existence since 1818.

The Manchester Club had had two or three premises, penultimately at a site south of the city. In 1857 one of those very cultural activities that were felt to mark the rise of a regional capital was held there: it was the Art Treasures Exhibition, one of the first provincial festivals of its kind, modelled, with royal patronage, on the Great Exhibition of 1851. Grudgingly the cricketers moved. They left what was to become the Royal Botanical Gardens and later the White City greyhound stadium, and re-formed a few yards further south. At a lease of £1000, a splendid real estate investment, they established themselves at what was to become the famous Old Trafford cricket ground.

Despite the proximity of Liverpool and a thriving Merseyside and of several other cricketing centres in south and east Lancashire, the Manchester Club and the county club remained solidly coupled. Nowhere in the history of the counties is the predominance of a city over a county club as marked as with Lancashire. The Manchester Club paid the expenses of county matches, provided all home matches were played at Old Trafford; it employed the professionals who played for the county; it selected the county team; and, on almost all its own outings, the Manchester Club fielded the county side.

The names that are recalled from Lancashire's antiquity in the beneficent thrall of Manchester are S. H. Swire, the organizing genius of this exercise in duality, and the Rowley family – for, like Middlesex or Gloucestershire, Lancashire had its seminal kin-group – in particular E. B. Rowley, Lancashire's first captain. Professionals were introduced, but, at first, amateurs were more prominent, and the subscribing membership grew. After Manchester's bravura pioneering in novel industrial habits, the town's 'shopocracy' mellowed a little, its radical tradition became subdued, and its parvenu members began to ape the lordlings of the south. Richard Cobden, founder and personification of Manchesterism, mourned the fact that these erstwhile souls of independent self-help had degenerated into 'the toadies of a clodpole aristocracy'. Part of this transformation of Manchester man into Lancashire gentleman, this switch from fierce individualism to conservatism, was, therefore, the creation of a county cricket club.

However, the competitive flame still burned brightly. It was not sufficient to have any old county club: it had to be an excellent one, and one that could bear comparison with the more aristocratically patronized clubs of the south, as well as their rivals among the woollen mills and iron foundries across the Pennines, and also among the hosiery trades and coal-pits of Nottinghamshire. Thus, after playing and beating Middlesex in their début county match in 1865, Lancashire set about building a team of which their membership might be proud. They were less bothered, in an area which owed much to incomers and inventions, by the narrow restraints of birthplace, about which Nottinghamshire and Yorkshire hugely concerned themselves; they grew even less anxious about providing cricket as such for the membership. Their purpose quickly became the creation of a team that the membership would watch and enjoy.

Professional bowlers were sought, such as Alec Watson, who, at a time when football 'professors' were crossing the border to join north-western clubs, migrated from Scotland. His off-breaks brought him just over 1300 county wickets, and he easily remains top of the all-Lancashire bowling averages. George Nash, John Crossland and William McIntyre were other successful and stalwart paid bowlers. Richard Barlow took over 700 wickets, and was distinctly an all-rounder, but he is chiefly recalled in legend and verse for his prudent stone-walling. He scored 8000 runs for Lancashire, often taking an unconscionably long time about it, and, in first-class cricket, he carried his bat no less than eleven times for Lancashire. He was obsessed with cricket. He toured Australia three times and never missed a match; he umpired for as long as he had played; and he surrounded himself in his home with cricketing memorabilia.

The team was lifted by the fluent work of Richard Pilling, 'the prince of wicket-keepers', a title too easily bestowed on some but, by all accounts, well merited in the case of one of the first world-class wicket-keepers, who died of consumption at the age of only thirty-five. These paid players supported amateurs such as the clergyman-schoolmaster, Vernon Royle, king of cover-points; and the lawyer, A. G. Steel, a fine

athlete, and, apart from Ken Cranston, Lancashire's chief amateur all-rounder.

This XI was galvanized into action by 'Monkey' Hornby, who captained England as well as Lancashire, and who exerted a tremendous influence on the county's cricketing fortunes for generations. Aggressive, even intemperate, in manner, he joined with the bearded and lugubrious Barlow in a well-balanced opening partnership, made memorable by the poem 'At Lord's' by Francis Thompson, a partnership in which amateur explosiveness was tempered by professional caution. In an era of fewer matches and fewer runs, Hornby was Lancashire's first player to pass 1000 runs in a season, but his major purpose was, by thorough but fair-minded discipline, to instil a sense of teamwork into the county side. In this, he was emphatically modern in approach, and nowhere is this better demonstrated than in his insistence on competent and zealous fielding.

The season of 1878 was an important one. The Australian and Gloucestershire games at Old Trafford were attended by huge crowds, among the biggest seen in the provinces, an authentic illustration that the county clubs had to provide spectator entertainment as well as just a sporting venue for the subscribing members. In 1879, in a pleasing finale for E. B. Rowley, Lancashire had shared the Championship with Nottinghamshire; in 1880, Hornby took over and Lancashire truly emerged as a premier combine. They took the title in 1881 and shared it with Nottinghamshire in 1882, losing only one county game in those two seasons.

Lancashire suffered problems with residential qualifications and with the throwing controversies of that era, both, directly or indirectly, the consequence of seeking to procure a team commensurate with the area's matchless economy. This was unsettling, but, although Hornby never led Lancashire to another Championship success, he never led them poorly, and, throughout this Victorian heyday, Lancashire were always near the top of the table.

Archie MacLaren was heir to the Hornby heritage and his favoured son, although he lacked some of Hornby's completeness as a captain, and saved many of his best feats for the international scene, especially the arena of Sydney. He has become a hallmark for Edwardian grandeur, his imperious effrontery in attack and tight-lipped valour in defence all but a self-parody of pre-1914 values. He was also the most efficient slip fielder of that generation. The regal flow of his batting was never better seen than when he scored 424 at Taunton against hapless Somerset. The bowling and fielding was none too hot (although Somerset contrived to bowl twenty-five five-ball overs an hour during this marathon) but the boundaries were not restricted and the ground not pristine. Most important of all, it was the first time that a target of 400 had been achieved in the first-class

game. Although matched on a few occasions on the harder tables of Australia and the sub-continent, this was never approached in English conditions until the prodigious Hick topped 400, also versus Somerset, also at Taunton, in 1988. Because the pioneering breakthrough, like Roger Bannister's four-minute mile, is the most arduous, it is possible to regard MacLaren's achievement as the most splendid batting perfor-mance, statistically speaking, in the history of county cricket.

Archie MacLaren shared with his friend and mentor, W. G. Grace, the flaws of mortal clay: theatrical and aristocratic in play, off the field he could be irksome as well as disorganized. None-theless, from the stand, he was and must be judged Lancashire's finest batsman and one of England's greatest. He scored 15,000 runs for Lancashire, and proved to be a knowledgeable if somewhat obstinate and unlucky captain. He was in good company, as the Edwardian summers beckoned. He was to be enjoyed in fruitful association with another amateur of verve, R. H. Spooner, a great cover-point and a driver of grandeur, while his partnerships with John Tyldesley may rightly be seen as the most sublime token of amateur and professional batsmen in concert. Drawn from different classes, joined in mutual respect, they became the golden prototype of that Edwardian cross-class divide. J. T. Tyldesley betrayed none of the polite diffi-dence of his civil manner when at the crease, where, like some frenzied assassin, he committed the most grievous assaults on fearful bowlers. It is sufficient to say that, in what is regarded as England's best-ever Test XI in 1902, he was the only professional bat to be included. With 32,000 runs, he is the county's second highest scorer.

The main bowlers were Walter Brearley, the brash, opinionated fast bowler, and Arthur Mold, with 1543 victims off his strike bowling, the county's third best attacker, at an average of about 15. Albert Ward and George Baker presented rational contributions as honest profes-sional batsmen. Then there was Johnny Briggs, far and away Lancashire's best all-rounder, for he is the only one to have scored over 10,000 runs

SOMERSET COUNTY CRICKET GROUND,
TAUNTON, JULY 15th, 16th & 17th, 1895.

SOMERSET v. LANCASHIRE.

LANCASHIRE. First Innings.		Second Innings.
1 A. C. MacLaren c Fowler b Gamlin	424 *	
2 Ward c R. Palairet b Tyler	64	
3 Paul c Gamlin b L. Palairet	177	
4 Sugg c Wickham b Woods	41	
5 Tinsley c Gamlin b Woods	0	
6 Baker st Wickham b L. Palairet	23	
7 Briggs not out	9	
8 C. H. Benton c and b Fowler	43	
9 Smith c Trask b L. Palairet	0	
10 Hallam c Fowler b L. Palairet	6	
11 Mold c R. Palairet b Gamlin	0	
B 9, l-b 4, w 1	14	

	Total....801 †		Total....

1-141 2-504 3-530 4-637 5-732 6-738 7-792 8-792 9-798 10-801
1- 2- 3- 4- 5- 6- 7- 8- 9- 10-

SOMERSET. First Innings.		Second Innings.	
1 L. C. H. Palairet b Briggs	30 b Mold		4
2 G. Fowler c Sub. b Hallam	39 c MacLaren b Mold		46
3 R. C. N. Palairet c Hallam b Mold	2 st Smith b Briggs		7
4 H. T. Stanley c Smith b Briggs	8 c Smith b Mold		12
5 R. B. Porch run out	18 c MacLaren b Mold		1
6 S. M. J. Woods c Smith b Mold	11 b Briggs		55
7 Dr. J. E. Trask c Ward b Mold	11 c and b Mold		26
8 Tyler not out	15 b Briggs		41
9 E. W. Bartlett b Briggs	4 c Mold b Briggs		6
10 Rev. A. P. Wickham b Mold	3 not out		0
11 Gamlin st Smith b Briggs	0 hit wkt. b Briggs		0
L-b 2	2	B 4, l-b 4	8

	Total....143		Total....206

1-71 2-73 3-73 4-94 5-107 6-121 7-122 8-132 9-137 10-143
1-5 2-61 3-61 4-83 5-150 6-151 7-187 8-206 9-206 10-206

Umpires—J. Wickens & F. N. Lowe.   Scorers—T. H. Knight & S. Lunt.
* RECORD for highest Individual Score in First-Class Cricket.
† RECORD for highest Innings in County Cricket.

95 The scorecard showing Archie MacLaren's mammoth score against Somerset in 1895.

96 Lancashire's leading all-rounder
at the turn of the century, Johnny Briggs.

and taken over 1600 wickets; indeed, he stands second only to Statham in the county's list of wicket-takers. A rotund funster, he is considered by many to be Lancashire's best-loved cricketer, and he was much mourned when he died, aged only thirty-nine. He was nicknamed 'Boy' Briggs, in part because he refused to grow up, and threw himself into cricket with a kind of childlike energy. He never despaired: buoyant and inexhaustible with his left-hand spin; instantly on the batting attack; venturesome and courageous in the field.

This strong side always batted well at a time when there were powerful rivals around. They won the Championship twice, their rapid run-making undoing their opponents and leaving time for their dismissal. In 1897 they started and finished in fine style, while, in 1904, they raced through that dry summer, scoring 80 and 100 runs an hour, and were unbeaten.

Lancashire went off the boil a trifle as the First World War approached, but the years beyond that conflict were to prove the most compelling in the county's saga. They were always efficient, first under Myles Kenyon, later under that notable all-rounder, Jack Sharp. Then Major Green, a strict disciplinarian, assumed command, knocked what could have been an awkward squad into ideal shape, and carried off the trophy in all three years of his captaincy: 1926, 1927 and 1928. Seventeen victories in 1926 enabled them to outpace Yorkshire; in the moist summer of 1927 they barely scraped home, but lost only once; but 1928 – a summer of glowing warmth – left them unbeaten and with fifteen wins, giving Lancashire their most clearcut Championship ever. Led by Peter Eckersley, they were joint second in 1929, and then carried off the 1930 Championship, another year of dampness, another year of no losses.

Few counties have exhibited such conscious teamwork. The grinding down of the opposition bowling; the marked acceleration as the innings wore on; the safe if not electrifying fielding; and the balanced bowling. E. A. McDonald, the classic Australian pace bowler, averaged 150 wickets a season over those five years, and Lancashire depended heavily on his effortless and exacting speed and accuracy. He took over 1000 wickets for Lancashire. His counterpart in typology and character was Richard Tyldesley, the corpulent, protesting slow bowler, who took almost 1500 wickets for the county. They were supported by Frank Sibbles, Len Hopwood and the excellent all-rounder, Jack Iddon. In the early 1920s, Cecil Parkin, perhaps the most naturally talented of cricket's comedians, had entertained magnificently and bemused hundreds of batsmen with his guileful bowling: in what amounted to four full seasons, he took not much short of 1000 wickets; but it was his virtuoso comic routines that so delighted his myriad fans.

The batting was in capable hands. Harry Makepeace and Charlie Hallows formed one of the best known of opening partnerships, the former obdurate in the extreme, the latter occasionally forgetting himself sufficiently to indulge in the sleekest of shots. Frank Watson contributed virtuous husbandry of the same mould, and the three of them played, in total, over 1300 times for Lancashire, and amassed among them some 70,000 runs. Ernest Tyldesley turned out to be Lancashire's most productive bat, a handful of runs ahead of his brother, John. With nearly 39,000 first-class runs, he is the only Lancashire bat to have scored 100 top-class centuries, and his county average of 45 is Lancashire's best. A neat, comprehensive and sedate performer, he was much admired for his pleasant, orthodox style.

The Lancashire fielding for once lacked a world-beating cover-point, something that has been a Lancashire speciality from Royle, Spooner and Briggs to Paynter, Washbrook, Lloyd and Fowler. But what they did have, rather rarely in the county annals, was the wicket-keeping of George Duckworth. Typically Lancastrian, appropriately so as Lancashire enjoyed their prime time, Duckworth had 922 victims for the county, twice as many as his nearest Lancashire rival. An astute judge of cricket, he was the most attacking of wicket-keepers, and his voluble, accusatory appeal was a famed trait of cricket between the wars.

This team, one of the most workmanlike in the story of county cricket, began to creak and age. The 1930s were not propitious, although, to general surprise, Lancashire did win the Championship again, in 1934. Sussex were overtaken on the run-in as Lancashire rallied well in the closing stages. In the last two years before the second war, Len Wilkinson was an overnight revelation as a leg-spinner, but he never recovered his form after the war. The one player to emerge and to concentrate a colourful England and county career into the 1930s was the popular left-hander, Eddie Paynter, as fleet of foot in the covers as he was compulsively the assailant as a

97 George Duckworth

batsman. The model of the perky, diminutive bat, he played innings long as well as brisk, and stands, to the surprise of some, fifth in the world Test averages and second in the England Test averages. He was Lancashire's main hope in the pre-war years, as he carved 20,000 silvery runs from his intensely packed and brief career.

Paynter and others never resumed county cricket after the Second World War; Jack Iddon was killed in a car crash, just when some felt he might take up the captaincy; while others, such as A. E. Nutter and Buddy Oldfield, went to different counties. In spite of this, Lancashire rallied solidly in the immediate post-war years, and were very difficult to beat. For a couple of mesmeric seasons, Ken Cranston, playing with the spirit of a club cricketer, captained the XI, and, incidentally, swept himself into the England team, but it was under Nigel Howard (who captained England in India) that they shared the Championship with Surrey, Lancashire's last touch of the purple.

Cyril Washbrook was now at the peak of his long and honourable career, during which he played exactly 500 times for the county. The demands of cricketing expediency and the calls of spectacular entertainment were beautifully mixed in his brand of confidence, tenacity and courage. The premier cover-point of his day, he was but marginally behind Hutton, Compton and Edrich as a superb Test and county batsman, and, in scoring 34,000 first-class runs, he is third to the Tyldesleys in the Lancashire listings. His 1000 runs in each of twenty seasons is a county record, and his towering hook and shattering square cut remain etched in the memory of post-war cricket-lovers.

He was partnered by the dry and technically flawless Winston Place, and these two provided a sound base for the fighting qualities of Geoff Edrich, a canny number three, and of John Ikin, most chivalrous of cricketers. A little later the Australian, Ken Grieves, brought his pugnacious batting and street-wise leg-spin to Old Trafford. These three, with Malcolm Hilton (one of four left-hand spin bowlers around at that time: the others were Bill Roberts, Bob Berry and Eric Price), formed a cordon of close catching that has

98 Cyril Washbrook

perhaps not been matched, as a group, in county cricket. It was they who delivered the *coup de grâce* to many of the 171 batsmen whom Roy Tattersall dismissed in 1950, and, indeed, to the 1000 and more he dispatched for Lancashire during those years. It was, to be sure, on helpful Old Trafford pitches that this loping, pensive off-spinner wrought these deeds of destruction, and he did so with the minimum of fuss.

The post-war years saw the concluding chapters in the careers of Lancashire's two honest-to-goodness fast bowlers, Eddie Phillipson

99 Brian Statham

and T'Owd Chain-horse, grafting Dick Pollard. But 1950 heralded the emergence of Brian Statham, most accomplished of bowlers of the highest pace, and the converse in temperament of the conventional fast bowler. Quiet, gentlemanly, conscientious, he bowled very fast and with impeccable line and length to become Lancashire's leading wicket-taker, with 1816 victims, and 2260 in all first-class games. Unluckily for Lancashire, he was less fortunate in his county than his national partners, until, late on, the robust Ken Higgs – with over 1500 wickets: fourth in the Lancashire list – made his redoubtable mark. Statham, with seventy Test appearances and 252 Test wickets, is Lancashire's most-capped England player, and it may be said of him, quite simply, that, beyond MacLaren, Washbrook and Clive Lloyd with all their flair, he is the best cricketer ever to have played for Lancashire.

Although the county team held together reasonably well for some years, there never seemed any likelihood of recovering the kind of momentum or organization of earlier decades. Some pleasing cricketers adorned these tarnished ranks, among those who spring most readily to mind being Alan Wharton, Geoff Pullar, Peter Marner and Tommy Greenhough, one of the last of the dying breed of leg-spinners. Discontinuities of leadership; disaffection among players, with too many leaving for fresh fields; failures of management, with key figures – for instance, Frank Tyson and Basil D'Oliveira – slipping through the net: all these factors contributed to the decline of Lancashire over the next forty years. Rarely, until the late 1980s, under the spirited captaincy of David Hughes, did they challenge for the Championship; too often for Old Trafford tastes were they to be found propping up the rest.

However, there was one glitteringly bright spell, and that a most thrilling one. In the 1970s, Lancashire produced one of the most exciting and well equipped one-day XIs there has been. They won the first two John Player Sunday competitions in marvellous fashion, in 1969 and 1970, the second of these being especially telling. In that same year they began their domination of the Gillette Cup. They beat the fancied Sussex combination by a margin of 6 wickets, Harry Pilling batting at his inimitable best. In 1971 they defeated Kent by 24 runs in an historic encounter, with their captain, Jack Bond, pulling off an all but fictitious catch to oust Asif Iqbal, when that worthy seemed to be winning the match single-handed. The next year, 1972, saw Lancashire beat Warwickshire by 4 wickets. After a poorish start to a tall challenge, Clive Lloyd smote his way amazingly to 126, said by many to be one of the finest innings ever played at Lord's. In 1974 Kent won a low-scoring and rain-spoiled final by 4 wickets, but, in 1975, Lancashire returned to deal comprehensively with Middlesex, defeating them by 7 wickets. They then lost by 4 wickets to Northamptonshire in 1976, and that marked the end of those seven years crammed full of success. Well led by John Abrahams, Lancashire won the Benson and Hedges Cup in 1984, but, despite scoring 242, were easily beaten by Sussex in the 1986 NatWest final. The glory days were fleeting and gone.

These finals apart, there were thrills and spills galore in the earlier rounds which would not have disgraced the *Hotspur* or the *Magnet*. This was the fifth and last great Lancashire side, and it was optimistically and sympathetically led by Jack Bond. The opening bats were those resilient professionals, Barry Wood, also a useful change bowler, and David Lloyd, who captained Lancashire after Bond. Sometimes, to take advantage of his eager attacking play, Farokh Engineer opened, and, needless to say, that ebullient Indian's wicket-keeping was a major factor in Lancashire's success. The squirrel-like accumulation of tiny Harry Pilling, the first player to score 1000 runs in the Sunday League, neatly amassing runs, while others lunged and scooped, was another asset. Then there was Frank Hayes, who, although he never fulfilled the flamboyantly ambitious promise created for him, was a handsome and glorious striker of the ball, and stands eighth in the all-time Lancashire batting averages. There were valuable little contributions from such as John Sullivan and Andrew Kennedy, while the quick bowling was variously in the competent hands of Peter Lever, Ken Shuttleworth and Peter Lee. To balance that, there was the shrewd, miserly slow bowling of the veteran, Jack Simmons, still weaving his webs in 1989, and David Hughes produced all-round performances that were, on occasion, critical.

The ringmaster of this virtuoso one-day circus was Clive Lloyd, the West Indies captain and one

100 Clive Lloyd

of the more far-sighted overseas investments by a county. Behind the innocence of the large-lensed spectacles, the floppy sun-hat and the gangling gait lay the most ferocious power, a controlled belligerence that could crucially change the direction of a match in minutes. As well as his mighty exploits in instant cricket, he scored heavily in Championship cricket, ending second only to Ernest Tyldesley in the county averages. Moreover, he was as deadly in the field, and, with Hayes, Hughes and the others his satellites, it is difficult to imagine a side which hemmed in and harassed opponents as did this one. Fielding was its crowning glory and its vital weaponry.

Yet, since the 1950s and as the construct of cricket altered, Lancashire seemed blighted. Only in very recent times has David Hughes, in liaison with that astute coach, Alan Ormrod, brought about a revitalization. They were the first winners of the Refuge Assurance Cup in 1988, beating Worcestershire in the play-off final, and next year they won the Refuge Assurance League. In 1990, as well as being sixth in the Championship and second in the Sunday League, they became the first team to win both cup finals. Worcestershire, in the Benson's, and Northamptonshire, in the NatWest, were swept aside with airy contempt. David Hughes had at his disposal the opening pair of Graeme Fowler, a breathtaking fielder, and Gehan Mendis; the explosive Pakistan all-rounder, Wasim Akram; Neil Fairbrother, batting as if in the footsteps of Paynter; the bowling of Paul Allott and Phillip DeFreitas; the capable Mike Watkinson; the emerging young wicket-keeper, Warren Hegg; and the thoroughbred promise of Michael Atherton, established in the England Test team during 1990. Unluckily, 1991 did not see the promise fulfilled. Lancashire came second in three competitions – the Benson's final, the Refuge League and, narrowly, the Refuge Cup – and deteriorated sadly in the Championship.

A Lancashire select XI would alight tidily on the peaks of their history, touching on the golden age of MacLaren, arching through the 1920s, and ending with the post-war delights of Washbrook and Statham. Indeed, Statham and McDonald would provide one of the most dangerous opening attacks on this ethereal county scene, while Johnny Briggs and George Duckworth are unrivalled as all-rounder and wicket-keeper. From Hornby to Atherton, a quarter of Lancashire internationals have been opening bats, but few would cavil at the choice of MacLaren and Washbrook, with the Tyldesleys and Eddie Paynter to follow. Parkin might just edge out Tattersall from the right-arm slower bowling department, and, in the absence of an outstanding left-hander and with a lengthening tail, one might opt for another all-rounder, possibly preferring the leg-spin of A. G. Steel to the more orthodox bowling of Ken Cranston. The fielding, especially the out-fielding, would be superb, and MacLaren needs must be captain: Archie MacLaren, Cyril Washbrook, Ernest Tyldesley, J. T. Tyldesley, Eddie Paynter, A. G. Steel, Johnny Briggs, Ted McDonald, Cecil Parkin, Brian Statham and George Duckworth.

EIGHT

Leicestershire

An advertisement for mountain spring water boasts how the liquid drips slowly for years through the soils, before emerging in all its wholesome glory. The history of Leicestershire cricket is not unlike that process. For nearly a hundred years it was a quiescent, even dormant, force, as if gathering energy for its vigorous putsch during the 1970s.

Entering the Championship along with several other late candidates in 1895, Leicestershire made only single-figure placements in that competition on eleven occasions before 1965, seven before the Second World War and four in the subsequent twenty seasons. A third place in 1953, under the leadership of Charles Palmer, was the best achieved by Leicestershire before the mid-1960s. However, since 1966, the reverse has been broadly true, for the county has only dropped into double-figure placings in six seasons, although this includes a disastrous sixteenth in 1985 and 1991.

During the 1970s, Leicestershire enjoyed, with Ray Illingworth at the helm, a victorious decade. The Championship was won for the first and only time in 1975, with Yorkshire and Hampshire pushed into second and third position. Although, perhaps strangely, Leicestershire have never appeared in the Gillette/NatWest final, they have more than compensated for this by their authoritative displays in the Benson and Hedges Cup.

They won the introductory tournament in this competition in 1972, beating Yorkshire comfortably by 5 wickets. They were beaten in the final by Surrey, with a 27-run margin, in 1974 but returned the next year to defeat the strong Middlesex XI by 5 wickets. Ten years later, in 1985, they beat an equally powerful Essex combine, once more showing a preference for the cushion of 5 wickets. In between times, they enjoyed themselves in the John Player League, and, apart from several other useful perfor-

101 Charles Palmer of Leicestershire leaving with Len Hutton for the 1953–54 MCC tour of West Indies.

mances, they were Sunday champions in 1974 and 1977. That meant five titles in the 1970s but only one in the 1980s. By 1991 the county, having lost Gower to Hampshire and DeFreitas to Lancashire, looked to the all-rounder Chris Lewis for uplift but he has now left for Nottinghamshire.

Cricket had been played in Leicestershire for years, with representative matches against Nottinghamshire arranged in the decade either side of 1800; and a roughshod form of county structure was known in 1820. The Wharf Street ground in Leicester was proudly believed to be one of the finest in the country but, in the 1850s, it fell before the builders' invasion, as Leicester underwent its Victorian boom. However, a Leicestershire Cricket Association was developed; an enclosed ground was found at Grace Road, and in 1879 a county club was formed.

Leicestershire, in its present establishment, is not one of the golden oldies, and enjoyed a relatively brief apprenticeship before being granted first-class status. Indeed, Leicestershire is a straightforward example of an English county of no great size, but centred on a county town of due significance. The county's population is a little more than 800,000, and Leicester's own populace numbers over a quarter of a million, a third, that is, of the county's total. Although Leicestershire move around a little – Melton Mowbray, Hinckley – Leicester has always been the undisputed base, at least five times as big as any other urban community in the county.

With the Quorn Hunt on the one hand and the mines on the other, and with Leicester's own urban history, ranging from its furniture concerns to its influx of ethnic minorities, a major influence, it is a mixed county, and one in which first-class cricket did not take root too happily. Rather like many a hunt, Leicestershire have been reliant on rich patrons, among them Sir Julien Cahn, who also organized his own XI, and was inclined to borrow Leicestershire stars to bolster it when those worthies might have been more gainfully employed supporting the county cause he sponsored.

Until the more creative and external financing of the modern era, Leicestershire had rarely enjoyed much solvency. Through the 1950s, like many other counties, they sought democratic rather than aristocratic patronage by the infinitely patient device of the football competition, with many giving a little a week, rather than the glad-handed days of the past when one or two gave massively. This helped salvage Leicestershire from probable bankruptcy.

The ground has been a further problem. Leicestershire played at Grace Road until 1900, and then had to transfer to Aylestone Road from 1901 to 1939. They moved back to Grace Road in 1946 (and have remained there since), when an electricity works was extended to trespass on the Aylestone Road ground. However, it was 1966, with money a trifle easier, and with the Leicester education authority moving its amenities from Grace Road, before Leicestershire were able to buy the venue outright and develop it.

Leicestershire started their first-class career, schoolboy-yarn style, with a cracking win over Surrey, an extremely tough side at the time. Thereafter they lapsed, and suffered sixty years in the wilderness. It was not that they lacked good players: it was more to do with an inability to recruit sufficient of the precise type and pattern to create a formidable outfit. C. E. de Trafford, captain from 1890 to 1906 and thus leading the county initially into the first-class fray, was a boisterous walloper of a cricket ball; Arthur Woodcock, briefly and around the start of Leicestershire's top-grade history, was the very fast bowler; and Arthur Pougher was, about the same time, one of the country's most efficient all-rounders. Cecil Wood, who captained Leicestershire for three seasons just before and after the 1914–18 war, was a diligent opener, who carried his bat seventeen times for the county, a staggering record, including the only instance in first-class cricket of a man batting throughout both innings and scoring two centuries. That was against Yorkshire in 1911. Another to catch the eye, if for a different reason, was the lay preacher, Albert Knight, who knelt and prayed before the start of his innings. His earthly reward was 18,142 runs. J. H. King, with 22,000 runs and 1100 wickets, was a productive all-rounder of the same period, and, after Astill, Leicestershire's most competent all-round player.

Between the wars Leicestershire were well served by two or three faithful retainers, who loyally and usually uncomplainingly, carried out their duties in a most efficacious manner. These were men who saw none of the power and little of the glory, spending long years at the frustrating business of shoring up feeble teams.

W. E. Astill soldiered on from 1906 to 1939. Scoring a little light of 20,000 runs and, with his leg-breaks, capturing well over 2000 wickets, he is Leicestershire's fifth best bat and by far their leading bowler. There was George Geary, with 11,688 runs and 1759 wickets, who carried a similar cross from 1912 to 1938. His gruff advice when asked by a baffled and greenhorn captain about a bowling change – 'put the bloody clock on

and let's all go home' – is of the stuff of legend. They were assisted by N. F. Armstrong (19,000 runs and almost 600 wickets), the hostile H. A. Smith (over 1000 wickets), a useful wicket-keeper-batsman in Tommy Sidwell and not many others. C. S. Dempster, the New Zealand batsman, captained the side from 1936 to 1938. George Geary played fourteen times for England, and Ewart Astill nine times, but, prior to the 1960s, Leicestershire players had picked up only another ten or so caps among them.

Les Berry overstrode the war, his career beginning with Leicestershire in 1924 and continuing until 1951. This personification of profes-

102 & 103 W. E. Astill (left) and George Geary, Leicestershire's hard-working all-rounders.

sional application is Leicestershire's heaviest scorer. He has a little over 30,000 runs to his distinctive credit, embracing forty-five centuries and 1000 runs in each of eighteen seasons, both also county records. Having scored 1000 in 1925, he proceeded to pass that mark in every first-class season available from 1928 to 1950.

He was accompanied by a troupe of stout-hearted comrades in the post-war years, and they sustained Leicestershire through what, without their influence, might have proved even more parlous days. There was Maurice Tompkin, an upstanding, straight-driving batsman, who died tragically early; and Maurice Hallam, a remarkable fielder and prodigious scorer, second only, with 23,000 runs, to Les Berry. Vic Jackson made a splendid all-round contribution with nearly 15,000 runs and over 900 wickets, while C. T. Spencer, an opening bowler, took some 1300 wickets. Jack Walsh, the Australian wrist-spinner, created a cricketing analogue of the 'Enigma Variations'. Although occasionally erratic, he is said to have been one of the most baffling bowlers ever, and his esoteric skills earned him 1127 gullible victims.

Gradually, at the bank and on the pitch, Leicestershire righted themselves, and thus the 1970s team evolved. It was cannily led by Ray Illingworth, with lots of Yorkshire and international experience to inform him, and with mid-order runs and useful off-spin to secure an all-rounder's place in his own right. There were attractive runs from the Rhodesian, Brian Davison; all-round utility from J. C. Balderstone, and, later, P. B. Clift; and competent batting assistance from Barry Dudleston and N. E. Briers. J. F. Steele and Jack Birkenshaw were capable all-rounders, and Roger Tolchard not only took the honours as wicket-keeper (his 887 victims make a Leicestershire record) but also scored nearly 14,000 lively runs.

In 1975 David Gower made his début. His England caps (over one hundred by 1991) outnumber the gross sum of all Leicestershire Test appearances, bar only those of Illingworth, who played in thirty-one of his sixty-one international matches while wearing Leicestershire colours. Even with reduced first-class play, David Gower has scored over 20,000 runs, over 7000 of them in Tests. His relaxed and effortless aplomb is joyous to behold, save when its fragility appears lackadaisical.

This one major successful side was built on Spartan rather than Athenian lines. If it did not have the quirky character of some of its predecessors, it was shaped on honest-to-goodness though not unattractive lines. It had, in summary,

104 Les Berry

105 David Gower

bowling batsmen and batting bowlers: it had no evident weakness, apart perhaps from a pace bowler of world class. Runs were scored at a brisk rate, and wickets were taken expeditiously. David Gower added the blush of flair to that trusty countenance. Now, sadly for Leicestershire supporters, he has departed for Hampshire.

An intriguing Leicestershire convention has been their offer of cricket's equivalent of political asylum for refugees from other counties, especially since registration was eased. Often these *émigrés* arrived for a year or two at the end of their careers, and even a random sample provides a fascinating picture of shelter sought and granted: Lancashire, with Alan Wharton, Peter Marner, Brian Booth, Ken Higgs and Ken Shuttleworth; and Yorkshire, as well as Illingworth, Jack van Geloven, Gerry Smithson and Willie Watson, provided several such veterans. Charles Palmer came from Worcestershire, while B. R. Knight of Essex, Tony Lock of Surrey, and Peter Willey of Northamptonshire have been other Test players to arrive at Grace Road.

It confuses the already difficult task of selecting a representative XI for Leicestershire, but it is intended to rely on those whose primary career was spent with the county. Even that leaves a problem with the captaincy, for both Palmer and Illingworth, Leicestershire's most distinguished commanders, both prefaced their incumbency with connections elsewhere. Still, it might be urged that Palmer's, so to say, palmiest years were with Leicestershire, whereas Illingworth was already an England star before he was drawn there. Les Berry, a certain England player had he lived in most other periods and luckless in his choice of contemporaries, must open the batting, accompanied, no doubt, by the prudent Cecil Wood. David Gower would obviously take another batting place. From the immediate post-war days, Dempster, Hallam and Tompkin would compete to join them, but several efficient all-rounders present themselves from relative antiquity to the modern era. J. H. King and Ewart Astill (one of the first to break the golden rule of amateur captaincy: he was skipper in 1935) would be the chief contenders.

Although the pace bowling has only lately been prominent, the supporting attacks have been excellent. The Australians, Walsh and Jackson, must be chosen, and their residential qualifications were as good as anyone's, while George Geary would be an automatic choice — and all three were capable bats. Roger Tolchard would be an equally obvious selection as wicket-keeper.

If this proved to be a team bereft of extremely hostile bowling and lacking some style in the batting, it would prove combative right down the order, with no tail over which to fret. It would bowl with aptitude and worldly skill, and field with panache: Les Berry, Cecil Wood, David Gower, Maurice Hallam, Charles Palmer, Maurice Tompkin, Roger Tolchard, Ewart Astill, George Geary, Jack Walsh and Vic Jackson.

NINE

Middlesex

The landless gentry might well serve as a contradictory soubriquet for Middlesex. A club which, certainly until the Second World War, had boasted a handsome lineage of crack amateurs, suffered, from its inception in 1864, two geographical problems: one to do with its ground; the other to do with its catchment.

Even in and since the middle ages, Middlesex, overwhelmed by the potency of London, has found difficulty in securing proper acknowledgement. The City of London was never included in the shire as such, and the Local Government Act of 1888 removed the districts of Middlesex closest to London for inclusion in the new London county. Middlesex was the second smallest county, only Rutland being smaller. The Greater London Reorganization of 1965 more or less erased Middlesex, and the 1972 Local Government Act completed that obliteration. Something of a postal district was all that remained. Many counties had altered shape or found their headquarters in foreign parts: Middlesex eventually had no homeland at all.

The seven Walkers of Southgate sound like a campanological title and have taken on the stuff of folk-lore. This septet of bachelor brothers created Middlesex in the same way that the Grace family shaped Gloucestershire. Some preliminary county matches were arranged by them, and some of them were played on the ground laid at Southgate by the cricketing Walkers.

In the December of 1863, with the Hon. Robert Grimston in the chair, a provisional committee was formed, and this led to an inaugural meeting at the London Tavern in February of the following year. Middlesex was then believed to be the only cricketing county without a county club, and, despite some opposition, presumably from those who thought that London had cricket a-plenty, one was enthusiastically begun.

The Cattle Market ground, Islington, was at the same time leased as the club's first ground, but this venue, down the Caledonian Road, was evacuated after quarrels with the lessor in 1868. Lillie Bridge, West Brompton, was used in 1871, but otherwise the club was homeless and in troublesome financial straits. In January 1871 in Holborn a special general meeting was called to debate the position, and its meagre attendance voted seven to six to save Middlesex from extinction. It was a momentous decision. From 1872 Middlesex transferred to the Prince's Ground, to the rear of Harrods, and played there for five seasons.

During this time MCC had occasionally tried to cajole Middlesex into using Lord's in order to boost the first-class programme there. Middlesex had shown scant interest, being naturally anxious to sustain their independence, but, with arguments breaking out over the use of the Prince's Ground and in the knowledge that (like the Islington ground) it would soon be developed, they acceded to the invitation in 1877.

The connection with Lord's and with MCC has been so interwoven that it is sometimes forgotten that, for thirteen years, Middlesex tried to exist without that liaison. Very occasionally Middlesex leave Lord's for a home match, and, since 1980, Uxbridge has been the favoured site. Whatever the satisfying advantages, there is little doubt that autonomy was threatened by the merger. No contract was officially agreed until 1899, and there was often an ambivalence about the relationship. Middlesex were at times organized as little more than a section of MCC, and it was 1950 before full-time staff were separately appointed. The distinction between the ground-staff and the county was sometimes blurred: Fred Titmus's début in 1949 led to a complaint that, as an MCC 'ground boy', he had no agreement with the county.

The restricted geographic area of Middlesex, its

terrain vanishing like the Cheshire Cat in *Alice*, and its setting at the heart of the capital, which attracted many cricketers from far rather than near, resulted in the extensive use of the residential qualification, much to the contempt of some other counties, especially Yorkshire. For example, Bill Edrich, released by Norfolk in 1934, had the expenses of his London qualifying period defrayed by Middlesex; and, over the years, the county has provided a resting-place for a most cosmopolitan circle of cricketing acquaintance.

The better side of all these troubles was that the teeming life of the metropolis attracted cricketers of all stations and nationalities, and MCC could often supply first-class experience to men awaiting eligibility. Right through to the 1940s, Middlesex enjoyed the services of dazzling amateurs, chiefly attacking batsmen in the Corinthian vein, few of them, sadly for the sake of balance, much of a hand at bowling.

By dint of a small fixture-list and of only one lost out of eight matches played, at a time when fewest losses was the key, Middlesex were deemed premier county in 1866, the first of their many successes. In 1878, in what *Wisden* declares the only 'undecided' Championship, commentators are usually agreed that Middlesex, with a modest record of three victories in six games, were most deserving of the title. Then, in 1903, one of the worst summers on record, Middlesex won the third of their pre-1914 titles, again rather luckily, their eight wins from a relatively small fixture-list giving them 77%. Yorkshire, with thirteen wins but many more games, mustered only 44% and were third.

For the first twenty years of their history Middlesex were led by Walkers; first, Vyell Walker, reputedly a most judicious captain and a lob bowler of devastating effect; and next, Isaac Walker, the best bat among the seven brothers. In 1885, A. J. Webbe took over the captaincy, and held it with kindly good nature until 1898; he was an exhilirating batsman, almost the equal, in 1887, of W. G. Grace himself. There were others, among them A. E. Stoddard, something of a matinée idol in the 1890s among cricketers, a venturesome bat and a handsome man, who, for

106 A. E. Stoddart

all his prowess, did not quite fulfil the high public aspiration held for him. The fragile Francis Ford, one of three cricketing brothers, and the dashing Timothy O'Brien contributed to the motley. There were also the brothers Lyttelton and the brothers Studd. C. T. Studd was regarded as one of the most accomplished of all-rounders, but he devoted his life to missionary work abroad.

This amateur cavalcade, at once dazzling, and, because of many distractions, irregular, lacked, like most amateur-oriented teams, bowlers. Apart from the swerve bowler, J. T. Rawlin, Middlesex, around these years, leaned totally on Jack Hearne. Hearne enjoyed an exceptionally lengthy career from 1888 to 1923, his rhythmic, nippy medium-pace being just about the county's sole assault force. His long travail earned him 3061

107 Jack (J. T.) Hearne

wickets, and he is one of only four bowlers in the history of cricket to have taken more than 3000 wickets. This tally included 100 wickets in each of fifteen seasons.

Part way through his remorseless stint, he was reinforced by the popular Australian, Albert Trott, a mighty if incautious hitter and a very effective bowler. Twice he achieved the remarkable double of 200 wickets and 1000 runs. He starred in the 1903 Championship side, which was captained by Gregor MacGregor, thought by many to be England's best-ever amateur wicket-keeper. This team also included G. W. Beldam, a consistent scorer, and B. J. T. Bosanquet, inventor of the 'Bosie' or googly, who, apart from the novel puzzlement caused by his bowling, was a useful bat. It is a fascinating comment on the sociology of cricket that the googly, most exotic and often most extravagant of deliveries, was the creation of an Edwardian toff, almost all other bowling developments having been introduced by professionals. A macabre end-piece to this first phase of Middlesex history is that Stoddart and Trott, unalike socially and culturally as chalk and cheese, each chose to shoot himself.

After a couple of a weak years, Middlesex rebuilt their team, very much on the same lines, and were always in the top six prior to the First World War. Following a depressing performance in 1919, they became classic champions in 1920 and 1921, and remained powerful for another eight years.

The first of these titles crowned the captaincy of Pelham Warner, for he had been skipper since 1908. The Championship was clinched in a fashion that would have been scoffed at had it been fiction. At 6.20 p.m. on the final day of an absorbing 'derby' match, Surrey were bowled out 55 runs short of the Middlesex challenge, and Plum Warner was chaired from the field. Middlesex won fifteen of their twenty fixtures, and, in 1921, under F. T. Mann, they won thirteen out of twenty. The end to that campaign was not dissimilar. This time Surrey were themselves straining for the title, and it was 6.05 p.m. on the last day of the last match before Middlesex hit off the mountain of 322 runs required.

The dedication of Sir Pelham Warner, as player, captain and administrator, became a by-word. His loyal devotion to cricket was religious in its intensity, and he came to be seen as the high priest of the the 'holy game'. By no means a robust or imposing man, he brought to the oversight of cricket the very characteristics that distinguished his own batting: an unobtrusive and precise tidiness, and an orthodoxy geared to conservatism. Thus Pelham Warner, if he had little of the charisma of the high priest, was a diligent keeper of the ark of the convenant. He embodied the spirit, touched on in Part One of this study, which saw the golden age of cricket as the ultimate in mood and address, and believed it should, at all costs, be preserved. No one did more to guarantee the continuing existence of first-class cricket in England; conversely, no one did more to ensure that it continued without evolutionary change.

The Middlesex XI, which Warner captained with his customary sanguinity of judgement, was a well balanced side, not least in its professional complement, for now the paid players were four or five in number. The unpaid members still shone: G. T. S. Stevens, another leg-spinner; C. H. L. Skeet, a sound opening bat; and Nigel Haig, who later captained Middlesex, a most worthy all-rounder, with over 12,000 runs and over 900 wickets for the county. Along with Warner and the hard-thrusting Frank Mann, they were a valuable coterie of players, but they needed the tougher professional support provided by Harry Lee, a somewhat graceless but abundantly productive opening bat; F. J. Durston, a quick bowler who turned to off-breaks towards the end of his career and captured over 1000 wickets; H. R. Murrell, capable stumper and wily assessor of opponents; and, of course, the evergreen Jack Hearne. Although he only played for a relatively few seasons before the First World War, space must be found to praise the exuberant efforts of Frank Tarrant, another Australian, subjected, like Trott, to some antagonistic jibes about his Middlesex birthright. He took just over 1000 wickets and scored over 12,000 runs during his cheerful spell with the county.

During the inter-war years Middlesex hopes rode chiefly on the younger Hearne and on Elias Hendren, who thankfully attracted the nickname of Patsy for all practical purposes. The former is one of the leading all-rounders of English cricket. Although critics complained that impending illness made him husband his strength, that his batting was too defensive, and that his slow-medium spin bowling was too erratic, he managed to out-bid these fault-findings with 1839 first-class wickets and 37,252 runs. J. W. Hearne three times had 2000 runs and 100 wickets in a season, and he played twenty-four times for England.

Hendren played fifty-one times for England, with a Test average of 47 with the bat, second only to Compton in the list of those Middlesex players who have represented their country. In E. W. Swanton's phrase, a 'squat, homely figure', Patsy Hendren was no aristocrat among batsmen, but his watchful zeal, his immaculate footwork and his ebullient temper combined to make him one of England's most successful and most popular cricketers. Only Hobbs and Woolley surpass his career sum of 57,611 runs, at an average of 50, which, remembering that the Lord's wickets were seldom flawless, adds even brighter lustre to his career.

There was a troubled patch in the early 1930s, including a sixteenth position in 1930, but again the ranks reformed and rallied. Although some amateurs were finding it difficult to play regularly, Middlesex enjoyed the services of G. O. Allen, the fast bowler; Ian Peebles, a teasing leg-spinner in that pleasing Middlesex tradition; and, in R. W. V. Robins, an all-round sportsman and audacious leader. One set of twins – Hendren and Hearne – was replaced by another when Bill Edrich and Denis Compton began their dashing partnership. Jim Smith, a quick bowler and legendary slogger; Jim Sims, a lugubrious spin bowler; and the elegant Jack Robertson were their professional fellows. Fred Price was the able wicket-keeper. Lifting their sights to third in 1935, Middlesex next pursued and harried Derbyshire in 1936 and Yorkshire in 1937, 1938, 1939, and again in 1946 for the title. Playing

108 G. O. Allen

The stage was set by the formidable opening act of Robertson, that most debonair of stroke-makers, and Syd Brown, no mild striker of the ball himself. Compton and Edrich then performed like two theatrical knights in their delectable prime: Compton, the Olivier, the maestro of daring and brilliant improvization; Edrich, the Gielgud, the epitome of faultless and tireless formalism.

Records tumbled giddily. Compton, with 3816 runs, and Edrich, with 3539, in that glorious summer stand first and second in the world list for a season's takings. Robertson had 2760 and Brown 2078 runs, and they shared in nine century opening stands. Middlesex scored forty-two hundreds that year, as they raced to nineteen dynamic wins out of twenty-six matches played.

Middlesex were third in 1948 and then they shared the title with their old and not always

109 R. W. V. Robins, who led Middlesex in their splendid Championship campaign of 1947.

attractive cricket, they were five times runners-up.

The historic events of 1947 are well known. After an uneasy start, the summer settled into a gloriously sunny one, and many regard it as the best of all cricket seasons. Runs galore were scored, and yet wickets fell with almost equal abandon. All the talents were on view, but, in vivid style, Edrich and Compton excelled in attack. The Championship is normally decided by bowling. Middlesex denied that truth by *blitzkrieg*, so that their bowlers – Jack Young, the neat and stocky left-hander, and Laurie Gray, a persevering fast bowler, in company with Sims, Robins, Edrich and Compton – had ample leisure to remove shell-shocked opponents. For instance, an innings of 537 for 2 in a single day at the Oval still left two whole days to demolish Surrey twice.

amicable rivals, Yorkshire. Frank Mann's son, George, another example of Middlesex's astonishing incidence of filial and fraternal connection, was captain for a couple of seasons (as well as captaining England), and other players included Denis Compton's brother, Leslie, as wicket-keeper, Harry Sharp and A. W. Thompson, pushing their capable way into the batting strength, and the Cambridge players, J. G. Dewes, the batsman, and John Warr, the quick bowler, both of whom played for England.

However, in due course the team aged and fell apart at the seams. Denis Compton, with nearly 39,000 runs to his mercurial credit, and Bill Edrich, with nearly 37,000 on his gallant account, ended their careers. They had proved themselves world masters. Compton's eighteen centuries in 1947 (six of them against the stunned South Africans) remains a record, but it was the manner of the achievement – carefree and blithe against a canvas of austerity – which makes the memory so pleasant.

The period of revival was longer this time. It was to be 1976 before the title returned to Lord's. It was not all sackcloth and ashes, for Middlesex struggled eleven times into the top six, and they were rarely pushed near the bottom. But, by their own exacting criteria, it was the county's longest ever phase of sporting despondency. Until 1971, when Mike Brearley began his triumphal reign, the captaincy was chopped and changed, and this was a department of the game where Middlesex had usually enjoyed a judicious stability.

Middlesex continued to be represented by talented players. Eric Russell scored 23,000 cultured runs; Peter Parfitt, in pugnacious style, scored almost as many and served England on thirty-seven occasions; J. S. E. Price thundered away off his long run; and John Murray, as balanced as any ballet dancer, was a graceful wicket-keeper. His 1527 dismissals in all matches place him second only to Bob Taylor in the world rankings. Around this time, Alan Moss, one of the county's finest fast bowlers, took over 1000 wickets, while Fred Titmus, the chirpy off-spinner and another England regular with fifty-three caps, was outstanding. He shuffled along in his

economical manner to play more times for Middlesex than anyone else, and, in addition to his tally of 2830 first-class wickets, he scored over 17,000 runs for the county.

But there was neither harmony nor vitality. Middlesex were slow to adjust to the modern era, without lordly amateurs smiting the ball disdainfully around the sward and bringing authority to the leadership. Although J. M. Brearley was not a noble batsman, rarely rising above competent county standards, he certainly had the breeding for captaincy. His authority, unlike that of some of his predecessors, was not an appendage of social class, although that perhaps played its part. It was based more on his cerebral approach to the design and conflict of the game and on his profound fascination in the motivation of colleagues. That said, he scored just over 25,000 first-class runs, and so could never be ridiculed as a 'passenger' captain. Brearley thus became some sort of guru figure, a Bertrand Russell among captains.

The formula took four or five years to perfect. Mike Smith and Clive Radley, Graham Barlow and Roland Butcher formed the backbone, with Brearley, of the batting; and, from 1980, Paul Downton was a hard-working wicket-keeper-batsman. Soon Phil Edmonds and John Emburey, left-hand and right-hand, were to dominate the England as well as the Middlesex spin attack. For Middlesex their joint brands of classical slow bowling earned them some 1600 or so victims. What was lacking – the age-old Middlesex weakness – was fiery fast bowling. Over these years Alan Jones, Mike Selvey, the West Indian Wayne Daniel, Vintcent van der Bijl for two seasons, Norman Cowans and Simon Hughes were among those who provided the solution. Wilf Slack, whose premature death all mourned, came into the side as a resourceful opening bat, while, from 1975, Mike Gatting developed his solid county and international career. He has proved to be a merciless slayer of any bowling of less than the highest class. At times Middlesex fielded full sides of well-nigh international talent, and, in one game in which the Australian, Jeff Thomson, played, the whole XI were Test players.

None of these personages was as mesmeric to watch or as blessed with gifts as the leading lights of previous Middlesex XIs, but all were utilitarian and efficient, so much so that, under the scholarly eye of Mike Brearley, the sum of the parts made a well-integrated whole.

A bare recital of their achievements is sufficient to mark them out as one of the most successful county sides ever. They won the Championship in 1976, with eleven wins out of twenty played; they shared it with Kent in the following year; they won the crown outright in 1980 and 1982; and then, with Mike Gatting in command, they took it again in 1985 and 1990. By then they were able to call on the skills of the world-class West Indies opener, Des Haynes, as well as the rising talents of Keith Brown, Mike Roseberry, Phil Tufnell, Mark Ramprakash and Angus Fraser, the last three now capped by England.

Turning to the one-day competitions, Middlesex, after many years of failure, lost both the 1975 finals – to Leicestershire and Lancashire – by large margins. Then, in 1977, Radley's batting secured a victory over Glamorgan, and, in 1980, Brearley's innings of 96 not out ensured a win over Surrey, both in the Gillette Cup. In 1984, under Gatting, Kent were defeated in the Nat-West Trophy, Radley again playing the decisive innings, and, in 1988, that cup was lifted again, at Worcestershire's expense. Warwickshire just defeated them in the 1989 final. In two very exciting contests for the Benson and Hedges Cup, Middlesex beat Essex by 4 runs in 1983 and Kent

110 Middlesex celebrate the 1982 Championship. With Mike Brearley (*left*) are Mike Gatting, Clive Radley, Richard Ellis, Paul Downton, Wilf Slack and Neil Williams.

111 Angus Fraser

by 2 runs in 1986. Finally, in 1990, they won the Refuge Assurance Cup.

Thus Middlesex have won thirteen titles since 1976, and this makes them one of the most successful of modern sides. In truth, they have been one of the most consistent teams for a century and a quarter, although, curiously, they have never managed to win the Sunday League. It is true that changes of leadership and personnel have periodically caused dislocation: Middlesex occasionally stumbled, and were sixteenth in the county table in 1987 and fifteenth in 1991. Nonetheless, with its London base and its advantageous, if somewhat ambivalent, relationship with Lord's and MCC, Middlesex have always had resource and motive to recover and reestablish metropolitan ascendancy. Jack Robertson, Alan Moss and John Murray might cavil at the provincial view that Middlesex players, *en fête* at Lord's, receive preferential international treatment; but it is plain that the cricket establishment has watched most of its cricket at Lord's, and, in turn, one supposes, ambitious hopefuls are drawn there. It is certain that many Middlesex cricketers have exotic birth-places, miles distant from St John's Wood, and, observed more perhaps by an aloof MCC membership than a domestic, fanatical support, Middlesex assume some of the character of an old-style select XI.

The sustained magnificence of Middlesex cricket, especially the *élan* of its middle-order batting, means that an array of stars press for choice in an All-Middlesex XI, an exhibition XI of glittering worth. Compton, Edrich, Hendren and Jack Hearne would be automatic selections – and

that takes care of all but the opening batsmen. Think what fine performers, from Webbe and Stoddart to Russell and Gatting, are thus omitted. The older Hearne must appear as chief bowler, while Fred Titmus might narrowly push out John Emburey for another slot. Rather than a left-hander, such as Jack Young or Phil Edmonds, the strength of the tradition might demand justice for a leg-spinner. Jim Sims, who took 1200 wickets and more for Middlesex, might fill that place. The fast bowling, as with many counties, is more problematic, but, of the possibilities, G. O. Allen, who took 81 wickets for England, and Alan Moss, most effective, in terms of figures, of the county's quicker bowlers, might be the lucky duo.

However, Middlesex have had great batsmen who could bowl, with young Jack Hearne an all-rounder of the highest class, Denis Compton ready to oblige with his beguiling chinamen, and Bill Edrich willing to open the attack, presumably with Allen. The gentlemanly John Murray would keep wicket, and his batting would be an asset. The fielding would be smart, although, in early times, this was not a Middlesex virtue.

That leaves the opening pair, and Jack Robertson should be one of these. Leaving aside the daring Robins and Pelham Warner, results point to the chess master, Brearley, as captain – and he could open the batting, completing a team which, typically of Middlesex, is characterized by a brilliance of batting that tends to make the bowling seem a trifle pedestrian: Jack Robertson, Mike Brearley, Bill Edrich, Denis Compton, Patsy Hendren, J. W. Hearne, John Murray, G. O. Allen, J. T. Hearne, Jim Sims and Fred Titmus.

TEN

Northamptonshire

The midland county of Northamptonshire is of much the same size as Leicestershire, and its cricketing life – doleful struggle, and then some post-war joys – is not dissimilar. It has not been, historically, a lucky county. The Yorkists defeated the Lancastrians just outside the county town in 1460, which seems a geopolitical mislocation, by which time Northampton was in decline, having prospered mainly in the 12th century. Because it embraced the parliamentary cause in the Civil War, the town castle and walls were razed at the Restoration, and much of the town was destroyed by fire in 1675. Northampton's situation deep in the Nene valley caused the Grand Junction canal and later the London Midland Railway line to by-pass it, although branch links with both were afterwards constructed. In the 19th century the Northampton shoe industry flourished manfully and the town thrived. Eventually, in the 1960s, decisions were taken to expand the town. With a population now of 156,000 it stands as by far the chief urban settlement of a largely agricultural region.

A county club was organized in 1820 and restructured in 1878, but it was 1905 before Northamptonshire competed in the Championship. It had been decided to reduce the number of qualifying matches to twelve, and, with the encouraging assistance of Derbyshire and Sussex, Northamptonshire just managed this. Winning two of those dozen games, they finished thirteenth out of the sixteen, although several counties were playing as many as twenty-eight matches.

Until the 1950s nothing much went right for the unfortunate Northamptonshire club, eagerly although officials and players strove. They were in the bottom three on no less than nineteen occasions, and they were rock bottom ten times, an unenvied saga of dismal failure.

Practically all their home matches were played at the Wantage Road ground, a pretty rudimentary arena, shared with Northampton Town, a football club that has known more failure than success. In later years, Northamptonshire have taken the commendable step of carrying first-class cricket, not only to other sites in the county, such as Kettering, Rushden and Wellingborough, but to other counties – to Bedford, to Luton, and to Tring in Hertfordshire. Decent crowds have rewarded this initiative.

The only release from Northamptonshire's captive gloom was in 1912. It was a moist summer and a triangular tournament between England, Australia and South Africa meant lots of Test calls for others. There was a plethora of draws, but Northamptonshire, using only twelve players, and welding this injury-free band into a collective force, won ten of their eighteen games. They ended an extremely close second to Yorkshire. Although their fixture-list was not as long or as strong as some, they lost only one. It was an exciting performance by a lowly club. They were fourth the following season, and these two were the halcyon years.

No club has been more reliant on one player than Northamptonshire were on George Thompson ('the Northampton Nugget') in the early years. He bowled and batted his heart out in the cause of the Tudor Rose, labouring to bring the county to first-class status and then to maintain it there. He took over 1000 wickets for Northamptonshire, eight times reaching 100 in a season, and he scored nearly 9000 runs in his genuine, thorough-going fashion. There were few to share the burden. The West Indian, S. G. Smith, qualified in 1909, and his all-round contributions were welcome. He was the first Northants player to top 1000 runs in a season and to complete the double. The fiery bowler, 'Bumper' Wells, made life uncomfortable for many batsmen, so that the county's bowling

112 V. W. C. Jupp, Northamptonshire's
captain between the wars.

was adequate. It was the batting that often proved insufficient. Even in 1912 no one reached 1000 runs, although in 1913 four managed this.

Between the wars there was not even the relief of a rare visit to the head of the table. Two or three players kept the flag fluttering as proudly as they were able. Claude Woolley, Frank's brother, scored more than 15,000 runs in a twenty-year stint, and J. E. Timms, Northamptonshire's second most prolific scorer, weighed in with over 20,000 runs. Once qualified after leaving Sussex, V. W. C. Jupp, a guileful off-spinner and faithful bat, inherited Thompson's all-round burden. His 13,000 and more runs and his 1078 wickets (the same total as that of George Thompson) were as manna in the desert. Jupp's ten doubles in first-class cricket position him third to Rhodes and Hirst in the 'doubles' league. A. E. Thomas was a whole-hearted fast bowler, who took over 800 wickets for his county, but Nobby Clark was the brusque spearhead of the attack. Reaching high pace and obtaining a handful of England caps, he became Northamptonshire's leading wicket-taker with a tally of 1097 victims.

Bad luck persisted. A. H. Bakewell, a most promising batsman of national calibre, had his career curtailed by a road accident. He passed 1000 runs in the eight seasons he played. Then the Second World War claimed the life of the young captain, R. P. Nelson, whose steadiness as batsman and skipper was another grave loss.

Does a captain stay longer when success more constantly beckons, or does a team benefit greatly from stable rule? Unlike, for example, Middlesex, who have tended to enjoy long tenures of captaincy, Northamptonshire have had no less than twenty-seven captains. Before 1949 no one captained the side autonomously for more than four years. Freddie Brown and Keith Andrew each held the office for five years, and then, in modern times, Geoff Cook dashed all records with an incumbency, completed in 1989, of nine seasons. This disorder and interruption at the helm can scarcely have helped Northamptonshire cricket. It is certain that, when commentators spoke of counties merging or losing first-class status, Northants was one that was often in their minds.

The county's chief asset for a long period from just before the Second World War until the late 1950s was Dennis Brookes. A methodical craftsman, he is their only batsman to score 30,000 first-class runs. He scored 1000 in no less than seventeen seasons, and this included six sums of 2000, while his seventy-one centuries also form a county record. Time and again he opened the batting, and stood, defiant and alone, like the sentry at Pompeii.

113 A. H. Bakewell

114 The Australian George Tribe bowled consistently well for Northamptonshire after the Second World War.

115 Dennis Brookes

In 1949 efforts were made to reinforce his stalwart efforts. Local businesses helped financially, and players were drafted in from other counties and from the leagues. A. E. Nutter and Buddy Oldfield arrived from Lancashire, and Fred Jakeman and Des Barrick from Yorkshire. All were batsmen, though Nutter and Barrick could claim to be all-rounders. Succour came from overseas. George Tribe and Jack Manning were, respectively, unorthodox and orthodox left-hand spinners, and a third Australian, Jock Livingston, a fleet-footed batsman, made up a formidable antipodean threesome. George Tribe completed the double in seven of his nine summers with Northamptonshire, and he became the fourth and last bowler to capture 1000 wickets for the county. Raman Subba Row, the Surrey and England opener, transferred to Northamptonshire, while, among the local talent, Brian Reynolds caught the eye. He scored over 18,000 runs for the county. The Lancashire-born Keith Andrew joined the side in 1953, and, with 800 dismissals, became the county's most successful wicket-keeper. He was, in every way, a splendid servant to the county.

The arrival of Freddie Brown, of Surrey and England fame, to captain the team galvanized everyone into spirited action, and, under his dominating control, Northamptonshire revived. They became a much less vulnerable side, and, in 1957, the dutiful vigil of Dennis Brookes was rewarded when, as captain, he led the county to second place in the Championship. It was galling, with fifteen wins, not to catch all-conquering Surrey, but it was the best result since 1912.

Everyone played well. Five batsmen obtained their 1000 runs; Tribe and Manning had 100 wickets apiece; and another left-hander, M. H. J. Allen, had seventy-six victims. Frank Tyson, another Lancashire lad, was the hostile opening bowler, and he took 86 wickets, his best season's haul for the county. His is a career which was pressed intensely into a brief and spectacular international cameo. The lifeless Northampton pitches reduced even his awesome pace, and Tyson ended with something over 500 wickets for his nine seasons.

116 Keith Andrew

That team was fourth in 1956 and 1958, and then, six years later, after some middling seasons, Northamptonshire had another mini-series of attainment: third in 1964 and second again in 1965. There were further anxious seasons, and then, in the 1970s, came their most consistent run: fourth in 1972; third in the next two years; and, after eighth position in 1975, second once again. Then came the bad years again, with a bottom place in 1978, something that had been avoided since 1948. Thereafter, since 1982, they have rested easily enough in the centre of the county table.

117 Freddie Brown, whose enthusiastic captaincy
galvanized Northamptonshire after the Second World War.

Four second places and no title: that is Northamptonshire's frustrating and unprepossessing record. There have been some compensations in one-day cricket. In their first visit to Lord's for a final in 1976, they defeated strongly-fancied Lancashire and carried off the Gillette Cup. Then, in 1980, they beat the holders and favourites, Essex, by 6 runs to win a thrilling Benson and Hedges final.

But here again ill-luck has dogged the Northamptonshire path. In the Gillette Cup Somerset beat them in the 1979 final with a comfortable 45 runs margin, while, in the first NatWest final in 1981, Northamptonshire suffered excruciatingly sad fortune. It was nip and tuck the day long; the scores finished level; but Derbyshire had lost fewer wickets. In 1987 cruel luck attended the county in both finals. In the Benson's, Northamptonshire, with David Capel's 97 outstanding, gathered together the respectable score of 244 for 7 – and Yorkshire reached the same score, but with only 6 wickets down. In September, Northamptonshire had Nottinghamshire reeling at 84 for 5 in a match marred by rain.

Larkins, with 87, had led a forceful display, and 228 for 3 in the allotted 50 overs looked safe. But Richard Hadlee scored heavily, and, when play resumed on the Monday, they took the NatWest Trophy. In 1990 an out-of-sorts Northants were drubbed in the NatWest final by Lancashire. Neither have Northamptonshire, in spite of some cavalier essays, won the Sunday League: so two cups and a shoal of near misses is the résumé of the county's history.

During these last thirty years, when registrations, including those of overseas players, have become easier, and when finances have been more efficaciously managed, Northamptonshire have been served by dozens of high-grade players. They have never, as in pre-war days, looked uneven and all but totally reliant on a Thompson, a Timms, a Jupp or a Brookes. They have sought their specialist overseas players mainly from the sub-continent: B. S. Bedi, the sagacious left-hander, and the exuberant all-rounder, Kapil Dev, from India; the quick bowler, Sarfraz Nawaz, and the all-rounder, Mushtaq Mohammed, from Pakistan. More recently, the off-spinner and magnificent field, Roger Harper, and the fast bowlers, Winston Davis and Curtly Ambrose, have been recruited from West Indies. Mushtaq was perhaps, on figures, the most profitable of these signings, for he made nearly 16,000 runs and took well over 500 wickets for the county.

A notable group of productive batsmen have represented Northamptonshire over this period. David Steele, with over 18,000 runs, became a popular anti-hero when, bespectacled and white-haired, he dared the vehement might of Lillee and Thomson, when Australia were pulverizing England in 1975. He is also the county's leading catcher, with 469 to his credit. Several others have represented England, chief among them Allan Lamb, of South African lineage, who has played over seventy times for England, and in many one-day internationals. His pugnacious survival as an international cricketer makes him far and away the county's most capped player, and he has already scored some 15,000 runs for the county. He has captained the side since 1989.

Other valued batsmen have been the high-scoring R. M. Prideaux, Wayne Larkins, R. J. Bailey and P. J. Watts, the last a useful bowler as well. The main all-rounder, until his departure for Leicestershire, was the determined Peter Willey, who made over 13,000 runs and took nearly 500 wickets. He won twenty caps while with Northamptonshire and his all-round role is now filled by David Capel, who has already played on occasion for England. Bowlers have been less to the fore. B. S. Crump and J. D. F. Larter were mainstays in the 1960s, and, in 1963, they each took 100 wickets. Crump stands sixth in the county's bowling honours with 807 victims, and the speedy, if rather ungainly, Larter played ten times for England.

Geoff Cook, despite his bouts of ill-fortune, proved to be a captain and cricketer of solid measure. In spite of fewer first-class opportunities, he is second in Northamptonshire's batting list behind Brookes; he is second on the catching list, with 355 such dismissals; and he is fifth in the register of appearances. It is a proud record. He is now playing an important part in the organization of Durham's first-class venture.

As a final melancholy testimony to the impoverished fortune that haunts the county, recall the case of Colin Milburn. Just as Bakewell was severely injured (and the amateur, R. P. Northway, killed) in a car accident, so did Milburn, that portly hard-hitting bat and consummate close fielder, lose an eye in a car crash in 1969. He was also a decent change bowler, and his forcefulness had won him nine England caps. It was another tragic blow for the most unfortunate of counties.

The dogged skills and determined attitude of Geoff Cook prompt one to propose him as captain of a Northamptonshire select XI, with Freddie Brown his only rival. Dennis Brookes, of course, could open with Cook, although this means omitting Milburn, and the next batting choices would go to Allan Lamb, J. E. Timms and Jock Livingston, who averaged a sprightly 45 during his eight seasons with the county. Like George Tribe, he was unlucky to have to compete with probably Australia's best-ever group of players –

and George Tribe must certainly be included. Two other all-rounders might be Thompson and Jupp, tributes to the abiding Northamptonshire convention (at least, until recent decades) of one man tottering under the weight of the county, not unlike Sinbad burdened by the Old Man of the Sea on his shoulders.

Although George Sharp, for nearly twenty years in modern times, and B. W. Bellamy, for much the same duration prior to the Second World War, merit mention, Keith Andrew must fill the wicket-keeping berth, and the two fast bowlers would be Frank Tyson and Nobby Clark, their leading wicket-taker, said to be so testy that even the songbirds flying overhead felt the lash of his tongue. In sum, then, the team would be: Dennis Brookes, Geoff Cook, Allan Lamb, Jack Timms, Jock Livingston, George Thompson, George Tribe, Vallance Jupp, Keith Andrew, Frank Tyson and Nobby Clark.

ELEVEN

Nottinghamshire

Where many counties' origins are sketchy and misty, Nottinghamshire's are full and detailed, with the team stepping forth in complete maturity, rather like the humanoid emerging, direct and adult, from the egg in Shaw's *Back to Methuselah*.

The 'laying out' of Trent Bridge by William Clarke in 1838 was, of course, the focal point. Cricket in and around Nottingham was already well established, with huge crowds assembling on Nottingham Forest to watch important matches. Originally a bricklayer, William Clarke became a publican, and he ran the Trent Bridge Inn, congenially adjacent to the ground. The involvement of inns and innkeepers is well illustrated in the tale of other counties, but, in Clarke's case, his actual control and domination of the cricket itself was crucial. From 1846 he organized the famous All-England XI, and this most influential of the exhibition troupes was based on Nottingham and on Nottingham players.

As elsewhere, Nottinghamshire club cricket had spawned some primitive county combats, with, for instance, Sussex, and there were also games with the Sheffield, Leicester and other major clubs. It is, at this distance, difficult to assess where club and county separated and where conjoined.

What, at this stage in mid-19th century, was critical was the quality and the quantity of Nottinghamshire professionalism. Aristocratic patrons were not so plentiful in the east midlands as in the south and west country, and cricketers had had to organize matters as best they might. Conversely, as was described in Part One, the peculiar character of industrialism in these parts was conducive to the development of professional play, and, in turn, this may have made patrons unnecessary rather than merely absent. The hosiery and other local trades, reliant on piece-work, had neither the limiting and possessive ties of agricultural rhythms nor the numbing regimen of the factory, thus men could adapt their time (as framework-knitters, for instance) more flexibly to cricketing requirements. Moreover, these were independent souls, whereas the early professionals in the southern counties were often the retained servants of the large estates.

William Clarke was a master – and a very dictatorial one – rather than a servant, but, amid the carefully pressed folds of Victorian social fabric, he was not a gentleman. The Nottinghamshire professionals were, then, 'industrial' as opposed to 'agrarian' in origin, being tradesmen in an autonomous way of business. Apart from their role in the exhibition XIs nationally, they were to the fore in international touring, for Alfred Shaw and Arthur Shrewsbury were heavily involved in such enterprises, as well as being partners in a Nottingham cricketing business.

However, socio-economic factors do not entirely explain the ascendancy of the Nottingham professionals. In the forty-five years before the First World War, Nottinghamshire supplied the world with cricketers and coaches, with, it has been calculated, approaching 400 of them a year fulfilling engagements at schools and clubs, at home and abroad, as well as composing a county team and often much of the national team. Granted that the social environment was propitious, one must seek some explanation in the form of cultural emulation. Once the models, earning money and wallowing in prestige, were manifest, then hundreds were anxious to indulge in the cricketing craze, so that, very quickly, it became as normal as a Welshman becoming a chorister or a Gurkha tribesman a soldier.

It is, therefore, the sheer quantity of Nottinghamshire cricket which is vital. Sutton-in-Ashfield, producing professional cricketers as lavishly as Hong Kong now produces toys and shirts, even ran to its own Professional Cricketers Friendly Society, a fitting demonstration both of the numbers involved – there were perhaps six dozen professionals from that district – and their acceptance, with a Friendly Society, of industrial working-class mores.

Spurred by this momentum, Nottinghamshire began and survived for some time mainly as a professional combine. The ground was, unlike most other county venues, initially in professional hands, and so was the captaincy. It is a mistake to think that the vogue for amateur leadership, at county or national level, is more than a parvenu habit, snobbishly adopted toward the end of the century. Nottinghamshire were captained by professionals until J. A. Dixon skippered the side from 1889 to 1899. In that latter year, when the Australian Test series was extended to five matches, Headingley and Trent Bridge joined the Oval, Lord's and Old Trafford as Test grounds, a singular token of the respect in which Nottinghamshire cricket was held.

It had been a remarkable period. At this time, Nottinghamshire's density of population was – at about 700 a square mile – on a par with Hampshire, Essex, Kent or Derbyshire. Nottingham itself was a good-sized city, but it was not much bigger than Leicester, while Bristol was larger, and Birmingham was three times as populous. Nottinghamshire had made their mark by and through the impetus of a self-created reputation.

It is superfluous to add that, throughout these decades, Nottinghamshire, once county cricket picked up its stride and the exhibition teams began to pall, were the pre-eminent county. In the twenty-six seasons between 1864 and 1890, Nottinghamshire won or shared the Championship on fifteen occasions, and were otherwise usually in urgent contention. Only Yorkshire's predominance between the wars may be compared, and, in all those seasons, Nottinghamshire were only three times out of the top four.

The county was as rich in players as plum pudding in fruity comestibles. William Clarke himself was a shrewd under-arm bowler, and his successor, both as captain of the All-England XI and of Nottinghamshire, George Parr, was known as 'the Lion of the North'. Strong and commanding, he fielded outstandingly and threw over 100 yards, while, from his crouched batting stance, he swept to leg in a manner still judged by many to be unsurpassed. He was replaced by the unmatchable Richard Daft, quick-footed and essentially upright in his individual style, and amazingly contemptuous of fast bowlers on the then fiery pitches. Later Alfred Shaw captained Nottinghamshire. Known as 'the emperor of bowlers', he was a natural round-arm bowler of slow medium-pace and deadly accuracy. In first-class matches he took a little over 2000 wickets at an average of 12, which, by that criterion, makes him the most successful bowler in history. Astonishingly, he had fewer runs scored off him than he bowled overs.

Other Nottinghamshire experts from those early times included Joseph Guy, a most elegant bat; James Grundy, a fastish bowler of compelling directness; R. C. Tinley, the pacy lob bowler; John Jackson, 'the Demon', a popular player and terrifyingly quick bowler, who collected nearly 2000 wickets in seven years; George Wootton and J. C. Shaw, the two talented left-hand bowlers; and 'Mad Charlie' Brown, the excitable but adroit wicket-keeper.

As some of that group of exceptional cricketers faded, others, equally talented, were their glorious substitutes. Fred Morley, his career curtailed by accident and premature death, was for ten years England's finest opening bowler, while Dick Attewell was the stock bowler, with 1302 wickets to his credit from his exploitation of off-theory. The highly competent Wilfred Flowers was the first professional to complete the cricketer's double; William Barnes was an attacking bat of international repute; W. H. Scotton became legendary as the epitome of prudent stone-walling; and affable Mordecai Sherwin, with 800 stumpings and catches, was rarely absent, and never less than excellent behind the wickets.

The crowning glories of this imperious array were William Gunn and Arthur Shrewsbury. At their peak both George Parr and Richard Daft, although in contrasting styles, had each been the nonpareil of English professional batsmanship.

Now Gunn and Shrewsbury mounted the rostrum. Billy Gunn, exquisitely balancing the mellifluous and the powerful, rarely hit the ball aloft, and pursued the classic tradition in regal manner. No more need be said of Arthur Shrewsbury than that he was W. G. Grace's choice as the greatest batsman he had known. He was never, like Gunn, robust, and, ultimately, he took his own life, believing himself to be afflicted with a fatal disease. Solemn of disposition and of infinite patience, Shrewsbury shaped himself on the classical lines of his mentor, Richard Daft. His immaculate technique included the clever use of pads, and it is still claimed that, on difficult wickets, he remains the most effective combatant there has been. Both Shrewsbury and Gunn scored over 25,000 first-class runs apiece, and only two or three others of those who played most of their cricket in the Victorian era passed this landmark, for fixtures were less frequent and pitches less placid. Shrewsbury and Gunn, in massive partnership, were to that period what Hobbs and Sutcliffe were to the pre-war, and Edrich and Compton to the immediate post-war, eras.

Gradually, as county cricket became more stable, Nottinghamshire fell into line constitutionally. Nottingham Old Club, then the leading local outfit, had flirted with county status in the 1840s, but Clarke's machinations had not helped. The prestige and money that came from a middle-class membership were vital. From about 1860, John Johnson, a solicitor from the city, became honorary secretary of the county club, and, in effect, constructed it. In concert with Joseph Hickling, tenant of the Trent Bridge Inn, he began the improvement of the ground. The usual panoply of committees was slowly established, and the professional hegemony was diminished.

There was a trial of strength in 1881, the year of the notorious 'schism', when the seven principal 'pros' struck, following a decision by the Nottinghamshire secretary, Captain Holden (a very unpopular figure with the players), not to allow them to organize a match outside the club's jurisdiction. Matters of contract – whether engagements should be by the season or by the game – and

other conditions were raised as well. Although Shrewsbury and Shaw, the ringleaders, held out for the whole of the season, the other five gradually yielded, and it is interesting to recall that the Nottinghamshire authorities were stiffened in their resolve by the encouragement of the other counties, who were fearful that labour disputes might spread.

That was, effectively, the last players' rebellion until the age of Packer, and it signalled the end of that peculiar form of independent professionalism inaugurated by William Clarke. A further factor was the club's long-term lease of the ground about the same time. It has been said that the appointment of amateur captains, such as John Dixon and the hyper-enthusiastic Arthur Jones, was intended to brighten the cricket. Yet, plainly, and to the delight of those of egalitarian persuasion, Nottinghamshire cricket was never again as authoritative as when these Victorian giants strutted the fields of England and paraded their virile prowess.

There were many years of relative decline, with just the exceptional year of 1907 to gladden east midlands hearts and minds, for Nottinghamshire, under A. O. Jones, won a further Championship, with fifteen victories and no defeats. In the wet summer of that year, the medium pace of Dusty Hallam and the nippy leg-breaks of Tom Wass proved devastating. They took almost 3000 wickets between them, and the next best bowler was William Gunn's nephew, John, with but 25. His brother, George Gunn, topped the batting averages, and his carefree genius, his seemingly casual approach to the most testing bowling, was wonderfully entertaining. James Iremonger and Joe Hardstaff were two other doughty performers, while, in 1911, Ted Alletson captured the imagination with his renowned 189 at Hove. He added 142 in forty minutes, the last 89 in fifteen minutes, in perhaps the most ferocious display of hitting county cricket has witnessed.

The inter-war years were sterling years for the county, apart from the summers just prior to the Second World War. Until 1937 they were almost always in the upper part of the table, occupying second place in 1922, 1923 and 1927, when they

118 George Gunn.

119 A. W. Carr

unaccountably lost to lowly Glamorgan on the last day of the season. Under A. W. Carr's spirited command, Nottinghamshire were always on the attack, and the team was even in tenor and talent. The arrival of Bill Voce, an extremely fast left-arm bowler, and Harold Larwood, according to many judges the premier pace bowler in history, gave the team the sharpest of cutting edges. In 1929 they again won the title after an interesting contest during a fairly dismal summer. W. W. Whysall and the veterans George Gunn and Wilf Payton led the batting, while Sam Staples and Fred Barratt assisted in the attack.

The bodyline row had repercussions for Nottinghamshire: Voce and Larwood, under Carr's leadership, occasionally used short-pitched leg-theory, and there was trouble when the Australians visited Trent Bridge. After a brief constitutional crisis, A. W. Carr forfeited the captaincy against a canvas on which all the counties condemned 'direct attack' bowling. Harold Larwood, most perfect in action of all fast bowlers, soon retired. In his relatively short career he had taken some 1200 wickets for his county at the frugal average of 16. Voce played on for several seasons, and took over 1300 wickets for Nottinghamshire: Larwood, like Wass, represented the mining interest, which, as in Derbyshire, was now a fruitful source of the county's cricketers, replacing the old textile tradition. With Walter Keeton and Charlie Harris as batsmen and Harold Butler as fast bowler, Nottinghamshire were still a solid side. There now emerged Joe Hardstaff's son, Joe Hardstaff junior. A gifted athlete, brave and handsome, he became one of England's most admired batsmen. He would have adorned any team in any period. He had a career aggregate of nearly 32,000 runs, second to George Gunn (35,000 runs) of Nottinghamshire players. Next in the list comes Reg Simpson, as debonair in style as Hardstaff or Joseph Guy, with over 30,000 runs. In the years after the second war, he was both the mainstay and the most attractive player in the county XI.

These were sad years for Nottinghamshire, and Simpson captained them for a decade, with only Arthur Jepson giving much bowling assistance. The Trent Bridge wickets were lifeless and the bowling was lacklustre. The South Australian leg-spinner, Bruce Dooland, joined the county's ranks for five years in the mid-1950s, and, given his prolific wicket-taking, their fortunes lifted

120 Harold Larwood

slightly. Nonetheless, in the quarter century after the war, Nottinghamshire were in the bottom three thirteen times, and fourth place in 1968 was easily their best performance.

The special registration of overseas players seemed to be Nottinghamshire's salvation, for they were able to secure the one world-class player, Gary Sobers, sought by all. Although contributing some glorious all-round displays, Gary Sobers did not entirely transform the county's cricket. There were some other capable hands – Mike Harris, Brian Bolus, Mike Smedley, Norman Hill and Deryck Murray, the West Indian wicket-keeper – but the bowling was poor. Nor did Nottinghamshire fare well in the newer one-day competitions.

It was to be the 1980s before the county really pulled themselves together, with Ken Taylor as manager and the South African, Clive Rice, as captain. In 1981, after a bad start to the season, they won nine of their last eleven matches and held off a strong Sussex challenge to win the Championship. Again, in 1987, with this time Lancashire the close contenders, Nottinghamshire took the title – two in the decade, after a long spell with nothing to celebrate. They were narrowly second in 1984.

Nottinghamshire eventually managed to win the Sunday League in 1991, while their revitalized 1980s' side made four cup final appearances. Two were lost. They folded drably to Somerset in the 1982 Benson's final, and were haplessly defeated by 9 wickets, while, in the NatWest final in 1985, they lost a high-scoring encounter by a bare run to Essex. Their first success in one-day competition came in 1987 when they won the NatWest Trophy. Northamptonshire always looked the likely winners, but Clive Rice and Richard Hadlee turned the match in its last phase, and Nottinghamshire won by 3 wickets. In 1989 they won the Benson and Hedges Cup for the first time, defeating Essex with a four off the last ball.

Nottinghamshire owed much to Clive Rice for his leadership and all-round ability, but there is little doubt that Hadlee, the New Zealand fast-medium bowler and forcing bat, was the chief architect of these successes. He was a dedicated cricketer of genuine world stature and the most successful bowler in Test match history. His serious devotion to the Nottinghamshire cause stood in stark contrast to the colourful but flashy

121 Joe Hardstaff junior

contributions of some overseas stars. In 1984 he was the first to do the double since the coming of one-day cricket and the reduction of first-class play.

Before and over these years the sunny and mercurial talent of Derek Randall was on show. An acrobatic fielder and, when on song, a glorious bat, his indigenous sparkle made him very popular. Chris Broad, once of Gloucestershire, and R. T. Robinson opened the batting, and, like Randall, they became England players of some experience. Bruce French was a tidy wicket-keeper who also appeared for England, so that, with a mix of efficient county talent, the side was strong in all departments.

That said, and with the team enjoying decent results after overlong in the cricketing wilderness, it is curious to watch their reliance (like most

122 Clive Rice

others) on international support, often eked out with imports from other counties, for Nottinghamshire, over many years, had strongly upheld the principle of county birth as the only rightful qualification. It is akin to a nation which is firmly adherent to the tenets of free trade – until circumstances alter and it appears less economically viable, and then, of a sudden, protectionist and mercantilist ideas are totally acceptable.

All in all, Nottinghamshire has a pretty uneven history. The derring-do of Wass and Hallam, of Larwood, Voce and Hardstaff, of Simpson, Randall, Rice and Hadlee is authentic enough in all conscience, but, compared to the grandeur of the county's Victorian past, it amounts to little.

This creates an all but insuperable problem when, by way of summary, a team of Nottinghamshire greats is contemplated. It would be

123 Derek Randall

feasible enough to select one from the 20th century – George Gunn, Joe Hardstaff junior and Reg Simpson are the county's leading run-makers, and Derek Randall might make a fourth specialist bat. A. W. Carr could captain the team with his customary energy, and he scored almost 19,000 runs for the county; and A. O. Jones, with over 20,000 runs, might be an extra batsman. Voce and Larwood would, inevitably, open the bowling, with Bruce Dooland their leg-spinning foil. Arthur Jepson, who took 1000 wickets for them, might be the stock bowler, while Tom Wass or Dusty Hallam, whose careers spread over the turn of the century, would ensure breadth and incisiveness in the attack. French would probably keep wicket. This leaves practically the whole of Victoria's reign from which to pick a Nottinghamshire select XI from those whose careers fell mainly in those years. By reversing the rose-coloured spectacles, it is possible for modern sportsmen to be amused at the antics of their forefathers, a hazardous attitude, for cricket is essentially a Victorian game which, in its *modus operandi*, has not altered unduly. Indeed, in some ways (manicured pitches, shorter boundaries, improved equipment) the balance has shifted in the other direction. The Nottinghamshire

pioneers helped create the game and were among its supreme protagonists. After all, there is a limit to the variety possible in the delivery and projection of a ball over a 22-yard span. There is no doubt that these superb performers would astound us today, were they joyfully re-incarnated.

Arthur Shrewsbury and William Gunn would open the batting, with Richard Daft and George Parr dancing attendance, each of them, in his prime, the major English batsman – and this in a period when amateurs were usually the leading run-makers. The bowlers would be Alfred Shaw, John Jackson, Fred Morley and Dick Attewell, with Mordecai Sherwin as wicket-keeper. The two other places might go to the steady all-rounder, Wilfred Flowers, and, as insurance against unlikely collapse, the stolid defender, W. H. Scotton. In Clarke's absence, Alfred Shaw might be appointed skipper.

What is, lastly, intriguing is that, if one attempted to combine the two into one team, only four of the later group would challenge convincingly, thus: Arthur Shrewsbury, William Gunn, Richard Daft, Joe Hardstaff junior, George Gunn, Alfred Shaw (captain), Bruce Dooland, Mordecai Sherwin, Harold Larwood, Dick Attewell and John Jackson.

TWELVE

Somerset

An informed glance at the populations of the county catchment areas reveals that Somerset has easily the smallest potential support. The home counties of Middlesex and Surrey draw on the London region with its teeming populace of, at a conservative estimate, 8 millions. Lancashire, Yorkshire and Warwickshire, the last set in the populous West Midlands conurbation, might tap totals of 5 or so millions in the first two cases, and over 3 millions in the third instance. Then there is an abrupt drop to a group of counties whose environs are each inhabited by around 1½ millions. These are Kent and Essex (both of which might also draw on the Greater London area), Gloucestershire, Glamorgan, Hampshire and Sussex. There is a further gradation: three counties in the North and East Midlands are each surrounded by a million people or a little less – Nottinghamshire, Leicestershire and Derbyshire. That leaves three counties. Worcestershire, in its new bracket with Herefordshire, touches about 600,000; Northamptonshire – hence doubtless its commendable essays in extra-parochial fixtures – weighs in at about 500,000; Somerset has a population of little more than 400,000.

That needs some explanation. It is the county's current population, and, by sensible order of the cricket establishment, counties must perforce act as if local government reorganization had never occurred. Were that spirited piece of wish-fulfilment to be accepted, one might recall to the Somerset cause those areas lost to Avon during the officious ravages of the early 1970s. For instance, Bath (population over 80,000) was and remains a proud arena for Somerset cricket. Nonetheless, one must accept that those Avon districts do look legitimately toward Bristol and the activities of Gloucestershire cricket. Bath is thirteen and Taunton forty-five miles from Bristol. As for Somerset, as she is now exhibited, Yeovil, with 130,000 inhabitants, is the largest

town. The districts of Mendip and Sedgemoor each approach 90,000 in population, while the sparser tracts of West Somerset offer succour and livelihood for only a few more than 30,000. That leaves the district of Taunton Deane with a populace of 86,000 – and the town of Taunton itself houses less than 40,000 souls. This is the most minute population, by region and by centre, to support a first-class county club. Several Minor Counties, again calculating by outlying districts and a core township, outstrip Somerset by considerable margins.

This must go a lengthy way toward explaining why Somerset, first, had an indecisive flirtation with first-class cricket, and, second, was something of a chopping-block for the richer counties, certainly until the grand equalization which, as Part One has described, pulled all counties up or down (depending on the value-system of the adjudicator) to a common level.

A succinct demographic account is probably necessary for any examination of Somerset's eccentric and, from one angle, uncharacteristic saga. With some worthy and one or two quite glorious exceptions, Somerset strictly has not been a rustic manifestation of Mummerset village greenery, played out on a higher, if not nobler, plane. Certainly until after the Second World War, Somerset relied on a procession of some-times ephemeral amateurs, stiffened by the inclusion of two or three robust, perhaps world-weary, professionals. So the team did not arise spontaneously from the artful practices of rural folk-games. If an older tradition informed their nature, it was that of the country house XIs, except that, even then, Somerset was a little more middle-class and suburban than that. School-teachers, army officers, city men on holiday – this was the stuff of Somerset cricket, with, in 1910, no less than thirty-eight names found on the team-sheets. From this inchoate, yet frequently high-spirited and entirely amiable discontinuity, it might be possible to decipher a 'character' of cavalier fluidity. However, to suggest that this, of itself, has any connection, geographically or socially, with Somerset as a political unit would be misleading.

Appropriately enough, an innovatory figure in Somerset's history was an Australian, one Sammy Woods. Expert rabbiter, rugby international, Victorian card, dangerous pace bowler, occasional batsman, inspiring captain and fielding slouch, he led Somerset intrepidly into some of their early forays in the County Championship. Somerset were formed in 1875, after some earlier comings and goings in the 1860s, and with the Lansdowne club to the fore. At a meeting at Sidmouth, chaired by the Rev. A. C. Ainslie, it was resolved to form a county club. It was, however, 1885 before Somerset took out a £50 annual lease on the ground at Taunton, although it was two years before it was fit enough for cricket. In 1890 the county defeated all its second-class opponents, and had, during the 1880s, welcomed occasional first-class opposition. In 1891 they brought the competition to nine in number, and, with five wins from twelve fixtures, Somerset, strangely enough, had one of their best seasons. With Derbyshire *persona non grata* in those years, Somerset thus joined the eight most firmly established counties.

For a year or two, before Sammy Woods's lengthier reign, Somerset were captained by H. T. Hewett, a mighty and demoralizing hitter. He opened the innings with Somerset's most elegant batsman, Lionel Palairet. Palairet was equable in manner and distinctive in classic execution, and his 14,000 runs for the county were not overtaken by a Somerset batsman until after the Second World War. Unluckily, he dropped out after 1904, and, while Somerset's amateurs were often glittering sparks, they often seemed to be easily extinguished. A couple of hard-working professionals struggled to maintain the county's equilibrium. E. J. Tyler, whose left-hand deliveries were slow to the point of inertia, took nearly 900 wickets, and he was steadfastly supported by G. B. Nichols.

124 Sammy Woods

In 1899 Len Braund was acquired from Surrey. An energetic cricketer, he became an England player and won twenty-three caps. Until the advent of Botham, he was Somerset's most successful all-rounder. His sprightly leg-breaks brought him and the county 684 wickets, and his sound batsmanship over 12,000 runs, while his fielding – he was then regarded as England's leading slip fielder – leaves him, with one exception, as Somerset's most successful poucher of catches, with 360.

Somerset's itinerant schoolmasters and clergymen continued to flare and fade spasmodically. They were fortunate to be captained before and after the First World War by John Daniell, a forceful character, who relished the typical Somerset problems of erratic batting, tepid bowling and unreliable fielding.

As might be expected, Somerset were subjected to some harsh drubbings. In one week in 1895 Essex scored 692 and Lancashire 801 against them. Yet, impishly, Somerset enjoyed the role of David or Jack, slaying a titanic Philistine here or discomforting a veritable Giant there. For instance, in 1892, Tyler's 15 for 96 defeated Nottinghamshire and deprived them of the Championship, while, under Woods in the early 1900s, there were famous victories over Yorkshire.

These occasional upsets to the form-book may have irked Somerset's self-styled betters, but they were rarely consistent enough to dislodge them from pre-eminent status, any more than the non-league club that knocks out a first-division club from the F.A. Cup ever actually proceeds to the Wembley final. Having risen to third, albeit well behind the two front clubs, in their second year, never again were Somerset to reach such heights for years. Sixth in 1894, seventh in 1902, fifth in 1919, and seventh three times in the 1930s: these were about their only sallies into the top half of the table, and, for the most part, Somerset were down among the dead men. They were bottom four times in the Edwardian period.

Yet between the wars, and although they must be listed among the worst five teams in the competition, they rarely collapsed completely

125 Len Braund

126 J. C. White

and were never bottom of the table. This was in spite of a cold financial climate, which afforded Somerset little chance of paying for many players and compelled them to rely on amateurs at a time when that strain was growing less virulent. The dashing play of P. R. Johnson and the polished approach of J. C. W. MacBryan stood out, but the most valued amateur was J. C. White. 'Farmer' White was a masterly left-hand spin bowler, who played fifteen times for England and captained both county and country. Depending on trajectory rather than spin, he had the stamina to bowl virtually all day, and his fruitful reward of 2356 first-class wickets places him high in the record of world bowlers, and, by many a hundred, makes him Somerset's most effective bowler. There was dogged assistance from the long-serving Ernest Robson, who is one of only four Somerset bowlers to take over 1000 wickets. He also scored 12,000 runs.

As finances improved and a more efficient nucleus of professionals was recruited, Somerset began to look in better shape. Frank Lee, a stubborn and honest opener, churned out over 15,000 runs, making himself one of Somerset's four top run-makers; W. T. Luckes, with over 800 catches and stumpings, proved to be one of England's most competent wicket-keepers; and Arthur Wellard and Bill Andrews provided straightforward pace to head the attack. Wellard, famed for his big hitting, scored over 11,000 runs as well as taking over 1500 wickets, becoming Somerset's second most successful bowler. There were also the able seamers of Bertie Buse and the deceptive spin of Horace Hazell.

In 1935 Harold Gimblett made his *Boys' Own* début, hitching a lift on a milk float at the start of his journey from village to first-class venue, and scoring a century in little over an hour. With dazzling assault, he continued in like vein, and he remains the only Somerset bat to have reached 20,000 first-class runs. This included 310 against Sussex in 1948, Somerset's best individual score until 1985. His co-existence with several great batsmen, his eschewal of safety first, and maybe a lack of single-mindedness combined to deny him more than a paltry three Test caps. His biography

127 Harold Gimblett

somehow personifies the myth and reality of Somerset cricket. Authentically, he elevated the breezy, wholehearted antics of the village green to a first-class level, and yet, behind that rubicund mien, lay a man who, eventually, was sick, hypochondriac and suicidal.

In the first season after the second war, Somerset amazed all when their honest-to-goodness bunch of pre-war professionals lifted the county to fourth place, their finest hour since 1892. It was delusive. Money was short; captains were many; amateurs were sporadic in appearances; and results were deplorable. Somerset were bottom in four consecutive years. They probably came nearer leaving the first-class scene than any county at this bleakly critical time.

By the end of the 1950s, however, Somerset became more professionalized, and reinforced their ragged brigade with overseas players. These included P. B. Wight, of British Guiana, whose tally, just short of 17,000 runs, puts him second only to Gimblett in the batting honours; Colin McCool, the crusty Australian veteran; and his countryman, Bill Alley, who scored only 300 less than Wight, and whose 3000 runs in 1961 shattered many Somerset records. Geoff Lomax, once of Lancashire, proffered steady all-round help, while H. W. Stephenson's talented wicket-keeping – he had over 1000 victims in a worthy career – was a decisive advantage. Graham Atkinson, an obstinate opening bat, who later went to Lancashire; B. A. Langford, who took nearly 1400 wickets with his off-spin; the quick bowler, Ken Palmer; and Johnnie Lawrence, an adept leg-spinner, were other fine contributors.

Burly Maurice Tremlett exploded on to the cricketing scene, his sterling medium-pace and doughty hitting confounding Middlesex in their 1947 Championship-winning year – another example of Somerset giant-killing. Inexplicably, he declined sharply as a bowler, but settled down to orthodox batting, scoring 15,000 runs for the county and becoming its first professional skipper. Later, Roy Virgin became one of Somerset's most consistent batsmen. He scored over 15,000 runs for the county, and, at much the same time and with much the same aplomb,

128 A young Ian Botham, batting for Somerset in 1974.

Mervyn Kitchen totted up about the same number of runs.

These were all notable names, and results did improve. The county was third in 1958, in 1963 and in 1966 – yet, in other years, there were poor placements, including last position in 1969. Still, it was an improvement, and, in the 1970s, Somerset wisely imported two wily campaigners, Brian Close of Yorkshire and Tom Cartwright of Warwickshire.

Nonetheless, Somerset were to save their brightest years for the last ten seasons or so. The arrival of Ian Botham more or less coincided with the employment of the West Indian stars, Joel Garner and Viv Richards. None of these three, as the conventional chairman might say, needs any introduction.

Ian Botham, a world-class all-rounder by any standards, with his superb attacking batting, brilliant slip fielding and often destructive bowling, has had his exploits, vocational and otherwise, lauded and, on occasion, jeered from the house-tops. The immensely tall Garner was one of an incandescent series of lethal West Indian fast bowlers, and Richards, of course, was the Hammond or Bradman of his era.

Although distracted by the inexhaustible flow of international commitments, this trio introduced excitement. There were valid, if less thrilling, contributions from others, such as Peter Denning, Vic Marks, Peter Roebuck and Brian Rose. When, in the mid-1980s, Botham, Garner and Richards departed and went their separate ways, not in the merriest of atmospheres, the Australian Steve Waugh and the assured New Zealand bat, Martin Crowe, came into their own. In 1990 and 1991, with Chris Tavaré, once of Kent, the captain, and the South African Jimmy Cook brimming with runs, Somerset's batting looked sound enough, but they lacked penetration in attack.

It has to be reported that the gifted threesome – Botham, Richards, Garner – while charging the air with sporting electricity, did not bring many achievements Somerset's way. Ian Botham scored under 9000 runs, but at an average of over 30, and took nearly 500 wickets in his thirteen Somerset seasons; Joel Garner took over 300 wickets; and Viv Richards averaged just less than 50, as he gathered well over 14,000 golden runs. But this was not all translated into tangible achievement. From 1976 to 1984 Somerset did enjoy their best run in the Championship, only once slipping from the upper berths, and rising to third in 1981. But they plummeted to bottom place in 1985 and climbed only a notch higher in 1986. Somerset have yet to win the Championship.

Their one-day record is much more heartening. The lively talents of Somerset's best-ever team combined well to win the John Player Sunday League in 1979, and there were several other brave essays in this competition. Somerset then won the Benson and Hedges Cup in consecutive years, 1981 and 1982. Going in second each time, their strong batting gave them exceedingly easy victories, Surrey falling by 7 wickets in the first and Nottinghamshire by 9 wickets in the second of these encounters. Somerset had been beaten by Kent by 32 runs in the 1967 Gillette final, but now the Botham-Richards partnership prevailed twice. In 1979 the Gillette Cup was captured at the expense of Northamptonshire by 45 runs, and, in 1983, in the NatWest Trophy, Kent lost to Somerset by 24 runs.

These moments of glory were enjoyed by jubilant Somerset fans, several of them in yokel attire and swigging cider. Five titles in five years constituted a flamboyant triumph, concentrating all of Somerset's successes into the last five per cent of their first-class history.

Somerset have seldom, if ever, fielded a team of Somerset-born players, and there are only two or three of the current squad with that birthright. Somerset teams – and it is no vice in itself – have been banded together without pedantic adherence to geographical locations. From the days of Sammy Woods, they have conducted themselves in the way that almost all counties now do. In that sense, they have been not unlike the ancient exhibition XIs of the mid-19th century.

The essential difference, of course, has been that the exhibition teams, like the medieval friars, were mainly mobile, whereas the counties, like the monks, have been chiefly static. Somerset, on that parallel, have taken monastic vows, quartering themselves principally at Taunton, and supplying cricket to the locals. Somerset, then, have long been an example of what most counties have become: exhibition teams with a domestic hearth.

Some of this is evident when an all-time Somerset XI is paraded. The rapier of L. C. H. Palairet and the bludgeon of Harold Gimblett would make for a complementary opening partnership, and they would be followed by Roy Virgin and P. B. Wight. A string of splendid all-rounders would come next: Ian Botham, Len Braund, Bill Alley and Arthur Wellard, while H. W. Stephenson would be asked to keep wicket. B. A. Langford might balance the bowling with his teasing off-spinners. There would be left-hand spin from the captain, J. C. White, holder, with 381, of the Somerset catching record. Only Langford of this team totalled less than 10,000 first-class runs, and the fielding, especially in the slips, would be very sound. So, in spite of a relative lack of success over 100 years, Somerset would not be embarrassed, were a Wellsian time-machine invented capable of organizing a county competition over the centuries: Lionel Palairet, Harold Gimblett, Roy Virgin, Peter Wight, Ian Botham, Len Braund, Bill Alley, Arthur Wellard, H. W. Stephenson, J. C. White and Brian Langford.

THIRTEEN

Surrey

No county has a richer history than Surrey. Middlesex, with its MCC and Lord's connections, may have the more metropolitan and regal disposition, but, just as ancient British families are said to look scornfully down on the parvenu traits of English royalty, so might Surrey claim equivalent status.

In such a bustling county, so close to London, it is no surprise to find representative cricket played during the 18th century, and, after the collapse of the Hambledon club, its Surrey-born members retired to their heritage. Not for the last time, Surrey's hegemony was complete and enduring. Throughout the years of the Napoleonic Wars, they were supreme. William 'Silver Billy' Beldham, the greatest all-rounder of his period; William Lambert, the noted single-wicket player who fell foul of the authorities with regard to fixing; and Edward 'Lumpy' Stevens, to whose bowling exploits we owe the implanting of the third stump – these were among the leading lights of cricket's pre-history.

But there was no focus of ground or organization, for such representative sides were strictly reliant on wagering patrons. By 1810 Surrey's long series of games with and, usually, victories over the All-England XI and others had passed, and, for over thirty years, it was the prosperous clubs of the county which held the interest. Richmond, Godalming, Dorking, Chertsey, Reigate, Farnham, Mitcham, Epsom . . . the list is lengthy, and many of these were a cut above the average village club, with the cricket by no means casual or ill-disciplined.

Perhaps the most notable of this host of well-to-do clubs was the Montpelier CC, based chiefly at Walworth. In 1844 that bane of cricket clubs, the entrepreneurial builder, caused them to depart from their Beehive ground and seek fresh quarters. An oval-shaped market-garden, some ten acres in dimension, at Kennington was alighted upon, and William Baker, a Montpelier member, negotiated a lease of £120 a year with the agreement of the Duchy of Cornwall. No less than 10,000 turves were transported from Tooting Common, and the Oval was very quickly a reality.

At this time London was largely to be found on the northern banks of the Thames, and the railway had only just begun to push across the river. There were green meadows and hillocks where soon there would be intense development, but Surrey was a busy county, with many active townships, and a thriving population. As early as 1855, the Metropolitan Management Act demanded the retreat of the Surrey borders towards Croydon, and so, for almost all its days, the Oval has been outside Surrey proper.

With the ground already in use, the Montpelier club, mainly through the medium of William Ward, arranged meetings in August and October of 1845 at the Horns Tavern, for many years its headquarters. Surrey club cricketers in general were invited to assist in the formation of a county club, and the Hon. Frederick Ponsonby, later the Earl of Bessborough, offered his noble support. Thus Surrey were formed, and, along with Lancashire, they are the only first-class club, if *Wisden* is to be believed, to have suffered no constitutional renewals nor vicissitudes of re-organization since that inaugural date.

Not that such political propriety was without its alarms. The programme was initially modest, and the ground was managed by Mr W. Houghton, the Montpelier president, and, from a cricketing viewpoint, mismanaged, so much so that there were fears of losing the lease. John Burrup, the business-like Surrey secretary, negotiated a deal which transferred lease and management to the club itself, and, since 1854 and until 1989, with the creation of the Foster's Oval, ground and county flourished. The world-famous gas-holders arrived in 1869 to mark the insidious spread and sprawl of urban man and to add an ambience of industrial distinction to the venue. In 1901 the jangling trams, which, for fifty years, were almost as famous as the gas-holders, first ran. The pavilion was erected in 1858, and, by 1861, the membership was almost touching 1000.

On this most solid foundation, the second of Surrey's series of distinguished XIs developed. In 1856, 1857, 1858 and 1859, they won twenty-six out of twenty-nine games, and lost only two. Their captain was F. P. Miller, a splendid driver and excellent out-fielder; and Fred Burbidge, who succeeded Miller as captain, and C. G. Lane, a sound player of fast bowling, were his viceroys. The principal professionals were the nervy but quick-footed Julius Caesar; William Caffyn, a wristy bat and positive bowler, variously nick-named 'Terrible Billy' or the 'Surrey Pet'; and H. H. Stephenson, a fast breakback bowler, strong batsman and excellent wicket-keeper, who, like Caffyn, was much involved in early forays to Australia. Tom Sherman and William Martingell did much of the quickish stock bowling, and the opening bats, Tom Humphrey and Harry Jupp, prefaced what was to be something of a Surrey speciality – a powerful duo to start the proceedings. Both were tiny, with their flowery Victorian soubriquets – 'the Pocket Hercules' and 'Young Stonewall' – testifying to their difference of approach. In Tom Lockyer and then Edward Pooley the side was happy to include a wicket-keeper of international rank.

This team, as teams will and must, aged and grew tired, so that the 1870s and the early 1880s must be judged, the diligent graft of James Southerton apart, among Surrey's most discouraging summers. What must, however, be noted is the sterling work of C. W. Alcock, secretary from 1872 to 1906. Under his rule, Surrey began to find their feet once more.

Gradually, the inspiring leadership of John Shuter began to reap dividends. His amateur comrade, Walter Read, proved to be, to that point, Surrey's most prolific run-maker, and an entertaining one to boot. His namesake, the professional Maurice Read, was also an estimable and dashing batsman, while Harry Wood was the

129 H. H. Stephenson, a Surrey star of the 1850s and 1860s.

efficient stumper. But it was the inexhaustible stamina of Bobby Abel that really led to many adjustments and additions to the record books. Chiefly in steadfast partnership with Bill Brockwell, Abel matured into one of cricket's most dominant opening bats. 'The Guvnor' – the Oval has a penchant for nicknames – scored 33,000 first-class runs in his long career. He was small and duck-like in gait, but was untouchable as a technician. His twelve centuries in 1900 were then a record; and in 1901 his aggregate in all matches was 3309 runs, also a record at the time.

However, there was another individual reason for Surrey's new-found triumph: George Lohmann. His class was such that this blond and broadset fellow, wholehearted, perhaps too generous in what he attempted to offer the game he adored, sprang immediately to the fore. W. G. Grace and C. B. Fry assure us that he was the best medium-pace bowler there had been, his ingenious deployment of break and, particularly, pace, being shrewdly allied to his easy control of formal length. He was a cavalier batsman, and, it was then claimed, the best slip fielder that had ever lived. In a relatively short career of not much over a dozen years, he took 1841 first-class wickets, at an average of just under 14, an average only improved upon by Alfred Shaw and, marginally, by Tom Emmett among world bowlers. Lohmann's Test average of 10.75, from 112 wickets in eighteen appearances, easily makes him the leader in a list of international bowlers.

This glittering revival brought untold success to Surrey. Having been declared champions in 1864, and thereby, according to *Wisden*, the first semi-official title-holders, Surrey dominated the competition until the turn of the century. Assuming the leading role from Nottinghamshire, they won the Championship in 1887, 1888, 1889 (jointly with Lancashire and Nottinghamshire), 1890, 1891, 1892, 1894, 1895 and 1899. Fifth in 1893 was their worst position over this jubilant phase. It was a pre-eminence similar to the one rapturously enjoyed by Surrey fans in the 1950s, and, although briefly recorded, it amounted to a considerable act of perpetual mastery. Between 1887 and 1899, out of some 250 county fixtures

completed, Surrey won no less than 160, with only 44 defeats, a record of superb attainment, especially when the prowess of two or three other counties is taken into the reckoning.

Continuity rather than the switchback of joy and demoralization attended Surrey about these times. As Lohmann, invariably overworked, fell away and died at the age of thirty-six, two more legendary figures had already emerged to form a deadly pair of opening bowlers. One was W. H. Lockwood, a little temperamental, but perhaps with that seasoning of inequanimity spicing his undoubted artistry. With a long, loping run and flexible action, he had the undefinable gift of satanic bounce, and confused the greatest of his opponents. In the famous Manchester Test of 1902, he took 11 for 76 against Australia.

The other was Tom Richardson, the yardstick for all antecedent English fast bowlers, just as Lohmann is the model for all medium-pace bowlers. Richardson had courage in the heroic mould to align with his immense physical power, but it must have been the third ingredient – a rhythmic, flowing action – which enabled him to bowl at high pace over lengthy periods and with unsurpassed excellence. He relished bowling and was a most chivalrous sportsman, and yet still his phenomenal stamina provokes imaginings of the superhuman. He took 2104 first-class wickets, ten times having a bag of 100 wickets in the season, and, in his prime, 1894 to 1897, he averaged 250 wickets a season.

As Bobby Abel grew older, the Surrey tradition of opening batsmanship was nurtured by Tom Hayward. A friendly and unruffled man, Hayward's batting was similarly unhurried but authoritative and founded on imperturbable back-play. In 1906 he recorded 3518 runs, an aggregate that has been beaten only twice, by Compton and Edrich in 1947. Of those whose careers began in Victorian times, he was the first, after Grace, to reach 40,000 runs, and his life's total – 43,551 – is Surrey's second-best.

About this time Herbert Strudwick became the wicket-keeper, and he was destined to keep twenty-eight times for England, an enviable record for those days of infrequent Tests. It is

130 Tom Richardson

accepted that, historically, he is one of the best dozen keepers of all time, and, from 1902 to 1927 (and remembering the hiatus of the First World War), he accounted for 1497 batsmen; only Murray and Taylor have passed this remarkable figure. This makes him the most successful wicket-keeper of the pre-1939 era. The spin bowling of 'Razor' Smith; the support bowling of Walter Lees; the forcing play of E. G. Hayes; and, until one of those bitter differences of opinion that cricket clubs somehow never avoid, the lively all-round assistance of J. N. Crawford, loaned ready aid to the masters.

While seasons 1903 and 1904 are best forgotten, Surrey remained a power in the land through the Edwardian prelude to the First World War and, in 1914, they were again champions. Although cancelling the last two fixtures, as the war clouds grimly gathered in August 1914, they were officially awarded the title, and, in truth, won fifteen and lost only two games.

Between the two world wars the Surrey momentum was reasonably maintained, although the iron grip of Yorkshire was never dislodged, and Surrey's neighbours, Middlesex, normally outshone them. Nonetheless, Surrey dropped out of the leading eight on only four occasions.

Some of the pre-war players continued to shine, and Jack Hobbs, who made his début in 1905 and was still playing in 1934, was foremost among them. If Tom Hayward, with whom for ten years he joined in sublime partnership, had demonstrated that professional batting might be attractive and well composed, Jack Hobbs now reconstituted the mould of professional batsmanship. Serene, earnest, but by no means solemn, he epitomized that superior professionalism which, for instance, Hammond and Sutcliffe were to exemplify. Hobbs was the first paid cricketer to be knighted; his values were civilized and decent; and, in a commercial sense, he was instrumental in raising paid cricket from a trade to a profession.

He replaced Grace as the sporting personality most loved by the public, and he succeeded and, for many commentators, surpassed him as the master batsman. It was, and remains, a delight that so humane and dignified a sportsman enjoyed huge popular acclaim as well as ceaseless critical accolades. His success was based on his smooth fusion of classic method and natural aplomb. Turning to a parallel dichotomy, he impeccably straddled past and future, harmonizing the free-flowing cavalier abandon of the golden age with the more puritanical watchfulness of the post-1914 era. Successful in all conditions, and, it is agreed, Bradman's superior in difficult circumstances, only Grace and Hammond might rival him as England's finest. Not in any way a mechanical accumulator, he proudly preferred the testing and probing of great bowlers in important contests to the humdrum passages of normalcy. Even so, he stands alone at the head of the run-mart, with 61,237 runs, at an average of 50.65, and his 197 centuries comprise a record never to be broken.

Those who might, ornately, be described as the courtiers around that kingly presence were themselves gifted. Andrew Sandham, neat, even diffident in style, who succeeded Hayward as Hobbs's opening partner, was the perfect foil for Hobbs. His 41,000 and more runs makes him third in Surrey's batting honours, and he made 107 centuries and won fourteen caps. There was also Andrew Ducat, one of that happy band of footballer-cricketers, and a most consistent bat, while Douglas Jardine (whose controversial international deeds dwarf his relatively brief county activities) was both orthodox and valiant in his valued contributions. It all made for an immensely powerful batting line-up: in 1928, nine Surrey players passed the 1000-runs marker, an unheard-of achievement.

Among them was the captain, P. G. H. Fender, who led Surrey for a dozen years from 1921 with consummate *élan*. He endeavoured to combine deep powers of judgement with a quixotic affection for the experimental and risky, a rare enough compound in cricket or in life. Apart from the trusty H. A. Peach, a sort of Sancho Panza to Fender's Don, the Surrey bowling was woeful and the Oval wickets were trance-like in their calmness. Fender, as well as scoring briskly, conjured up devious bowling to mislead scores of batsmen,

and something of the same artfulness informed his captaincy. Thus, though the team was never strong enough overall to win the title, Fender contrived to keep Surrey in the hunt, and he is regarded by many as one of cricket's most intelligent captains.

He was replaced for a short while by Jardine; and then Errol Holmes, a forceful bat and forceful character, took over. As the 1930s drew on, other names emerged, among them that Surrey rarity, a left-hander, in the person of Laurie Fishlock, whose delightful footwork helped him to garner over 25,000 runs; and there was Alf Gover, a welcome and stirring addition to the bowling department, whose fiery assaults earned him over 1500 first-class wickets.

The war came, and the Oval was made ready to receive any German parachutists who might land. Then a few post-war seasons passed without many omens of Surrey's impending decade of grandeur. It was the phoney war before the all-out assault. Put briefly, Surrey now assembled one of the most efficient machines ever displayed in the County Championship, and they engineered a set of conquests over the 1950s that enabled them to lay claim to being the most effective county team of the post-war period. Having shared the Championship with Lancashire in 1950 and having dropped to sixth place in 1951, they then won, usually with contemptuous ease, the next seven Championships. No other county has enjoyed such an impressive reign of consecutive titles. And, of course, 1950 marked Surrey's first honours since 1914.

Their invincibility was Napoleonic, and, inevitably, a psychological dimension to their achievement. In winning twenty-three out of twenty-eight matches in 1955, they steamed away by a record margin, and, in 1956, they beat the Australians, undefeated by a county for over forty years, by 10 wickets.

Two factors, the opposite of those that characterized the inter-war years, conspired to help Surrey: they assembled a deadly group of bowlers and the Oval wickets gave them pertinent assistance, Some critics have scolded Surrey for their dependence on helpful pitches, and have

131 All-conquering Surrey, the 1956 champions. *Back row*: A. Sandham (coach), B. Constable, R. C. E. Pratt, M. D. Willett, K. F. Barrington, D. G. W. Fletcher, G. A. R. Lock, P. J. Loader, T. H. Clarke, M. J. Stewart, D. F. Cox, D. E. Pratt, J. C. Laker, R. Swetman, J. Tait (masseur); *front*: E. A. Bedser, A. V. Bedser, Marshal of the RAF Lord Tedder (president), W. S. Surridge (captain), B. K. Castor (secretary), P. B. H. May and A. J. McIntyre.

even suggested that the resultant one-sidedness became boring and led to lost attendances. This is unfair. The Surrey bowlers did plenty of damage on their travels, and, needless to say, other bowlers also had use of the Oval wickets. As for the crowds dropping away, that probably had more to do with the general decline in spectatorship for cricket and, in fact, for football too during this time. Few genuine fans really mind how devastatingly their heroes triumph.

Four bowlers joined to procure these great successes. Alec Bedser, powerful, controlled, tireless, thudded away at his stern medium pace, carrying England, as well as Surrey, on his burly shoulders. In England terms, he is challenged only by his predecessor, Lohmann, and by Maurice Tate as the country's leading medium-pace bowler. He took almost 2000 wickets, and his 236 wickets in fifty-one Tests stood as the record for some time, until, with more frequent Test matches, five Englishmen overhauled him. The other quick bowler was Peter Loader, un-

lucky that Trueman, Statham and Tyson collided with his career, but still capable of winning thirteen caps with his lively swing bowling.

The contributions of Tony Lock and Jim Laker need little more rehearsal. Tony Lock, his left-hand spin stinging and zestful, mocked and tormented batsmen from one end, while the lugubrious Jim Laker, the Mr Plod of spin bowlers, methodically plotted their downfall at the other. Together they constituted one of the most lethal spin duos cricket has witnessed, a pairing coloured by opposites of temperament, the former perky and volatile and the latter canny and perceptive. Both played approaching fifty times for England. Lock took more first-class wickets than any other Surrey player, some of them, of course, with other clubs. His total was 2844, including 174 for England. Laker had 1944 victims, with 193 in Tests, the best by any England off-spinner, including his magnificent 19 wickets in the 1956 Test against Australia. Excellent as Tony Lock was, Jim Laker, with his chary usage of

132 Jim Laker

age. With Cowdrey, he would be judged the best of English batsmen bred in the post-war era. Putting to scorn atrocity tales about the Oval wicket and its slow surrounds, he scored runs galore, their beauty somehow failing to chime authentically with his painful demeanour during his unhappy period as chairman of the England selectors in the 1980s. He made over 27,000 runs, and is one of only ten cricketers qualified to play for England with a career average of over 50. He won sixty-six caps and led England many times.

The motivator of this unshakeable force was Stuart Surridge, himself a useful all-rounder, but, beyond that, a daring general with a sardonic

133 Surrey's inspirational captain, Stuart Surridge, fielding close to the wicket.

angles and sheer strength of spin, must claim chief attention. When world XIs are chosen, one place is rarely disputed. Laker is probably the best off-spinner in cricket's long saga.

The batting was moderate for so unassailable a side. Constable, Fletcher and Clark provided a modicum of runs, and the tail, including Alec's twin brother, Eric Bedser, and the long-serving wicket-keeper, Arthur McIntyre, jogged along merrily enough. One batsman was outstanding, and that was P. B. H. May, later to captain Surrey and England with distinction. The shapely lines of his classical and graceful style evoked memories, in that last effusion of amateur batting, of the hatred of the draw. Five years captain – five years champions: that brooks no debate about successful leadership. Surridge was also an intrepid close-to-the-wicket catcher, and, with the agile Lock, formed a trap of enormous menace. This rather compensated for a pedestrian tendency in the rest of Surrey's out-cricket, for theirs was a celebrated series of victories in which constantly sharp bowling, unmatchable close catching and ebullient captaincy remained the keys.

The next thirty years were, maybe unavoidably, years of anti-climax, edging towards bathos. Subba Row, like F. R. Brown before him, had transferred to Northamptonshire and conducted himself sufficiently well to open the England batting. The admirable Ken Barrington, a Test and county batsman of indomitable application, held together the defence of both country and shire until the end of the 1960s, collecting nearly 32,000 runs in that unflinching and committed process. Micky Stewart and John Edrich formed another noted opening partnership, resolute and wary. J. H. Edrich proved eventually the more accomplished, making nearly twice as many international appearances as his famous uncle, Bill Edrich. With nearly 40,000 runs to his credit – only Boycott, Amiss, Graveney, Cowdrey and M. J. K. Smith of post-war batsmen have scored more – he was a decided asset. Stewart scored some 26,000 first-class runs. His son, Alec, was later to bat well enough to earn an England place himself, and he was appointed Surrey captain for the 1992 season.

Over that lengthy period of what might be termed ultra-modern cricket, Surrey fielded other likely lads. Among the bowlers, there were R. G. D. Willis, who moved to Warwickshire, R. D. Jackman, G. G. Arnold, and, from Barbados, Sylvester Clarke. Pat Pocock and Intikhab Alam were the pick of the slow bowlers. G. R. J. Roope, S. J. Storey, Younis Ahmed (later of Glamorgan), M. A. Lynch, A. R. Butcher (who also moved to Glamorgan) have shone as batsmen. The wicket-keeping of Robin Swetman, Arthur Long and C. J. Richards was always of good class. For the last two or three seasons Ian Greig made some headway as captain, assisted by a group of

134 J. H. Edrich

135 Ken Barrington

promising young players including the Bicknell brothers, D. M. Ward and G. P. Thorpe.

At times over these three decades Surrey have sunk uncomfortably, and they were sixteenth in 1978. All things are relative. In a score of seasons they have remained in the top half of the table: it is the vividly etched memory of the 1950s by which even the most praiseworthy endeavours are judged. The 1980s have, for instance, shown Surrey to be a resourceful side. Nonetheless, the proudest year was 1971 when Surrey were champions again, a pleasing reward for Edrich, Stewart and company. They enthusiastically held off the competition of Warwickshire and Lancashire, and it was a meritorious performance. They were also runners-up in 1973 and 1980, and enjoyed a sparkling campaign in 1991, when Waqar Younis took over 100 wickets with his explosive pace.

Surrey have also had some good times in the one-day contests. They twice made the Gillette finals, only to be defeated, by Yorkshire in a monumental trouncing by 175 runs in 1965, and by Middlesex by 7 wickets, another comfortable margin, in 1980. But in 1982, in the second of the NatWest finals, it was Surrey's turn to luxuriate at ease: Warwickshire were well beaten by 9 wickets. In 1991 they were just beaten by Hampshire in a nicely-balanced final. Surrey have played three Benson's finals and won one. In 1979 Essex won by 35 runs and, in 1981, Somerset won by 7 wickets. Prior to that, in 1974, Leicestershire lost to Surrey by 27 runs.

Surrey have never won the Sunday League, and so, since 1960, they have had one Championship and two cup wins to their credit, a little weak after the grandiose days of the last seasons of the 19th century and the martial conquests of the 1950s. For all that, Surrey must be judged one of the greatest of the seventeen counties.

Such has been the cavalcade of talent which has enlivened the Oval that the choice of a best-ever team is beggared by the opulent profusion of players inviting consideration. Even if one grudgingly rules out the old guard of Beldham, Caffyn *et al*, the problems are large, if pleasant.

Jack Hobbs is one of two or three undoubted selections, and his partner, picked from a long line of Surrey openers, would be Tom Hayward. Peter May would be the automatic number four, and Ken Barrington the likeliest number five. Most students of Surrey's life and times would expect Percy Fender to be elected captain, and he would fill the role of an eccentric all-rounder. Fans of both John Shuter and Stuart Surridge are entitled to feel a little aggrieved.

One might include Bobby Abel to bolster the batting, and stick to four bowlers, plus Fender. The trouble is that Surrey, while often short of bowlers, have had half a dozen world-beaters: Richardson and Lockwood; Lohmann and Bedser; Laker and Lock. One might argue till the cows come home, but perhaps the best solution would be Richardson, Lohmann, Bedser and Laker – with Herbert Strudwick more than happy to keep wicket for that brilliant array. It is a reluctant conclusion because of those sorrowfully omitted, but this Surrey team would conquer most: Jack Hobbs, Tom Hayward, Bobby Abel, Peter May, Ken Barrington, Percy Fender, George Lohmann, Jim Laker, Alec Bedser, Tom Richardson and Herbert Strudwick.

FOURTEEN

Sussex

Like Hampshire and Kent, the Sussex area has played host to cricket in its rural surrounds for long enough, but, like Hampshire and Kent, its representative county sides mustered around town life: in the case of Sussex, Brighton. Brighton, the metropolitan playground and the haunt of royalty, became a key town for the developing first-class game in England.

It is a fact that village cricket in Sussex dates back to the early history of the game, and Slindon, about four miles from Arundel and with Chichester a little further away, was especially noteworthy during the 18th century. Its captain was the Chichester surgeon, Richard Newland, believed to be the leading all-rounder in England at that time, and uncle and mentor of Richard Nyren, the 'general' of Hambledon.

Sussex enjoyed aristocratic patronage in those early years, in particular from the second Duke of Richmond, who was Charles II's grandson. He employed useful cricketers on his Goodwood estate, including the old original professional, Thomas Waymark, and was associated with Slindon's success. More royal patronage came from the Prince Regent, later George IV, who, in 1791, was to the fore in establishing the Level, afterwards known as Ireland's Gardens, as the venue for many matches. Later on, the Sussex wicket-keeper, Tom Box, was its manager, until, in 1848, Sussex cricket transferred to the Brunswick ground at Hove (though the Montpelier ground was also used). Then, in 1871, the Brunswick turf was moved to the present Hove ground, at Eaton Road.

In the worldly-wise and extremely accurate bowler, William Lillywhite, and his comrade, Jem Broadbridge, Sussex could boast the chief protagonists of the round-arm revolution, while John Wisden, a most effective all-rounder, was the mainstay of Sussex cricket, as well as a seminal figure in the development of the processes and mechanics of the cricket business.

In 1836 William Lillywhite leased the Montpelier ground and there were moves to raise funds for Sussex cricket. It was in 1839, however, that the Sussex county club was formally constituted. The Rev. George L. Langdon, first secretary of Sussex, was the leading progenitor, and the seal was placed on the inauguration of the club with a celebratory dinner at Pegg's Hotel, Brighton.

There was some reorganization in 1857, when, according to common practice, the committee was based on a division of the shire into districts, but, with its official origins in 1839, Sussex was to be the oldest of the first batch of senior county clubs. Despite its respectable heritage, Sussex has never prospered in the county competition. Until the late 1890s they were a poorish side, and were bottom or next to the bottom some fifteen times prior to the major expansion of the competition. During the golden age Sussex were a formidable team, and were runners-up in 1902 and 1903, and third in 1905. Still they could not carry off the title, and, between the wars, their record was not too distinguished. However, there were excitements hereabouts, for the county's strong batting led them to second place in 1932, 1933 and 1934. If the years of the oligarchs were dismal ones for Sussex, then the more democratic seasons of the post-war era brought them no greater success. Often Sussex had to mourn in quite lowly positions, and runners-up in 1953 and 1981 were their nearest approach to the elusive title.

Seven second places seems an unlucky record. The cricket statistician, Roy Webber, rules that, in 1875, Sussex should have shared the championship with Nottinghamshire and Lancashire, although that worthy's Sussex blood may have affected his usually impeccable mathematics. In 1932 and 1933 Sussex lost their way when reasonably placed, while in 1934 another victory – they won, in fact, only one of their last ten fixtures – would have clinched the title. Under

David Sheppard, Sussex ran Surrey close in 1953, but 1981 was the most frustrating year, when Nottinghamshire were only very narrowly the winners.

The controlled aggression of much Sussex cricket in the modern dispensation has enabled them to enjoy transports of ephemeral delight at instant cricket. Perhaps finding it problematic to settle early in the season, Sussex have never reached the Benson's final, but their endeavours in the Sunday League have often been invigorating. In 1982 their campaign was ultimately successful and they topped the table.

The Gillette Cup, however, became something of a Sussex speciality. They won the first two finals. In 1963 they managed to overcome Worcestershire by just 14 runs, and, in 1964, they routed Warwickshire by 8 wickets. Then they were beaten finalists on three occasions. In 1968 Warwickshire extracted their revenge with a 4-wicket victory; in 1970 they lost to a strong Lancashire side by 6 wickets; and, in 1973, Gloucestershire won by 40 runs. Then, in 1978, there was a further victory, when Somerset were comfortably beaten by 5 wickets. Sussex did not profitably turn their attention to the NatWest Trophy until 1986, when P. W. G. Parker's 85 laid the foundation for a 7-wickets win over Lancashire, whose commonplace bowling permitted a Sussex score of 243, then the highest by any side batting last in either of the two domestic finals. Thus Sussex have been seven times finalists, a splendid performance, and have been four times winners.

After that simple *résumé* of Sussex's most meritorious team exploits, one may relax and allow the story of the county's charismatic players to unfold, unhindered by the intercession of gloatings over paltry baubles. And, after the stirring deeds of 'Old Lilly' and Wisden, 'the Little Wonder', we must leap ahead to the *fin de siècle*, and that most attractive and diverting of all Sussex XIs, the one associated historically with K. S. Ranjitsinhji, afterwards the Jam Sahib of Nawanagar, and the polymath, C. B. Fry. They were both, needless to say, brilliant cricketers, but, more important, they personified much of

the character, eccentric yet pertinent, of the English county game in its maturing stages.

In a relatively short career of some dozen seasons, Ranji scored over 24,000 runs and averaged an impressive 56; his Test average was almost 45. He scored seventy-two centuries, including a remarkable fourteen double centuries, and twice scored 3000 runs in a season. C. B. Fry scored 30,000 runs, averaged 50 and scored 94 centuries (thirteen of them 'doubles'), over a slightly longer career, and that included 3000 runs in 1901. By world standards both men stand pre-eminent. Both, for instance, played in the first Test of 1902, when England fielded what many regard as her strongest-ever side. It is astonishing to find them in the same side at the same time, joining one another in perhaps county cricket's most fruitful pairing ever.

They complemented one another in ways not intelligible from the mere figures of their heavy scoring. Ranji was the perfect instance of the anglicized Indian princeling, devoting himself to the field-sports of the upper-class, whereas Charles Fry, fair and robust, was the quintessential athlete from that top drawer, with a wide range of sporting and intellectual interests.

They differed, too, in style. The Indian introduced a pagan aestheticism into his batting that, to honestly sweating bowlers, appeared to border on the occult. His eye was hawk-like and his deft reflexes were informed by a vividly sharp mind. The thinly threaded leg-glance and the gossamer fine cut, alongside immaculate driving, were his hallmarks, but one illusion was paramount. He gave every impression of spontaneous, magical genius, but, while obviously naturally talented, he was, as befitted his Anglo-Saxon commitment, dedicated to arduous practice.

C. B. Fry was something of the reverse: a gifted bat who made manifest a rational portrayal of careful analysis and objective self-control. Well organized backplay, supplemented by a searing on-drive, was his trade-mark, and the labelling is not idle, for one was the artist and the other the technician, undoubtedly lifted by the presence of illuminating genius. Fry was resolute in concentration and patience and his calculated on-side play was to be noted and copied by the modern schools of batsmanship.

Sussex were fortunate to surround these titans with other good players. Joe Vine, exhorted by the martinet Fry to forego his yearning for assault and dwell on stolid defence, coupled his 25,000 first-class runs with tempting leg-breaks and superb fielding in the country. The Australian captain, Billy Murdoch, and the bespectacled left-hander, E. H. Killick, supported him trustily, while Albert Relf's willing medium-pace gained him a career total only a little short of 1900 wickets. He accomplished the double eight times, making him the closest competitor to Maurice Tate as the county's best all-rounder. It was Tate's father, Fred – he took 1341 wickets for Sussex with his frugal off-breaks – and George Cox – 1810 wickets for Sussex in a long career as a left-hand spinner – who brought most succour to the hard-working Relf.

Sussex, predominantly a batting side and lacking fiery penetration in attack, especially on the placid Hove square, finally found a sharp opening attack in the years after the First World War. The gigantic bulkiness of Maurice Tate, some flavour of the village smith about him as he thundered towards the wicket, was allied with exemplary control and a fizzing velocity off the pitch. His black hair and large hands, his boyish mix of frustrations and good cheer, his unfailing vim – these traits added a gloss of happy feeling to his huge skill, so that, like Fred Trueman in later years, he was a most popular character. He took 2784 wickets in his career (2211 for Sussex); and he played thirty-nine times for England. He is certainly one of the three best medium-pace bowlers to represent the old country. A fine fielder and batsman, he did the double eight times, plus a ninth occasion on tour with MCC in India and Ceylon. He is one of only nine cricketers with over 20,000 runs and 2000 wickets in the first-class game.

His county captain and fellow bowler, Arthur Gilligan, rated fielding highly, and, leading from the front as one of the game's supreme mid-offs, he insisted that Sussex were never lacking in this regard. That amateur rarity, a quick bowler, he

136 A young Maurice Tate

took over 600 wickets for Sussex and batted with panache. He was one of several Sussex players to captain England.

He was well served by the long-standing opening bat, Ted Bowley, who scored over 28,000 first-class runs in vigorous fashion, and by T. E. Cook, who scored 20,000 runs. K. S. Duleepsinhji, Ranji's nephew and a glittering batsman, averaged over 50 for the county, but did not play regularly or for long enough. He holds the Sussex individual record of 333. A. F. Wensley and J. H. Cornford, with Bowley, were the main bowlers when Tate and Gilligan were done.

On either side of the Second World War, Sussex developed a highly responsible and capable bunch of journeymen, locked together in filial

137 & 138 John (left) and James Langridge.

relationship as well as sporting camaraderie. The Langridge brothers proved to be worthy sons of Sussex. John Langridge, with over 34,000 first-class runs, and James Langridge, with over 31,000, stand second and third in the ranks of Sussex run-scorers, and James also took 1500 wickets: sane and solid careers, if ever there were such. They dominated Sussex cricket, and served it with sensible dedication. John scored seventy-six centuries for Sussex and James topped 1000 runs twenty times, both county records.

George Cox junior, another son of a notable father, delighted with 22,000 runs and more for his county, while Jim and Harry Parks scored over 40,000 between them for Sussex, the former also taking nearly 800 wickets. There was still the amateur leavening. Hugh Bartlett, a hitter in the heroic mould, was a most popular and much-enjoyed cricketer, and his close friend, S. C. Griffith, that rare bird, an efficient but un-paid wicket-keeper, stood where Harry Butt, George Street and W. L. Cornford had once stood. Hubert Doggart impressed for a few seasons, but the two great post-war Cambridge products with Sussex connections were David Sheppard and Ted Dexter.

Sheppard batted only 192 times for Sussex, but his average of 43 indicates that he did so with polish and a wholesome lack of churlish restraint. A splendid close fielder as well as an assured bat, he led Sussex during 1953 in a campaign which took them close to the title. He was helped by Robin Marlar, the Cambridge off-spinner and, later, the Sussex captain, whose energetic approach to his craft produced plenty of wickets.

With sixty-two caps and 4500 Test runs, E. R. Dexter became Sussex's leading Test player, who captained England in several series. Seemingly aloof where David Sheppard was involved, and disdainful in batting mien where his illustrious predecessor had been whole-hearted, he caused older watchers to recall Edwardian glories. Upright in stature, all but scornful in his dismissal of the unoffending ball, he was also a valued medium-pace bowler. Between 1956 and 1970 he scored some 21,000 runs and took over 400 wickets.

139 David Sheppard

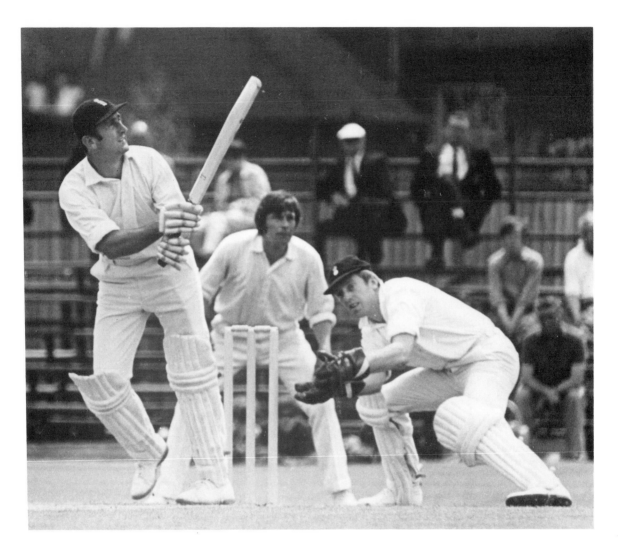

140 Ted Dexter

Both of these famous batsmen gave up the game earlier than their admirers would have wished. David Sheppard left to follow, as is well known, a clerical career, rising to become the Anglican Bishop of Liverpool, one of the last, perhaps the finest, illustration of cricket's liaison with the cloth. Ted Dexter also retired while in elegant command. Though not leaving so indelible a princely stamp as Ranji and Fry, these two, abetted by the able Marlar, drew a colourful curtain on the finale of amateurism in Sussex.

James Langridge had already given Sussex a taste of professional leadership, and now the all-professional game had arrived. J. M. Parks, nurturing the Sussex family tradition as the son of James Parks, turned out to be one of the county's most successful cricketers. Resourceful and well-built, if lacking the finesse of some of his county exemplars, he eventually managed to out-do them all, and, with nearly 37,000 first-class runs, became the most prolific of Sussex batsmen. Again, he appeared to the pedants a trifle gauche as a wicket-keeper, but, over his long career, 1949 to 1976, he trapped 1181 batsmen in first-class cricket, only a little behind the 1228 victims of the equally long-serving stumper of late Victorian and Edwardian vintage, H. R. Butt.

Parks was contemporary with Ken Suttle, whose 30,000 runs were acquired quietly, without fuss and with a pleasing neatness. Ian Thomson, a capable fast-medium bowler, took nearly 1600 wickets during much the same period, a genuinely impressive contribution in a county not over-blessed with bowlers. Alan Oakman, an adept slip, and afterwards Warwickshire's coach, and D. V. Smith were both workmanlike batsmen.

Dexter, Parks, Suttle and Thomson were involved in the early triumphs Sussex enjoyed in one-day cricket. As the ultra-modern day shimmeringly dawned, other players emerged. Tony Greig, tall, blond and athletic, proved to be an adroit all-rounder, his off-spin and batting enterprise providing Sussex with a dual asset. His involvement with the Packer régime when England's captain left many of cricket's audience hissing as if he were the demon king. On the other hand, his prowess enabled him to match Maurice Tate – and only six other Englishmen – in the rare Test double of 1000 runs and 100 wickets. John Snow took 202 wickets for England, leaving him seventh in the England list, and he is certainly the most successful bowler of high pace in the Sussex saga. Through the late 1960s and early 1970s, this lithe bowler generated bursts of destructive speed, and, with his rare hostility and intelligent control, he must be rated only just below the post-Edwardian quintet of Larwood, Farnes, Statham, Trueman and Tyson – and that is compliment enough.

There have been others – M. A. Buss, another Langridge, Richard, son of James, and, into the present, Paul Parker (now with Durham), C. M. Wells and Tony Pigott. There have been foreign reinforcements, among them Javed Miandad (later of Glamorgan) and the South African, Kepler Wessels, for a season or two. However, the overseas player most associated with Sussex is the brilliant Pakistani all-rounder and captain, Imran Khan. Few more vivid or effective cricketers have been seen at Hove.

Although Sussex cricket is spoken of warmly as of sunny disposition, which is fitting for its cheery seaside location, its internal processes have had a darker character, with occasional financial tight spots and constitutional wrangles over the captaincy. Sussex have rarely enjoyed continuous periods of uninterrupted leadership, as their wriggling string of captaincies testifies.

It is the more peculiar in that Sussex have provided England with several captains: Fry, Gilligan, Dexter and Greig. Sir C. Aubrey Smith, of Cambridge and Sussex, thereafter of Hollywood, captained England on the first South African tour, in the winter of 1888–89. In fact, Sussex could summon up from cricket's Elysian and earthbound fields a superb Gentlemen's XI. They would be fortunate in having varied bowling from Marlar, Dexter and Gilligan, as well as a wicket-keeper of Griffith's ability. Such a team might read: Fry, Ranji, Duleepsinhji, Sheppard,

141 John Snow

Dexter, Bartlett, Doggart, Arthur Gilligan, his brother Harold (a handy all-rounder and former Sussex captain), Griffith and Marlar. And that powerful batting would not require the great Australian, Billy Murdoch, or two amateurs – V. W. C. Jupp and P. G. H. Fender – both of whom left Sussex and did startling things, respectively, for Northamptonshire and Surrey.

Were the full Sussex staff paraded, several professionals would challenge for places, Jim Parks, his batting denying Butt the wicket-keeping slot, Maurice Tate, Albert Relf and the Langridge brothers among them. What a colourful and strikingly forceful team to represent a county devoid of any County Championship! The batting to number 10 is crushingly brilliant; there are Snow and Arthur Gilligan to open the bowling, Dexter and Relf to follow, and James Langridge to supply the spin. C. B. Fry would be the chosen captain, his cool intellect and precise authority perhaps being more in demand than the more inspirational talents of Gilligan or Sheppard: C. B. Fry, John Langridge, James Langridge, K. S. Ranjitsinhji, David Sheppard, Ted Dexter, Jim Parks, Albert Relf, Maurice Tate, Arthur Gilligan and John Snow.

FIFTEEN

Warwickshire

Outside the home counties and the south-west, the Industrial Revolution had a direct impact on the growth of first-class cricket. Why, then, was Warwickshire, focused on Birmingham and the sprawling array of West Midlands engineering and allied trades, a little slow to get off the mark and destined to join the first-class competition only in the second major phase of its development? It was a largely a matter of timing. The northern trio of Yorkshire, Lancashire and Nottinghamshire, plus the smaller entity of Derbyshire, underwent industrial change earlier. Manchester was the commercial capital of the 1840s and remained the leading provincial city for a decade and more. But soon Birmingham was to storm ahead, and, in population, in technology, in influence, become, as it still prides itself, Britain's second city. Etched in terms of personalities, where Manchester's shopocrats and millowners had been nationally represented by Richard Cobden and John Bright as Victoria came to the throne, it was towards the last quarter of her reign when Joseph Chamberlain – like Dick Whittington in London, he was thrice mayor – made the municipal state of Birmingham influential well beyond the boundaries of the city.

The town became a city as late as 1889, and then, as the dimension of its vehicle manufacturing expanded, it solidly became Britain's premier provincial city. It stands at the salient of an amorphously extensive conurbation embracing a population of over 2½ millions, including such industrial towns as West Bromwich, Wolverhampton, Coventry and Walsall. Where Birmingham alone houses a million souls, the actual county of Warwickshire has no more than half a million inhabitants.

As with most other counties, there had been desultory efforts early in the 19th century to set up county cricket there. There was a Warwickshire club which came to be known as the Warwick Gentlemen's club, for that was an exact description of its status and location. Colonel Jervis, its secretary, called a meeting at Leamington with a view to establishing a fully organized county club, and there was support from the Birmingham Cricket Association, from Coventry, and from Rugby, where, of course, the school had an interest in the game. This was, with tidy appropriateness, in 1882. Just as Birmingham was coming of political age, the county club opened for business.

It was, equally aptly, the secretary of the Birmingham Association, William Ansell, who indefatigably guaranteed Warwickshire's development. He was secretary of the county for twenty years, and was mainly responsible, in 1884, for leading the struggle to find a permanent home for the club and one where gate money might be taken. Edgbaston was the result. This urbane ground was opened in 1886, and later was to become a Test venue. It lost this distinction between 1929 and 1957, when expensive modernization saw Edgbaston securely on route towards being one of the best-appointed of any cricket ground in England. In 1988, 1989 and 1990 it played host to the Refuge Assurance Cup final, the first time domestic finals have been played away from Lord's. This might also be the point at which to mention that Warwickshire, as befits their thrifty commercial background, were about the first of the counties seriously to undertake the strenuous task of raising money through football lotteries and other such devices.

William Ansell, like Joseph Chamberlain, played a major role on the national stage. It was he who called the meeting in 1885 that led to a proposal that the senior counties should encourage their younger brethren with a game or two each year. Not content with that, he was very much to the fore in the fight to classify counties properly with a view to the advancement of some to first-class status. Warwickshire were a most powerful second-tier side and recorded good victories over top-class opposition, so that it was scarcely surprising to find them elevated in 1894 and first competing in the Championship a year later. It was a clear case of the second wave of industrialization creating a second wave of senior county clubs.

Though Warwickshire have never slid into the marshes of abject failure, neither have they possessed, judged by the highest standards, a dazzlingly successful team. They have won three Championships and four one-day trophies in 100 years of endeavour – and yet the community is heavy in population and prosperous in income. It is a valuable reminder that it is economic and cultural factors which intermingle to accelerate or retard the growth of a social institution, such as a county cricket club. There used to be an opinion expressed that the West Midlands area did not appear to produce many cricketers, and that is certainly evidenced in the alien derivation of many Warwickshire players. There have been occasions when Warwickshire have fielded an entirely non-Warwickshire side, and, of its famous 1951 Championship team, only two of the regulars were Warwickshire born. We have noted that, among others, Somerset have been untoward in this respect, but they, at least, had the decent excuse of a minute population.

The truth that few Warwickshire-born players have grown to first-class and Test status has easily led to the *canard* that some oddity of regional character appertains, whereby West Midlanders have a gauche genetic endowment, manifesting itself in unco-ordinated hand and eye. That, needless to say, is a nonsense. What the region has lacked has been a well founded tradition of cricketing involvement, relative, that is, to the metropolitan districts and the earlier industrialized areas of south Lancashire, what was the West Riding of Yorkshire, south Derbyshire and around Nottingham. Although there has been some excellent competition, league cricket in the region has not quite matched the longstanding value of the more northerly examples, nor have the local clubs earned quite the same prestige of some of their southern counterparts.

There was something neither fish nor fowl about early midlands cricket. This applied, too, to manufacturing in the Birmingham area. For a long time, and with some important exceptions, the typology was the small firm. Even in the early 1970s, Birmingham had some 1600 companies, each with a staff of less than a hundred. There was neither the ancient approach of the Nottingham hosiery trades, with men able to dovetail two professions, sporting and textiles, reasonably well, nor the factory formula of the north midlands, with larger-scale mill, mine or foundry often, whatever else, with a sizeable enough work-force to support societies or clubs, such as a cricket team. However, the structural arguments carry one only so far, and, once more, the factor of cultural momentum or inertia becomes crucial. Other intensely industrialized regions – Tyneside and Clydeside are instances – have not given rise to major cricketing fraternities, whereas other social manifestations – football is the prime example – are certainly to be associated with the rise of industry there.

The unrepentant cynic might harshly claim that its anonymous, sporadically grey and some-what dismal socio-economic terrain leaves the West Midlands an impoverished base for any civilizing tendencies of this kind, be they brass bands, choral societies, cricket clubs or football teams, although, *inter alia*, adherents to the causes of Aston Villa and Wolverhampton Wanderers might wish to enter the lists of that particular controversy.

If anything, Warwickshire, as an identifiable county, the birthplace of Shakespeare and the home of George Eliot, was curtailed and all but obliterated more emphatically than, for example, Lancashire and Yorkshire, for the centrifugal push of Birmingham and its urban satellites had already made something of a mockery of Warwickshire as a political entity by the turn of the century. Later constitutional formulations did no more than recognize this condition.

Warwickshire have had some poor times as a cricketing county. They had a roughish passage after the 1914–18 war, while a similar tough ride more recently watched them sink to rock bottom in the early 1980s. On the whole, however, they have jogged along in the diffident comfort of mid-table. They were first led by the Old Etonian, H. W. Bainbridge, a fine bat, who, after captaining his county in their opening first-class campaigns, was secretary for the amazingly long duration of thirty-seven years, from 1903 to 1940. E. J. Diver and J. H. G. Devey ensured the batting had some fire-power, while the burden of the bowling was carried by Sydney Santall. Over twenty years his willing medium-pace earned him over 1200 wickets for the county, Warwickshire's second best haul. The slow left-hander, Sam Hargreave, and the quick bowler, Frank Field, were his main associates. The county was fortunate in its wicket-keepers, with A. A. Lilley followed by E. J. 'Tiger' Smith, both of international repute. Between them they captured over 1400 stumpings and catchings for Warwickshire, and were equally consistent for England. With his brilliant career cut short by accident, the meteoric rise of the supremely assured young amateur, Frank Foster, boosted Warwickshire, if but for a brief spell. As captain, as fiery bowler and as attacking batsman, he gave his team much authority in the late 1900s.

For all this goodly talent, the most important figure in the early history of Warwickshire, and perhaps in the whole of that tale, was W. G. Quaife. He scored 36,000 runs in first-class cricket, and his seven caps seem a mockery – they would have been many more in any other era. Quaife had the build and manner of a slight youth, and yet his acute judgement and expert technique made him a miniature champion.

So in 1911 Warwickshire won the Championship. Several events, from the sinking of the *Titanic* to labour disputes and Anglo-Irish disorder, have been deployed to illustrate what George Dangerfield called 'the Strange Death of Liberal England'. In the cricketing world, Warwickshire's seizure of the pennant was the nearest equivalent to the ominous portents of the instability associated with the 1914–18 war. Pourers of cold water might argue that Warwickshire played only twenty fixtures; that they

142 Frank Foster

played few matches against the stronger teams; and that the initial introduction of first-innings points told in their favour (five teams actually won more games than Warwickshire), but still, for the first time, the title passed from the clutches of the aristos. Things were never, to coin a cliché, to be quite the same again.

It was to be some time before glory revisited Edgbaston. Fourth was easily their best position between the wars. Warwickshire appeared to fall, once more, between two stools; geographically

143 W. G. Quaife

and socially, they leaned neither to gentlemen nor to players. A rule-of-thumb might be that the further one travelled north, the less likely was one to find a team dominated by several brilliant amateurs, as opposed to several doughty professionals. Sussex and Yorkshire might, in this light, be observed as the opposite extremes of that spectrum. Warwickshire found themselves uneasily dropped in the middle, with no more than a few workaday players from either sector.

These were respectable rather than glorious times. F. S. G. Calthorpe, the Cambridge all-rounder, performed well, and L. T. A. Bates was another considerable bat, while Quaife, E. J. Smith and Santall soldiered on. The bowling rather depended on the pluck and stamina of Harry Howell, G. A. E. Paine and J. H. Mayer, all of whom took many wickets and Mayer well over 1000. They had no simple task, especially on the dull pitches of their home ground.

For most of the 1930s the county was captained by R. E. S. Wyatt, who won forty England caps and also led the Test team on occasion. He scored 39,000 runs at an average of 40, including eighty-five centuries, although some of this bounty was procured post-war in Worcestershire colours. He was the Trojan upon whom Warwickshire principally relied, and he rarely let them down, for he captained the side keenly and also took many wickets into the bargain. It is perhaps typical of Warwickshire's social conundrum that he was an amateur after the flesh of Fry rather than the spirit of Ranji. Determined, wary and hardworking, he was – and remains – a tremendous model of the rational virtues married to pleasing, not exceptional, talent.

After the Second World War, Warwickshire, afflicted with a rash of twenty-four amateurs on their 1946 teamsheets, speedily moved to resolve their social and geographic dilemma. They soon settled for an all-professional side with a regular professional captain. Tom Dollery was, in those post-war years, the first to obtain such a commission on an unqualified basis, and, knowledgeably in tune with the first-class game as he astutely and sympathetically was, he became one of the leading professional cricketers – indeed, there are many who would claim his powers of county captaincy have not been equalled in the professional ranks. An accomplished number five of the infinite adaptability that suits that fulcrum role, he scored some 23,000 first-class runs and was an extremely good county player. After they had twice been fourth in the preceding years, he led Warwickshire to their proudest Championship win in 1951.

144 R. E. S. Wyatt

It was, in every way, a more convincing performance than the 1911 achievement, and it was less reliant than the 1972 title on overseas reinforcements. Sixteen games were won and only two lost. The side was well integrated and well balanced. No one was brilliant. No one was moderate. Warwickshire lost no player to representative games, and they suffered few injuries, so that, unusually, they called on barely more than the regular XI. Each specialist fitted comfortably into his place in the scheme of things; each worked for the others and gelled smoothly into a well run team; an accent on keen and tidy fielding was the final gloss on that exposition of unity and cohesion.

The batting went on and on: Fred Gardner, lugubrious and dour, opened with Dick Spooner, a most effective wicket-keeper-batsman, and then, as well as Dollery, Jimmy Ord, Ray Hitchcock, Bert Wolton and Alan Townsend carried on the good work. Tom Pritchard, like Hitchcock a New Zealander, made an emphatic impression with his fierce left-hand pace, accompanied by the balding Charlie Grove, of medium speed and stately accuracy. With Gardner, they were the only Warwickshire-born players in the side. The spin bowling was in the bailiwick of Eric Hollies: small but stocky, tireless, economic, and, if not a prodigious turner of the ball, a leg-spinner of disconcerting character. As if to correct for the imbalanced length of the batting, Hollies was one of those popular heroes whose mammoth total of first-class wickets – 2323 – is more than the sum of his mouse-like batting. He played thirteen times for England and fourteen times took more than 100 wickets in a season.

It was a team that reached the acme of its utility when its members were advanced in cricketing years, and, therefore, its sense of substance proved quite flimsy. Warwickshire dropped back almost immediately; and for all but two seasons – they were sixth in 1954 and fourth in 1959 – their place was nearer the bottom of the table in the years up to 1960. They had entertaining players, such as the big hitter, Jim Stewart, the bustling opener, Norman Horner, and two stylish subcontinentals in A. H. Kardar, later to captain Pakistan and to become secretary of his country's Board of Control, and Billy Ibadulla. The quick bowler, Jack Bannister, later to be elected secretary of the Professional Cricketers' Association, took nearly 1200 wickets, making him Warwickshire's third most successful bowler, while Tom Cartwright, wheeling away with as nagging a length as any English medium-pacer of any era, took almost as many before completing his career elsewhere.

Then, from 1962, there were ten better years, culminating in Warwickshire's third Championship success, in 1972. They fought off the strong challenge of Kent, Gloucestershire and Northamptonshire, all of whom were playing powerfully around this time, and finished no less than 36 points ahead of the field. From 1957 to 1974, Warwickshire were captained first by Mike Smith and then by Alan Smith, two notables who

ushered the county into the age of avant-garde cricket with consummate intelligence. Bespectacled and gaunt, M. J. K. Smith was an unlikely Corinthian, but he captained England, for whom he played fifty times; scored nearly 40,000 first-class runs, chiefly through his distinct preference for the on-side; and pocketed scores of catches at short-leg. Alan Smith, a true all-rounder in that he kept wicket, batted well, and took over 100 county wickets, was to become a top-line administrator, and it was such organizational skills that made him a most efficacious skipper.

Mike Smith, in particular, was quick to grasp the new essentials of modern cricket, especially its one-day variation. Warwickshire were early protagonists in the Gillette finals. Having lost to Sussex by the large margin of 8 wickets in the second such final, they beat Worcestershire

145 M. J. K. Smith, surrounded by Warwickshire colleagues, holds up the Gillette Cup in 1966.

146 Dennis Amiss

comfortably enough by 5 wickets in the fourth, that is, in 1966. Two years later, in 1968, they revenged themselves on Sussex, this time by 4 wickets. Alan Smith, as captain and batsman, was prominent on both occasions. In 1972 Warwickshire lost to Lancashire by 4 wickets in an exciting and high-scoring final, and, in 1982, in the NatWest Trophy final, Warwickshire found themselves badly mauled by Surrey, who were easy 9-wicket victors.

Warwickshire have had little luck in the Benson and Hedges tournament (though they were runners-up in 1984), and, after several fine displays in their glory days without any ultimate success, they finally won the Sunday League in 1980, when their 3-day performances were poor. Indeed, they suffered the gross indignity of being last in 1981 and 1982, and rarely distinguished themselves during the 1980s. However, they just snatched the NatWest Trophy in 1989, winning boldly in the dying moments of their clash with Middlesex, and in 1990, with the Australian bat, Tom Moody, in brisk form, they were fifth in the Championship. This was a prelude to 1991, when, with the South African quick bowler, Allan Donald, in devastating form, they led the table for much of the summer, only to be overtaken by Essex at the last.

They had fielded bright and breezy teams in the 1960s and early 1970s. There was the stroke-making of J. A. Jameson and of Bob Barber, imported from Lancashire; while the quick bowling of David Brown earned him over 1000 wickets and an England place on twenty-six occasions. A major key in the county's success was, however, the dogged consistency of Dennis Amiss, whose technical impregnability, founded in careful limitation on risk, eventually enabled him to by-pass Mike Smith and Quaife and become the county's tallest scorer. He amassed well over 40,000 runs in all first-class cricket and notched over a hundred centuries. He finds himself, perhaps to his own surprise, in the top eleven run-makers of all time, and his resource and determination are exceedingly praiseworthy. Although he has not, like too many cricketers, lost seasons to one or other of the world wars, he has

played at a time of restricted first-class opportunity, and, all in all, his record is, for modern times, phenomenal. He has played fifty times for his country, but, somehow, he never emerged as a national hero, although his average of 46 belies that impressionistic view.

Bob Willis left Surrey and brought sharp impetus to the Warwickshire attack. His deeds were more to be relished on the international plane, for he played for England ninety times, an amazing feat. He was huge of heart and rangy of limb and his speed and resolution brought him the reward of 325 Test wickets, second only to Botham in the English list. Curiously, he has taken only a few more than that for Warwickshire, an oddity only in part explained by fewer county matches on the one hand and many more Test matches on the other. Although his ungainly style must, both on practical and aesthetic grounds, exclude him from that tiny *élite* of incomparable fast bowlers, no more committed cricketer was to be found.

During their modern years of favourable results, and until some bar was placed on the number of overseas players in any one team, Warwickshire were substantially leavened by awesome West Indian talent. From one angle, the county had much more justification than some, for the Birmingham area had become the habitat for many West Indian immigrant families, and the cultural norm was, if anything, less singular than, say, a South African playing for Northamptonshire or even a Scot playing for Kent. Whatever the arguments, four West Indians displayed their vivid skills with panache and sparkle at Edgbaston and elsewhere, and many, not all of them of Warwickshire persuasion, were enthralled.

Rohan Kanhai, with a county average of nearly 52, is, by that token, the county's supreme batsman, and his genuine power, little short of angry in the execution of his attacking shots, was often breath-taking. Alvin Kallicharran is, with 46 or thereabouts, second in those averages, and his handsome strokeplay has been a feature of Warwickshire cricket over many years. Lance Gibbs, the off-spinner, plied his craft with equal skill. He has the distinction of having taken more

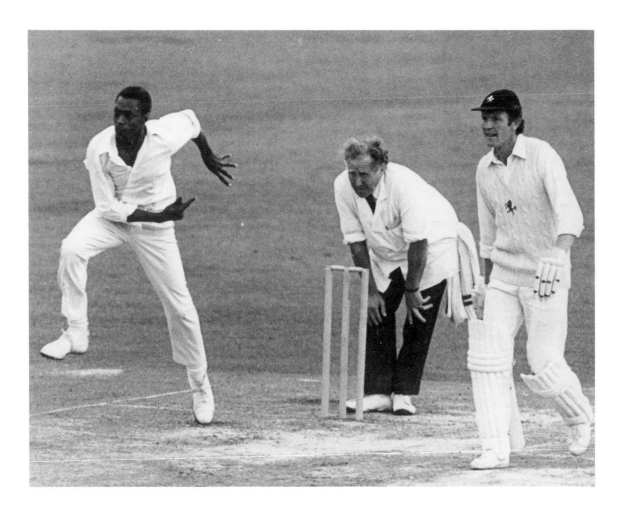

147 Lance Gibbs, a prolific wicket-taker for Warwickshire and West Indies.
Mike Denness is the batsman in the picture, Johnny Arnold the umpire.

Test wickets, with 309, than any other slow bowler in cricket history. Fourth, Deryck Murray, possibly the finest wicket-keeper produced by the Caribbean (he ranks seventh in the list of world Test dismissals), fulfilled those duties admirably for Warwickshire, after his spell with Nottinghamshire. In quantity, they were almost half a side; in quality, they were perhaps three-quarters of an average first-class team.

When, finally, one tries to pick a Warwickshire side without the aid of those great players, the task is a little easier than for some counties. This is mainly because five batsmen present themselves as an integral grouping, a little apart from the next bunch of run-makers. These are Quaife, Amiss, M. J. K. Smith, Wyatt and Dollery, and this would probably be the order in which, ethereally, they might appear. Warwickshire have lacked a little in classy all-rounders, but Quaife took 900 wickets in his 665 games for the county while Wyatt had 652 victims. That possibly means that no place would be found for the all-round energy and style of Frank Foster.

Once the inevitable Hollies has taken up his

undisputed place at number eleven, the bowling makes for some difficulty, mainly because Warwickshire have not had an off-spinner or a left-arm spinner to match the effortless guile of Hollies's leg-spin. Willis, on the strength of his undoubtedly splendid international performances, would take the new ball, along with Brown, who took just on 1000 wickets for Warwickshire, by dint of which he might marginally inch out the dangerous Pritchard. There might then be two stock bowlers. Santall would obviously be one, and the other would be Tom Cartwright. Something of an unsung star, with but five caps to his name, Cartwright took over 1500 first-class wickets, and, such was his thrifty approach, he tops the all-Warwickshire bowling averages with just a shade under 19. It is not a versatile attack; rather is it business-like and thorough-going, maybe in keeping with the matter-of-fact character of the West Midlands environment. The tail is a trifle shaky, but help is at hand. The wicket-keeper would be A. A. Lilley. He would most probably deny the wicket-keeping function to 'Tiger' Smith, for, apart from his thirty-five Test appearances, he schooled himself sufficiently to score some 13,000 runs for Warwickshire.

R. E. S. Wyatt might be invited to preside over this solid XI with his prestigious authority, and in the knowledge that, in Dollery and Smith, he would have two wise and devoted advisers. It is also a team that has another kind of balance in that it reasonably combines the best of the county's three happiest phases, just before the First World War, just after the Second World War, and around the 1960s and early 1970s: W. G. Quaife, Dennis Amiss, M. J. K. Smith, R. E. S. Wyatt, Tom Dollery, A. A. Lilley, Sydney Santall, Tom Cartwright, David Brown, Bob Willis and Eric Hollies.

SIXTEEN

Worcestershire

Rather like Somerset or Northamptonshire, Worcestershire is nearer than most to the romantic ideal of a county. Now merged with Herefordshire, that combined local authority area still musters only some 600,000 inhabitants, while Worcester itself, with a population of no more than 75,000, is one of the smallest of the county headquarters. Set, then, in rural landscape, Worcestershire has a genuine claim, in its origins, to be accepted as the model county of literary and aesthetic mode.

Its attractive ground at New Road conveys this impression pleasantly. The swiftly flowing Severn and the ageless charm of the cathedral have become etched on the soul of cricket lovers as symbols no less potent than the Oval's gasholders, Canterbury's encroaching tree or the smoke stacks of Sheffield. It became the enjoyable tradition for tourist teams to begin their campaign at Worcester, and a century or double century from Don Bradman became yet another emblem of Worcestershire cricket.

Although previous efforts had been made to organize county cricket before the actual foundation of the cut, Worcestershire officially opened for business in 1865, around the time when several other counties, such as Lancashire and Middlesex, were getting under way. During the 1890s they had a particularly successful time in their Minor Counties games, and, in 1899, they were invited to take part in the senior competition. They arrived alone, a year or so after the big bulge in membership, and became the fifteenth of that esoteric fraternity.

Their elevation owed much to the persistence and zeal of their then secretary, Paul Foley, but, more famously, they were blessed with the Foster brothers. Two or three other counties acknowledge a debt of gratitude to a founding family, Gloucestershire, Middlesex and Lancashire among them. None, however, could match the impact of the fecund Foster kinship. In American musical comedy, the seven brides were wooed by seven brothers; American vaudeville watched and wondered at the Seven Little Foys, a troupe of siblings. Worcestershire, in play and administratively, were succoured by the seven Foster brothers, unrelated to Warwickshire's talented captain of much the same era. Newspaper references to 'Fostershire' may have owed more to sub-editorial delight in word-play than to historical accuracy, but it was not a wholly imprecise label.

In spite of the idyllic surrounds, in spite of the even placidity of the square, in spite of the smooth quality of the outfield, and in spite of the inspiration of the Fosters, Worcestershire spent the first forty years of their first-class existence in something like durance vile. During this time they were in the last three or very near the bottom on sixteen occasions. Sometimes there was organizational crisis. In 1914 (the year Gloucestershire were also under threat) there was a proposal 'that the side be wound up'. The 1914–18 war acted as a breathing-space, and, although Worcestershire, uniquely, could not compete in the 1919 season, they managed to resume normal service in 1920: it is an ill wind . . . Basically, Worcestershire was far too small an area to support a first-class club, and their reliance on a sporting family and a couple of dedicated professionals proved inadequate.

By a mixture of ill-luck and ill-management, Worcestershire never quite achieved technical harmony. Several commentators have dilated on the fact that when the county enjoyed the services of a handful of valuable bowlers, these were frustrated by the feebleness of the batting, whereas, conversely, when there were several strong batsmen, they were disappointed by inadequate bowling.

Indeed, when one considers the talented cricketers available to Worcestershire over that first half of the century, it does seem surprising, even when allowance is made for shortcomings, that the county did not reach greater heights. At the beginning of the century, R. E. Foster, most gifted of the brotherhood, was rightly hailed as third only to Ranji and Fry in the amateur batting ranks. Gracefulness and assurance were allied in his displays of authoritative and brisk scoring, the drive, as ever in the golden age, to the fore. In a brief career he scored thirteen centuries and averaged 42 for the county.

Apart from his brothers, he was backed by amateurs such as W. B. Burns, a very quick bowler and no mean bat, and by G. H. Simpson-Hayward, the last and the most effective of the lob bowlers. His 400 or so wickets, several in Tests and including 5 for 17 for the Gentlemen against an extremely strong Players XI, must cause one to ponder whether under-arm bowling was dispensed with prematurely.

Their only moment of near glory was in 1907, when, with four Fosters on show, they tied for second place with Yorkshire behind the champions, Nottinghamshire. Worcestershire were always worth watching around these years for their venturesome and good-looking batting. In 1905, for example, H. K. Foster averaged 50, and his brother, R. E., a magnificent 92 for the county.

In the early 1930s there was a similar attractiveness about the Worcestershire batting, albeit accompanied by a similar poverty of placement in the Championship table. C. F. Walters moved, rather unexpectedly, from Glamorgan to Worcestershire, where he became secretary, and, on qualifying, captain. An England captain also, he played with some of the imperiousness of the Edwardian era and evoked memories of R. E. Foster. In 1933, for example, he scored 2165 runs for the county, including nine hundreds. Ill-health forced him towards early retirement, and thereby hangs an illustration of another source of Worcestershire ill-fortune. Their outstanding players often seemed to fall quickly. The great R. E. Foster, a diabetic, died in 1914, aged only thirty-six, and W. B. Burns was killed in the First World War. Maurice Nichol was a player of rich promise – scoring over 2000 runs in 1933 at an average of 46 – but he suffered, un-

148 C. F. Walters

complainingly, from serious health problems. He died in his hotel bed at Chelmsford during the Whitsuntide game with Essex in 1934. The Nawab of Pataudi did wonderful things for Oxford University and for Worcestershire, but he, too, fell ill in 1934, and, though returning as captain of All-India in 1946, was never the same power in the game.

These lamentably short-lived careers made a mockery of continuity and development, but they were partially compensated for by the long service of one or two stalwart professionals. One of these from the days of the Fosters was Fred Bowley, who notched 21,000 runs for Worcester in the first twenty or so years of the century. His comrade was the all-rounder E. G. Arnold, a bowler of consummate length and a batsman of regular soundness. He scored over 15,000 runs for Worcestershire and took over 1000 wickets, and these good figures included four doubles. From 1928 to the Second World War, H. H. Gibbons opened the innings, and, while overshadowed by C. F. Walters and the Nawab of Pataudi in artistry, he amassed plenty of runs – some 21,000 in all, including 2452 at an average of 54 in the run-riotous summer of 1934.

After service with Derbyshire Fred Root mono-polized the bowling from about 1923 to 1932. He bowled quickish in-swing to an arc of swooping on-side fielders. This predatory leg-theory, although scorned by purists, in that few dared to risk the off- or cover-drive when Root was wheeling away, brought this hard-working professional some 1500 wickets for Worcestershire.

The less fashionable counties have frequently depended on the dogged expertise and experi-ence of one or two hard-pressed professionals. Bowley or Arnold or Root would probably have cheerfully exchanged the swiftly flowing Severn for a Larwood or the ageless charm of the cathedral for a Hammond.

By 1939, however, the house of Worcester was a little more in order, and the county was seventh, its best position since 1907. Here again Worcestershire were a little unlucky. If the First World War gave them a chance to reform ranks,

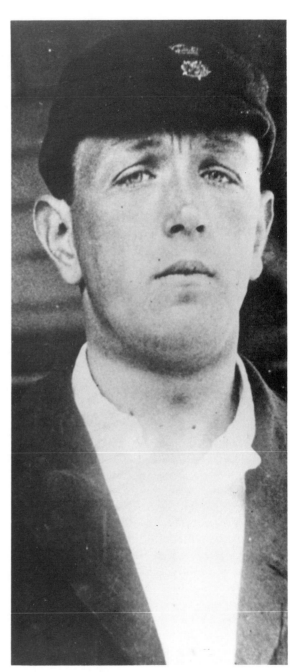

149 Fred Root in his Derbyshire days

that of 1939–45 split up a side which promised forthright results. Two who lost priceless seasons were Peter Jackson, the tireless off-spinner and fine catcher, and Eddie Cooper, the quietly efficient batsman.

Reg Perks was another, although he crossed the divide more effectively, and remains Worcestershire's finest bowler. Strong in stamina and controlled in delivery, he provided the attack with a snap and sting it had never hitherto experienced. He bowled great-heartedly from 1930 to 1955, and took 2233 first-class wickets, 2143 of them for his county. Only Tich Freeman, Derek Shackleton and Wilfred Rhodes have bettered his achievement of 100 wickets in each of sixteen seasons.

Reg Perks was something of a talisman, albeit a large one, in those years, and the county persisted in trying to field a side of workmanlike performers. There was Dick Howorth, a most amiable all-rounder, whose left-hand spin and determined batting brought him the rewards of 1345 wickets and over 10,000 runs. There was Roly Jenkins, of maritime gait and tantalizing leg-spin, and a spendid outfielder to boot. With them Worcestershire were third in 1949 and fourth in 1951.

However, the 1950s were not spectacular summers, and the results were below par. Still, the cricket was enjoyable. Peter Richardson, whose solid form earned him thirty-four England caps, scored 26,000 first-class runs, some of them with Kent towards the end of his cricketing life. Laddie Outschoorn, from Ceylon, George Dews, from Yorkshire, and Bob Broadbent, from Middlesex, were three other useful bats, while Hugo Yarnold had established his emphatic claim to be regarded until then as the best of all Worcestershire's wicket-keepers.

By now Worcestershire cricket was moulded around the commanding figure of Don Kenyon. Between 1946 and 1967 he accumulated 37,000 first-class runs, 33,490 of them for his county, a Worcestershire record. Powerful, consistent and dominant, he was one of that group of quite outstanding county players who, curiously, have not been able to display that quality on the international plane. Fred Root was another

150 Reg Perks

in that same category. No disrespectful criticism is intended: would that thousands of cricket-loving rabbits such as ourselves, just once in our feeble lives, might score twenty runs in the manner of Don Kenyon or bowl an over of Fred Root's leg-theory.

Don Kenyon eventually combined the authority of his opening batsmanship with that of the captaincy, and he was rewarded with Worcestershire's first triumphs in the county contest. In 1962 they were second, just pipped by Yorkshire, but a merry portent of the happiness to come to New Road. In 1964 they found themselves in a race with Warwickshire. Not until the very end of August was the race decided. Then Warwickshire lost to Yorkshire, while Worcestershire beat Gloucestershire by an innings and the crown was theirs. In 1965 Worcestershire were off to a dragging start, but they rallied with common sense and application, and thus won the title in consecutive years. In the last crucial game at Hove, Worcestershire lost wickets trying to reach a relatively low score, and ultimately managed it. The quality of the team was further underlined when they were second in 1966, just behind Yorkshire.

It was a side shaped more after the model of Perks than Foster. It was reminiscent of the Derbyshire champions of the mid-1930s and Dollery's successful post-war Warwickshire team. Alongside Kenyon was the solid batting provided by Dick Richardson, Peter's brother; by Ron Headley, talented son of the great West Indian, George Headley; and by Martin Horton, the valued all-rounder. But the cream of the batting, especially in 1964, was proffered by Tom Graveney. Worcestershire had a penchant for receiving political refugees in mature state from other counties: C. F. Walters had been one, and R. E. S. Wyatt another, for the latter had given much appreciated service to Worcestershire in the immediate post-war years. Thus it was that Graveney, in the ripe autumn of his fruitful career, stamped his exquisite style on Worcestershire cricket, and, in that one respect, lifted it above mere technical acumen.

The bowling was in the respectable hands of J. A. Flavell, who took over 1500 first-class wickets in a long life devoted to fast-medium bowling, while his chief partner was L. J. Coldwell, another sturdy combatant and shrewd swing bowler. Martin Horton and Norman Gifford were the crafty spin bowlers, the one an off-spinner, the other the obligatory left-hander. Norman Gifford threatened immortality as a cricketer and later moved to Warwickshire, having played a role in many of Worcestershire's successes. He took just over 2000 first-class wickets. Roy Booth was the wicket-keeper, and an efficient one, with his no-nonsense batting a fine bonus.

During Worcestershire's second title run, Basil D'Oliveira came to the fore. As gentle a sportsman as he was a mighty striker of the ball, he was also a dependable change bowler. The South African's story was destined to be unfolded more on the national and political front than on the county field, happily with a satisfactory ending. He won forty-four caps, which makes him one of Worcestershire's leading internationals, and he scored well over 20,000 runs for his adopted county. That said, he brought much authority to the middle of the Worcestershire batting order, and acquitted himself with admirable distinction.

Over the last score of years Worcestershire have remained reasonably in touch with the Championship hunt, although 1971, 1978, 1982 and 1983 were lean summers for them. To compensate for this, there were three more splendid Championships in 1974, 1988 and in 1989, and second place in 1979.

Although Worcestershire progressed to six one-day finals, they were not sufficiently lucky or skilful to take a cup. They lost the very first Gillette final to Sussex in 1963 by the slender margin of 14 runs, and then they were defeated by Warwickshire in 1966 by 5 wickets. Two losses in the Benson and Hedges competition followed. In very similar games in 1973 and in 1976 Kent were the victors, by 39 and 43 runs respectively. In 1988 Worcestershire were the favourites to beat Middlesex in the NatWest Trophy, and thus complete a unique treble, for they were county champions and Sunday League winners. Again, it

151 Basil D'Oliveira

was not to be. Worcestershire lost what proved to be a disappointingly low-scoring encounter, while, in the 1990 Benson and Hedges final, they were outplayed by Lancashire. Finally, in 1991, they succeeded in landing one of the cups, defeating a lacklustre Lancashire in the Benson's competition. As well as their success in 1988, Worcestershire had won the Sunday title in 1987, and, back to the time of Gifford and co., they had enjoyed an initial victory in this competition in 1971. They added a second trophy in 1991, beating Lancashire in the spirited Refuge Assurance Cup final by 7 runs.

Norman Gifford was an enthusiastic and sharp-witted skipper, and he was abetted in the palmy days of the 1970s by such as Brian Brain, the quick bowler, and Alan Ormrod, the opening bat. Overseas talent was beginning to play a major role. As well as Basil D'Oliveira, there was the West Indian pace bowler, Vanburn Holder, and the two New Zealand stars, John Parker and Glenn Turner. Turner was of particular value, remembered for his 1000 runs before the end of May in 1973, and scoring over 34,000 runs in all his first-class innings. It was an entertaining as well as a winning team, and they clinched the 1974 title with a 7-wickets victory over Essex as the rains fell.

Under the chairmanship of Duncan Fearnley, Worcestershire's more recent and excellent successes have also been the consequence of extra-mural recruitment, at home as well as abroad. The batting has been entirely dominated by the precocious genius of Graeme Hick, born in Harare, Zimbabwe, a tall scorer of confidence and accomplishment. His innings of 405 not out against Somerset in 1988 was only the second time an individual score of over 400 has been achieved in first-class cricket in England and the first since Archie MacLaren's 424, also against Somerset, in 1895. Such is the prodigious character of Hick's comprehensive talent that many are pleased to recall those late Victorian and Edwardian innings when noble batsmanship was the norm.

The sudden arrival of that cricketing phenomenon, Ian Botham, from Somerset in

152 Norman Gifford

1987 was dramatic, and, especially in the hurly-burly of the Sunday League, Botham was destructive with hefty bat and swinging ball. Graham Dilley, the England fast bowler, was signed from Kent, joining Neal Radford, born in Northern Rhodesia and brought up in South Africa, who was also capped for England. This brand of mature expertise gave Worcestershire an enormous boost, and their lesser known players have responded well. One might remark that few of them were Worcester born or bred. Phil Neale, the capable batsman and skipper (who stood down at the end of the 1991 season), hails from Scunthorpe, while the spin bowler, Richard Illingworth, and the promising wicket-keeper, Steven Rhodes, are both Yorkshiremen. The opening bat, Tim Curtis, who won a Blue and England caps and has now taken over the captaincy from Phil Neale, was born in Chichester though educated in Worcester; the lively all-rounder, Phil Newport, is from High Wycombe; and the support bowler, Paul Pridgeon, released in 1989, was born in Wall Heath. Ian Botham is a son of Heswall, Dilley a native of Dartford, and Tom Moody, who scored heavily for the county in the 1991 season, is an Australian. Indeed, of the main squad Martin Weston is the only Worcester-born player.

The results of the policy of searching high and low for the requisite ability is plain to see. Worcestershire are now one of the leading teams in the Championship, and there is little doubt they will remain in contention for the honours at all points and in most seasons.

Cricketers, especially in English conditions, appear to take time to come to their prime. From that angle, it does seem a trifle unfair that one county may have the anxiety and trouble of bringing a player to his peak and another enjoy the largesse of his maturity. The qualification period, although it has to be interpreted as restraint of trade and was, in the hands of some authorities, little short of feudal, did have the secondary benefit, perhaps by accident, of ensuring some continuity. Players had to wait and learn to belong, as opposed to the instant citizenship of modern times. The apprentice

153 Graeme Hick

and the journeyman often developed together, and many players, wherever born, gave long and diligent service. Worcestershire is a vivid example of the modern mode of adopting a kind of 'repertory' approach to cricket team-building, something like the practice of the Football League.

The alpha and the omega of the Worcestershire story is, therefore, that the county which began as the closest to a rural, scarcely populated shire, all but in the romantic tradition, is now the club which most nearly represents the new convention of scouring the nation and the world for a glittering cast of stars.

In between those two extreme poles, the history of Worcestershire has been a tale of two halves. There was the first forty years of mundane results, relieved by the mercurial beauty of often ephemeral efficiency, frequently in lonely isolation. The second fifty years have been times of much more solid consequence, characterized by sides, first, warily expert, and, second, vastly entertaining.

A Worcestershire XI for all its ages testifies to that dichotomy, drawing equally from both periods. R. E. Foster would lend his majesty to the batting, and, with the ever reliable Kenyon, that would make for an excellent and complementary opening pair. The old-world style of C. F. Walters and the youthful class of Hick (as he endured long years to make good his English qualification, it seems just to include him) would offer a similar blend at three and four. The all-rounders would be D'Oliveira and Howorth, rather closer in dates, but still suggestive of the new and the old. Hugo Yarnold, holding off the honourable challenge of Booth and Rhodes, would keep wicket and bat at number seven. The bowlers would be enlisted from across Worcestershire's time-lines. There would be Perks and Root to open the bowling, with the leg-spin of Jenkins and the left-hand attack of Gifford in attendance, recalling, of course, the alternatives provided by the all-rounders. With plenty of sage counsel from Foster, Kenyon and Gifford, C. F. Walters would probably be delighted to captain a side of such powerful batting and such wide-ranging bowling: R. E. Foster, Don Kenyon, C. F. Walters, Graeme Hick, Basil D'Oliveira, Dick Howorth, Hugo Yarnold, Roly Jenkins, Fred Root, Reg Perks and Norman Gifford.

SEVENTEEN

Yorkshire

It could have been some constitutional providence that guaranteed Yorkshire's position as last in any review of the counties such as this. Their ultimate alphabetic placement means that, meritoriously, they top the bill. The supporting turns have honestly entertained and had their moment; now the limelight glare is switched across to Yorkshire, far and away the star of the county circuit. With thirty-three Championships, only two of them shared, they have been twice as successful as any other county on that significant basis alone. The inter-war years marked the astonishing pinnacle of this astonishing record. In those twenty-one seasons, Yorkshire were fifth once, fourth twice, third four times, second twice and first twelve times. During those summers, the county won 330 of the 616 matches played, and lost a mere 49. It was, in fact, 1953 before Yorkshire knew the indignity of a slide into the double-figured positions – they were twelfth, and their previous low points had been eighth in 1889, 1891 and 1910.

On the whole, Yorkshire kept up the good work until well after the Second World War, and it has been only since the end of the 1960s that they have come to seem, by the previous standards of triumph, ordinary. Nonetheless, Yorkshire have not been by-passed entirely by the modern world of instant cricket and international cricketing relief. With an uncharacteristically cavalier display from Geoff Boycott, they took an early grip on the Gillette Cup, when, in 1965, they thrashed Surrey by the merciless gap of 175 runs, and in 1969 they defeated Derbyshire by a margin of 69 runs. Having lost to Leicestershire in the first Benson's final, that of 1972, by 5 wickets, they had to wait until 1987, when, in a most exciting finish against Northamptonshire, Yorkshire survived on level scores but having lost fewer wickets. They have also won the Sunday League, just once, in 1983, when everything else seemed

to be going wrong for the white rose. Still, four one-day titles, and no Championship since 1968, does mean that the last twenty or so years have been comparatively dismal ones for the county.

The reasons for Yorkshire's early momentum have been described in Part One, and they are similar to the causes of Nottinghamshire's Victorian renown. The primary and rudimentary industrialization of Yorkshire allowed trades to be coupled, so that semi-professional cricket soon became both possible and widespread. The economies of the small-scale Yorkshire townships, their livelihood often dependent not just on one trade but one manifestation of such a trade, next gave cultural support to the game. The one colliery or the one woollen mill or the one iron foundry was the fulcrum of life for its surrounding community, and this was even the case in the larger cities, frequently composed of several of these socio-economic communities. The social import of cricket thus grew, granting a sense of identification for the urban village or town, giving it at once a *raison d'être*, what W. S. Gilbert called 'an innocent source of merriment', and an ambition, in terms of local fame as well as finance, for the sporting young men in the community.

Writ large and in cumulative form, this became the context for Yorkshire cricket, a honeycomb of cricket-conscious communities. The economic wherewithal of the mill or workshop was the base both for domesticity and for its cultural outcrops in the chapel, the brass band, the choral society and the cricket club. Gradually, cricket embossed Yorkshire with its firm and enduring stamp.

Yet there had to be an extra reason why Yorkshire, more so than the other counties, appeared to have an additional cricketing drive. The answer is largely a quantitative one, for Yorkshire was and remains, in terms of its traditional ambit which is sanely retained for cricketing purposes, a very large area. The old adage boasts that Yorkshire has as many acres as there are verses in the Bible, while the present population of what used to constitute the Ridings, before the reorganization of the 1970s, is pushing 5 million. Only the more disparate London region surpasses that, and only by combining the various populations of the north-west may it otherwise be matched. It is wiser to visualize it as a region rather than a shire. In size, decorum and self-evaluation it more nearly resembles a small country. After all, New Zealand, with a population of only 3 million or so, deploys these days a more than respectable Test team.

This size fired the fierce clannishness of Yorkshire cricket, for, at its simplest, there were always plenty from whom to choose. The triumphs of their cricketers in turn fuelled the pseudo-nationalist emotions of Yorkshiremen, and so the wheel turned. Yorkshire, in the graphic phrase of an American general of the Civil War era, 'got there fustest with the mostest'. Cricket became, for Yorkshire, the banner of their proud superiority.

As with the unification of most nations, Yorkshire were beset by internal squabblings about where sovereignty should reside. Even after the formation of the county club, there were confusions as to whom to approach regarding fixtures. Bradford and York, for instance, rivalled Sheffield and made attempts to raise representative sides. However, Sheffield was the chief base, and it had been from fixtures between that town and Nottingham that more elaborate arrangements had arisen. It was Sheffield cricketers who had made the most noteworthy contributions thus far, James Dearman and Tom Marsden among them.

In 1855 the historic Bramall Lane ground was opened, leased at a nominal rent from the Duke of Norfolk, whose steward, M. J. Ellison, was Yorkshire's first treasurer and a dedicated president of the new club. This was formed in 1863, with a half-guinea subscription, and all the committee were from Sheffield. Intra-county rivalry and the professional schism of the mid-1860s restricted Yorkshire's beginnings, but then matters improved. There was a steady stream of talented players, including those great quick bowlers of ancient fame, George Freeman, Tom Emmett — one of the first of cricket's cards — and Alan Hill; the first pair in Yorkshire's amazing heritage of slow left-hand bowlers, Edmund Peate and Bobby Peel; such excellent batsmen as Ephraim Lockwood and George Ulyett; and a brave stumper in George Pinder.

Immediately one runs across the difficulty of analysing Yorkshire's history in summary form. Already ten players have been mentioned in cursory passing who might take on the best of practically every other county — and we have barely reached the 1890s. So rich have been the county's seams of talent that players who would rate a paragraph in the *résumés* of other clubs must be lightly disposed of in a sentence, and those elsewhere who might have earned a phrase may not be listed at all in these few pages about Yorkshire.

Nonetheless, those first years disappointed. In spite of these gifted players, results were frustratingly mediocre. Individual performances were pleasing, but the all-round effect was erratic and unco-ordinated. Not for the last time, the committee was volubly blamed, and, in the early 1890s, the club was overhauled to complete its liberation from the dominance of Sheffield members and officers.

It is unlikely that this was the only cause of Yorkshire's rejuvenation, which led to the winning of the county's first title since the official recognition of the Championship in 1890. This was in 1893, when twelve victories from sixteen games left them easy winners. In fact, Yorkshire had been declared champions three times before, during the prehistory of the Championship; that is, in 1867, in alliance with Nottinghamshire in 1869, and in 1870. It is also important to remember that one of the reasons Yorkshire fared uneasily in the competition was that they often played more matches than others at a time when 'least losses' was a key — Yorkshire at least gave themselves a chance of losing matches, where other counties kept their fixture-lists a little too trimmed.

With all this said, however, the fine accomplishment of 1893 is viewed by many as the realistic starting-point of Yorkshire's jubilant story. For those who would prefer a romantic tale of working-class heroism, these next sentences will make unfriendly reading. Yorkshire had relied on more or less all-professional teams, and there had been no answering response of spontaneous purposefulness and gallant *esprit*. The worker's co-operative (albeit governed by a bourgeois committee) had not proved effective. What did prove effective, however, over and above the reorganization of the club, was the aristocratic and authoritarian command of Lord Hawke. Hawke was a useful batsman. He took over the captaincy for the first time in 1883, was firmly established in 1886, and continued in the post until 1910, combining it with the club presidency from 1898, and continuing in the latter role until he died in 1938. Few have given such service to any county, even if he sometimes erred on the side of blinkered autocracy.

Hawke's main task was a civic one, that of imposing a discipline upon a troupe of Yorkshire professionals so that their overall performance might match their potential. He insisted on improved dress and deportment, and, faced with imbibers who had won the grudging admiration of others in a game where abstinence had won precious little ground, he sternly ordered due moderation.

The authority of Lord Hawke over the Yorkshire professionals, rather like the command assumed by A. N. Hornby over his Lancashire counterparts, created the classic amateur-professional dichotomy, which, until the 1960s, was to remain the essence of county cricket's internal structure. It was enough that the amateur was a competent cricketer, a decided bonus were he a crack player: what was important was the discipline he imposed and the unity of goal he produced. It was the traditional formula, also to be observed in other Victorian cross-class institutions, such as the army and the navy, the well-to-do household with its servant, or in some vocational dualisms, such as landowner and bailiff or factory-owner and foreman. The characteristic Yorkshire 'pro' became not

154 'Long John' Tunnicliffe, Yorkshire's opening bat and record catcher at the turn of the century.

only technically supreme in his trade, but he also developed a set of matching virtues. Conscientious, tenacious, relentless, sombre, with a value-system that was hard but just, he was imbued with a pride in his vocation that was illustrated by good standards of behaviour and dress, both on and off the field. All this was a decided change from the past, and it was, of course, circular in cause and effect, for the more serious-minded and careful the approach, the more the actual techniques were honed. In turn, this joint concern for craftsmanship and reputation was passed down from generation to generation.

This was a phenomenon evolving in more or less degree all over the country, but it was its Yorkshire manifestation that was the model illustration. Nor, truth to tell, was it an entirely satisfying and admirable phenomenon, bringing joy to the conservative flank of working-class romanticism. The virtues, in extension, became the vices, the sins of stultifying caution, of heavy and opinionated smugness, of affected bluntness and enervating solemnity. Nonetheless, it served Yorkshire well as a formulation for close on eighty years.

Henceforward, at least until the 1970s, Yorkshire cricket is a long and unadulterated yarn of celebration, crowded with the exploits of players of genius and near genius, the whole glossed with a kind of grim glamour.

In the years before the First World War, Yorkshire's fortunes were mainly in the hands of two all-rounders who, perhaps along with Gary Sobers, might claim to be the best in the history of cricket. George Hirst, showing the most wholesome traits of sturdiness and endurance, bowled his left-arm 'swerver' to perfection, and delighted in his pull shot to gather many runs. In 1906 he performed a unique double, something like a quadruple, when he became the only cricketer to score 2000 runs and take 200 wickets in a season, a feat which stands alone as the most comprehensive summer's work ever. All in all, he scored 1000 runs in a season nineteen times and took 100 wickets in fifteen seasons, including fourteen doubles. He took 2739 first-class wickets; he scored 36,323 first-class runs, including Yorkshire's highest ever, 341 against Leicester; and, as the most steely mid-off of his generation, he took some 500 catches.

Wilfred Rhodes, often in concert with George Hirst, mastered the technical know-how first of bowling and then of batting to the degree that he was able to sustain his superb level of joint authority longer than any cricketer in history. Dedicated and patient beyond belief, and maintained by practised rhythms that seemed never to exhaust him nor vulgarize his natural style, he is rightly hailed as the supreme professional cricketer. Like Hirst he stands alone, and for two achievements. He is the only player to have done the double sixteen times and he is the only bowler to have taken 4000 first-class wickets, 4187, to be precise, at an average of 16. He gathered nearly 40,000 runs, including 1000 in each of twenty-one seasons, and he took approaching 600 catches. Rhodes played in fifty-eight Tests (to Hirst's twenty-four) and became one of only eight Englishmen to do the international double of 100 Test wickets and a 1000 Test runs. As tribute to his stamina and his persistent talent, he is the oldest cricketer to have represented his country.

Before and during the performance of these zealous deeds there were other noted players. Yorkshire were blessed, as so often, with a productive pair of opening bats. Like a traditional variety double act, there was the squat figure of J. T. Brown and the extraordinarily lanky figure of John Tunnicliffe, both difficult customers to displace. Respectively, they scored some 16,000 and 20,000 runs for their county, and Tunnicliffe, with acrobatic slip fielding, took 665 catches, still a Yorkshire record. The mainstay of the batting was David Denton, who buffeted his way to 2000 runs in no less than five seasons, and whose career total of 37,899 was excelled at this time only by W. G. Grace, J. T. Tyldestey and Tom Hayward. He was famed for his glorious outfielding as well as for his daring batsmanship.

Ted Wainwright was a useful all-rounder, a trundler of huge off-breaks and a batsman of correct method. Schofield Haigh was a cheerful, zestful bowler, who took over 2000 wickets (including 100 victims in each of eleven seasons) and only his two great contemporaries and Fred Trueman and Ray Illingworth have passed that total of first-class victims in the Yorkshire story, though some of Illingworth's wickets were for Leicestershire. The mantle of wicket-keeper passed safely to David Hunter – his bag of 1253 catches and stumpings places him seventh in the all-time ratings, a marvellous record – and then to Arthur Dolphin. During the Edwardian era the all-round play of M. W. Booth and Alonzo Drake commanded attention, but, sadly, the one was killed in the First World War and the other died prematurely. Two other players now caught the eye. One was the popular Roy Kilner, who scored some 13,000 runs and took 858 wickets for Yorkshire; and the other was Edgar Oldroyd, who scored 16,000 runs. Both were spirited contributors to the county's cause.

155 F. S., later Sir Stanley, Jackson

Several precocious amateurs did play for Yorkshire alongside this batch of seasoned campaigners, and pride of place must go to that attractive all-rounder, F. S., later Sir Stanley, Jackson, the respected cricket administrator. Although his not overlong playing career suffered interruptions, he was an exceptional cricketer who did sterling work as an England regular, winning twenty caps, all against Australia. For Yorkshire, his medium-pace secured him over 500 wickets and his free strokeplay over 10,000 runs. Few cricketers have possessed such self-confidence and imperturbability.

After the three Championships of the 1890s, in 1893, 1896 and 1898, this Yorkshire side continued the new century in like vein, with a hat-trick of titles in 1900, 1901 and 1902, and then three more victories in 1905, 1908 and 1912.

Some of that older generation stayed on to support the team in the early inter-war years. During this period Yorkshire developed what must be judged the most successful team in the history of county cricket. Despite the general high standards of play and, in particular, the excellence of counties such as Lancashire and Middlesex, Yorkshire were a titanic force. They won the title in the first post-war year of 1919 and the last pre-war year of 1939. In between they had a run of four titles from 1922 to 1925, and then, after a short respite, they won the Championship from 1931 to 1933 and again in 1935, 1937 and 1938, making another hat-trick with the 1939 success.

Yorkshire had always seemed reasonably fortunate in keeping up the heritage of firm amateur captains, who knew both how to exert control when it was necessary and acknowledge the superiority of the cricketing talent they led. Neville Cardus tells the revealing anecdote of Emmott Robinson standing respectfully behind the captain's chair, as the county batted. A ball popped. 'Bring 'em in, Major', muttered the sagacious Robinson, and Major Lupton promptly declared. It was Brian Sellers who was the commanding figure among a series of such skippers. He captained the side from 1933 to 1947, and he did so with gusto, thrust and horse sense.

156 Emmott Robinson, the epitome of Yorkshire dourness

The team itself was individually brilliant in every department of the game, with bowlers to suit every occasion, and with so many fine batsmen that, eventually, two were left out of the squad of thirteen on a rota basis. Personal charisma and aptitude were welded so expertly that there was maximum collective effectiveness. Few cricket teams have matched Yorkshire's of this period for that enviable soldering of the one and the several. With three or four musketeers it was a difficult enough precept to entertain: with eleven cricketers of remarkable gift and independent mood it might have appeared well nigh impossible. Yet Yorkshire, under Brian Sellers, proved such pessimism false.

As ever, Yorkshire traded on the impact of a sound start, and wisely based their hopes on Percy Holmes and on the suave Herbert Sutcliffe. In 1932 they assembled 555 in an opening stand at Leyton against Essex, and it is salutary to note that, in so doing, they surpassed the 554 of their fine predecessors, Tunnicliffe and Brown. That 555 still remains the fourth highest stand in first-class cricket. Holmes, who scored some 30,000 runs, was the admirable foil for Sutcliffe. Sutcliffe has a total of 50,000 first-class runs to his name at an average of 51.95, and this includes over 4500 runs in fifty-four Tests at an average of just over 60, the only Englishman to achieve that mark. That average puts him seventh in the list of world first-class batsmen, and he is the highest-scoring Yorkshireman. He scored 149 centuries, and he made 1000 runs in each of twenty-four seasons. Herbert Sutcliffe was a living monument to concentration, having the priceless knack of rendering himself oblivious to the behaviour of the last ball as he measured up to the next. It was reflective of the prudent concern of the true professional craftsman, but it was also resonant of the sang-froid of the upper-class amateur. Sutcliffe, in fact, became, in his life-style and in his future business life, a pioneer of what the new cricket professional would aspire to be.

The doughty Leyland, left-handed and pugnacious and the scorer of 33,000 first-class runs, was the anchorman of the batting. Like his fellows, he was a shrewd student of the game, and

157 & 158 Two key players in Yorkshire's successes in the 1930s,
Maurice Leyland (left) and Bill Bowes.

the entrance of his broad frame on to the arena often spelt the death of hope to opponents of both Yorkshire and England alike. Arthur Mitchell, Wilfred Barber and Cyril Turner maintained these solid traditions, each proving to be fine servants of the club.

Strong and virile though the batting was, it was the bowling – as is more frequently the case with long-term victors in cricket – which was definitively lethal. Abe Waddington, for too brief a spell, exhibited the smooth fluency of his pacy action, and Emmott Robinson, the archetypal tyke, took nearly 900 wickets for Yorkshire with his astute control. Ellis Robinson succeeded him and had over 700 victims, and there was also the off-spin of T. F. Smailes. For many years George Macauley was the epitome of barely concealed aggression, and his mix of off-spin and seam earned him the splendid sum of 1837 first-class wickets.

In the second half of these seasons between the two world wars the attack came to rest on the complementary talent of Bill Bowes and Hedley Verity. With his high action and tall frame, W. E. Bowes rattled the ball stingingly around the batsman's midriff, with the occasional shorter pitched delivery for additional unease. Thoughtful in approach and skilled in control, Bowes ended with 1639 first-class victims, and was one of the premier quick bowlers of his generation.

Hedley Verity, academic and courteous and as chivalrous in attitude as he was masterful in technique, replaced Wilfred Rhodes as Yorkshire's left-hand spinner, and England's too. His command of the arts of flight, length and turn were such that in ten seasons he achieved 1956 first-class wickets at the thrifty average of a mere 14.90. Some fifty times in his relatively short career he took 7 wickets or more in an innings, and, of the four times a Yorkshire bowler has taken all 10 wickets, Verity was twice responsible; his 10 for 10 against Nottinghamshire in 1932 is the best bowling performance recorded in the Championship. It is said of Hedley Verity that he preferred the challenge of the great batsman on a perfect pitch to the rabbit on a tip, and thus, like several players in Yorkshire's illustrious past, he

transcended technical prowess and touched on art.

Sutcliffe and Verity were two of a number of 1930s players who, by example, brought a new respect and image to professional cricket. If the likes of Hirst and Rhodes had transformed cricket from a trade to a craft, then Sutcliffe and Verity were responsible for changing it into a profession. It was a sign of that alteration, as well as of some general revisions in the social order, that Verity and other professionals were commissioned when the second war came; that was practically unknown in the first war although Herbert Sutcliffe was a rule-proving exception, being commissioned towards the end of the first war. It is also worth noting that Sutcliffe was twenty-four before he played his first first-class match.

Hedley Verity died bravely in battle in Sicily, a grievous loss to both nation and county, and Bowes's torrid experience as a prisoner-of-war left him unable to be quite the same bowler again.

Between the wars Yorkshire were also outstanding in the field, another bequest from the days of Lord Hawke. All was menacing address, with few catches going begging. This was the hallmark of the complete machine, this aggressive and acute teamwork when fielding. Among men who were all top-class in this department, Arthur Mitchell, Brian Sellers and Cyril Turner stood out and glittered. The wicket-keeping passed from Dolphin to Arthur Wood, who worked with commendable good cheer as well as commendable safety.

In spite of tragic losses and incapacities, this team survived the Second World War, and, with Arthur Booth substituting gamely for Verity in 1946, Yorkshire won the Championship yet again. They shared the title in 1949 with the rampant Middlesex side, but then the ancient regime collapsed entirely. There was a decade of team building, and then Yorkshire entered into the third and final episode of their glory days. Apart from low places in 1953 and 1958, they were never disgraced, but, during the 1960s, they did look more akin to the pre-war Yorkshire sides. They won the Championship in 1959, again in 1960, in 1962 and again in 1963, and then again twice consecutively in 1966, 1967 and 1968. A thirteenth placement in 1969 was the real beginning of the lean years, with rock bottom struck in 1983, and only a runners-up spot in 1975 to lighten the lengthening gloom.

Len Hutton was, of course, the pride of Yorkshire in the early post-war years. His career ran from 1934 to 1960, so that he enjoyed much success with Yorkshire, as Sutcliffe's young partner, in the truly golden days of his county's cricket. Despite a bad arm injury, he sustained the promise of his early Test career, and then became England's first professional captain of the modern era. He scored around 40,000 first-class runs, including 6971 for England, and he averaged over 55 both for his country and in all first-class cricket. He also scored 129 centuries, and, if one adds a notional statistic to all that for the six lost wartime seasons, one may form an even more accurate measure of the maestro. Like the snow in the carol, he was, technically speaking, crisp and even; his balance and footwork were precise and perfect, and his cover shots one of the treasured memories of cricket lore. He illustrated a pleasing point about the best of Yorkshire cricket: however schooled the cricketer and however the combine absorbed the individual, the personality of genius glimmered through, so that Hutton at the crease was as unmistakable as he was inimitable. He daily proclaimed the excellent truth that cricket is at its most pragmatic when it is at its most artistic.

In Norman Yardley Yorkshire found the last of their considerable number of fine amateurs, a sprightly cricketer with bat and ball, who captained England as well as Yorkshire. He, too, had played before the war. Since that time there have been other all-rounders. Brian Close, he of the youthful Test début and twenty-two caps in all, had a long and lively career, the end-piece of it with Somerset. He scored 34,994 runs in all between 1949 and 1986, twenty times reaching 1000. He took nearly 1000 wickets for Yorkshire alone, and, in all cricket, this fearless and intrepid fielder snatched 813 catches. Another all-rounder, Ray Illingworth, had a similar kind of career, for, like Close, he captained both county and country, and moved to a second home, in his case Leicester. Illingworth, off-spinner and workmanlike bat, is one of only nine cricketers to have scored over 20,000 first-class runs and taken over 2000 first-class wickets.

The pick of the other batsmen since the war have probably been John Hampshire, with some 28,000 runs in top-class cricket; J. V. Wilson, who scored 20,000 runs for Yorkshire and took 525 catches; Phil Sharpe, most watchful of slip fielders, who added 18,000 runs to his 525 catches for Yorkshire; the stylish left-hander Willie Watson who scored 25,000 runs in all cricket; Frank Lowson, who became Hutton's opening partner; and D. E. V. Padgett, another to top 20,000 runs for Yorkshire.

There were also splendid bowlers to support this array of runmakers. Bob Appleyard had his career sadly curtailed – he was a talented bowler of off-cut and spin, and he took over 600 wickets for the county. Chris Old was a quick bowler who also took over 600 wickets for Yorkshire, and he added to this the goodly sum of 143 Test wickets in his forty-six international appearances. The grand left-arm tradition was maintained by Johnny Wardle, peremptorily sacked in 1958 for 'general misbehaviour', and by Don Wilson, if with rather less brouhaha, and nowadays by Phil Carrick. Wardle was a most ingenious bowler, as his 1846 wickets testify, and just over 100 of these were in Test matches. Wilson weighed in with over 1000 wickets just for Yorkshire, and Carrick achieved his 1000th wicket in the Roses match at Old Trafford in 1991.

Emerging from this gifted group as Yorkshire's leading bowler since the Second World War, and their most dangerous opening bowler ever, is Fred Trueman. His tally of 2304 first-class wickets is a remarkable aggregate. He was the first Test bowler to reach 300 wickets, closing on 307, and he must always be shortlisted when the game of picking world XIs is played. Strongly built, and with a most fluent action, he contrived to couple the roles of belligerent attacker and affable jester. Neither is easy on a cricket field. To perfect both parts and then compound them is otherwise unheard of, and Fred Trueman is remembered as much for his characterization as for his bowling – which is how it should be in a spectator sport.

159 Fred Trueman

With Close, Sharp, Wilson, Watson and Trueman himself to the fore, the Yorkshire fielding remained constant to the ancient principles. Once more Yorkshire found wicket-keepers who combined ability with longevity in the persons of Don Brennan, J. G. Binks (who had over 1000 stumped and caught between 1955 and 1975) and, more recently, David Bairstow. Martyn Moxon, the new captain, now tries to carry forward the Yorkist banner, guided by their coach and mentor, Steve Oldham.

That leaves the intriguing case-study of Geoffrey Boycott, who inherited the mantle of Sutcliffe and Hutton in the very position – opening the innings – where Yorkshire had always excelled. Both for England and for Yorkshire, there is no discounting the value and bounty of his contribution, for here, by the highest standards, was a world-class batsman of extraordinary circumspection and skill. The most capped Yorkshireman, with 108 Tests to his credit, during the course of which he scored twenty-two of his marvellous collection of 151 centuries and scored over 8000 runs, Boycott must stand comparison with any cricketer. He scored 1000 runs in each of twenty-six seasons, which has been equalled once and passed four times only in cricket's history. He is eighth in the world order with 48,000 runs, one position behind Herbert Sutcliffe, but, interestingly enough, he is the batsman with the largest post-war aggregate. Yet passions rage over whether his single-mindedness shaded out into undue selfishness, and much of the furore at, and much of the despondency over, the Yorkshire club was concurrent with his career, which ran from 1962 to 1986.

There had, of course, been other rows – Wardle's disagreement is a case in point – and it is debatable how much Boycott was the cause of argument and how much Yorkshire had become introverted and soured, numbed by their relative lack of success in the modern dispensation. Mention was made in the concluding section of Part One of the chauvinism of Yorkshire, and there is no need to repeat the detail. Yorkshire have, perhaps pluckily, perhaps shortsightedly, tried to retain the closest possible identity. By their own hard yardstick, against a backcloth of increased financial and technical equality, with one-day cricket and overseas assistance the norm, they have failed.

It is not for an outsider to intrude on these private griefs, even though the mourning has been overloud and the wailing overlong. Having first determined to recruit players reared and schooled, if not born, in the county, they suddenly decided, in 1991, to adopt the same registration tenets as everyone else, and, aided by Yorkshire Television sponsorship, they signed the Australian quick bowler, C. J. McDermott, for the 1992 season as their first-ever overseas player. It does appear that Yorkshire will now begin to make some accommodation with modernism, in an attempt to retrieve the grandeur of yesteryear, and to end the continual aggravation which had come, in part, from that very cloistered and inward-looking policy. This, however well it had served in the past, had become something of a political as well as a sporting liability.

But nothing can subtract from the richness of the Yorkshire story. When it comes to picking a Yorkshire side to represent that wealth of history, the surfeit of talent is overwhelming, with several players vying for the same position in a mythical world, let alone county or even national, XI. One might begin with a bare announcement of teams selected from before the First World War (and that without delving too far back into Yorkshire's antiquities), from the inter-war years, and from the seasons since the end of the second war. Allowing for some subtle shifts where players, as sometimes happened, won fame in two of these eras, something like the following might emerge:

Pre-1914	1919–1939	1945 onwards
Tunnicliffe & Brown	Sutcliffe & Holmes	Hutton & Boycott
Jackson	Leyland	Close
Denton	Mitchell	Hampshire
Hirst	Barber	Watson
Rhodes	Macauley	Illingworth
*Lord Hawke	*Sellers	*Yardley
Peel or Peate	Robinson	Old
Haigh	Bowes	Trueman
Emmett	Verity	Wardle
†Hunter	†Wood	†Binks

* captain † wicket-keeper

These teams (not necessarily in batting order) are composed of a fine pair of opening bats, solid further batting, including excellent all-rounders, a good captain, a medley of useful bowlers, including pace as well as the regulation left-hand spin, and a competent wicket-keeper. The genuine difficulty arises when one tries to refine further and find just one side. Choosing two openers from Sutcliffe, Hutton and Boycott is just as arduous as deciding between Verity and Rhodes. Trueman and Bowes make for easier selection to begin the assault, and Hunter should probably keep wicket, while Hirst must, of course, play. A cowardly solution would be to choose all three opening bats, and, recognizing that Yorkshire's left-hand has usually been superior to their right-hand spin, play both Verity and Rhodes. This eleven would read: Herbert Sutcliffe, Len Hutton, Geoffrey Boycott, Maurice Leyland, George Hirst, Wilfred Rhodes, Brian Sellers as captain, David Hunter, Fred Trueman, Bill Bowes and Hedley Verity. Illingworth and Macauley would share the twelfth man spot and either would be counted unlucky to be excluded. It would be an unthinking gambler who would wager against this team not defeating any of the other sixteen sides already chosen.

160 Yorkshire's trio of great opening batsmen – Geoffrey Boycott, Herbert Sutcliffe and Leonard Hutton – each the maker of over 100 centuries.

APPENDICES

Some Facts and Figures

APPENDIX 1
Foundation dates of each county club

	Foundation date of first known cricket organization in the county	Foundation date of present county club	Date of joining Championship
Derbyshire	1870	1870	(1871–87)1895
Essex	1790	1876	1895
Glamorgan	1863	1888	1921
Gloucestershire	1863	1871	1870
Hampshire	1849	1863/1879*	(1864–85)1895
Kent	1842	1859/1870*	1864
Lancashire	1864	1864	1865
Leicestershire	1820	1879	1895
Middlesex	1863	1864	1864
Northamptonshire	1820	1820/1878*	1905
Nottinghamshire	1841	1841/1866*	1864
Somerset	1864	1875	(1882–85) 1891
Surrey	1845	1845	1864
Sussex	1836	1839/1857*	1864
Warwickshire	1826	1882	1895
Worcestershire	1844	1865	1899
Yorkshire	1861	1863/1891*	1864

* Denotes year of major reorganization

APPENDIX 2
Championships and cups won since 1864

	Championships	Gillette/ NatWest	B & H	Player/ Refuge	Total
Derbyshire	1	1	0	1	3
Essex	5	1	1	4*	11
Glamorgan	2	0	0	0	2
Gloucestershire	4(1)	1	1	0	6
Hampshire	2	1	1	3	7
Kent	7(1)	2	3	3	15
Lancashire	12(4)	5	2	4*	23
Leicestershire	1	0	3	2	6
Middlesex	12(2)	4	2	1*	19
Northamptonshire	0	1	1	0	2
Nottinghamshire	19(5)	1	1	1	22
Somerset	0	2	2	1	5
Surrey	20(2)	1	1	0	22
Sussex	0	4	0	1	5
Warwickshire	3	3	0	1	7
Worcestershire	5	0	1	4*	10
Yorkshire	33(2)	2	1	1	37

Brackets = shared titles   * Includes Refuge Assurance Cup win
Included in the total

APPENDIX 3
Highest and lowest county scores

	Highest score	Lowest score
Derbyshire	645 v. Hampshire 1898	16 v. Notts. 1879
Essex	761–6 v. Leicester. 1990	30 v. Yorkshire 1901
Glamorgan	587–8 v. Derbyshire 1951	22 v. Lancashire 1924
Gloucestershire	653–6 v. Glamorgan 1928	22 v. Somerset 1920
Hampshire	672–7 v. Somerset 1899	15 v. Warwicks. 1922
Kent	803–4 v. Essex 1934	18 v. Sussex 1867
Lancashire	863 v. Surrey 1990	25 v. Derbys. 1871
Leicestershire	701–4 v. Worcester. 1906	25 v. Kent 1912
Middlesex	642–3 v. Hampshire 1923	25 v. Surrey 1885
Northamptonshire	636–6 v. Essex 1990	12 v. Gloucester. 1907
Nottinghamshire	739–7 v. Leicester. 1903	13 v. Yorkshire 1901
Somerset	675–9 v. Hampshire 1924	25 v. Gloucester. 1947
Surrey	811 v. Somerset 1899	14 v. Essex 1983
Sussex	705–8 v. Surrey 1902	19 v. Notts. 1873
Warwickshire	657–6 v. Hampshire 1899	16 v. Kent 1913
Worcestershire	633 v. Warwicks. 1906	24 v. Yorkshire 1903
Yorkshire	887 v. Warwicks. 1896	23 v. Hampshire 1965

† Batting one man short

APPENDIX 4
Highest Championship stands

Derbyshire	C. S. Elliott & J. D. Eggar v. Notts. 1947	349
Essex	G. A. Gooch & P. J. Prichard v. Leicester. 1990	403
Glamorgan	R. C. Fredericks & A. Jones v. Northants. 1972	330
Gloucestershire	W. R. Hammond & B. H. Lyon v. Leicester. 1933	336
Hampshire	R. M. Poore & E. G. Wynyard v. Somerset 1899	411
Kent	S. G. Hinks & N. R. Taylor v. Middx. 1990	366
Lancashire	F. B. Watson & E. Tyldesley v. Surrey 1928	371
Leicestershire	B. Dudleston & J. F. Steele v. Derbys. 1979	390
Middlesex	W. J. Edrich & D. C. S. Compton v. Somerset 1948	424*
Northamptonshire	A. Fordham & A. J. Lamb v. Yorks. 1990	398
Nottinghamshire	W. Gunn & A. Shrewsbury v. Sussex 1890	393
Somerset	H. T. Hewett & L. C. H. Palairet v. Yorks. 1892	346
Surrey	R. Abel & T. W. Hayward v. Yorks. 1899	448
Sussex	E. H. Bowley & John Langridge v. Middx. 1933	490
Warwickshire	A. I. Kallicharran & G. W. Humpage v. Lancs. 1982	470
Worcestershire	E. G. Arnold & W. B. Burns v. Warwicks. 1909	393
Yorkshire	P. Holmes & H. Sutcliffe v. Essex 1932	555

* Denotes unbroken partnership

APPENDIX 5
Highest individual scores and best bowling achievements

Derbyshire	G. A. Davidson v. Lancs. 1896	274	W. Bestwick v. Glam. 1921	10–40
Essex	P. A. Perrin v. Derbys. 1904	343*	H. Pickett v. Leics. 1895	10–32
Glamorgan	D. E. Davies v. Glos. 1939	287*	J. Mercer v. Worcs. 1936	10–51
Gloucestershire	W. G. Grace v. Yorks. 1876	318*	E. G. Dennett v. Essex 1906	10–40
Hampshire	R. H. Moore v. Warwicks. 1937	316	R. M. H. Cottam v. Lancs. 1965	9–25
Kent	W. H. Ashdown v. Essex 1934	332	C. Blythe v. Northants. 1907	10–30
Lancashire	A. C. MacLaren v. Somerset 1895	424	W. Hickton v. Hants. 1870	10–46
Leicestershire	S. Coe v. Northants. 1914	252*	G. Geary v. Glam. 1929	10–18
Middlesex	J. D. Robertson v. Worcs. 1949	331*	G. O. Allen v. Lancs. 1929	10–40
Northamptonshire	R. Subba Row v. Surrey 1958	300	V. W. C. Jupp v. Kent 1932	10–127
Nottinghamshire	W. W. Keeton v. Middx. 1939	312*	K. Smales v. Glos. 1956	10–66
Somerset	I. V. A. Richards v. Warwicks. 1985	322	E. J. Tyler v. Surrey 1895	10–49
Surrey	R. Abel v. Somerset 1899	357*	T. Rushby v. Somerset 1921	10–43
Sussex	K. S. Duleepsinhji v. Northants. 1930	333	C. H. G. Bland v. Kent 1899	10–48
Warwickshire	F. R. Foster v. Worcs. 1914	305*	W. E. Hollies v. Notts. 1946	10–49
Worcestershire	G. A. Hick v. Somerset 1988	405*	C. F. Root v. Lancs. 1931	9–23
Yorkshire	G. H. Hirst v. Leics. 1905	341	H. Verity v. Notts. 1932	10–10

* Denotes not out

APPENDIX 6
Highest individual aggregate runs, wickets and centuries in all first-class matches for the county

	Runs		Wickets		Centuries	
Derbyshire	D. Smith	20,516	H. L. Jackson	1670	K. J. Barnett	34
Essex	K. W. R. Fletcher	29,434	T. P. B. Smith	1610	J. O'Connor	71
Glamorgan	A. Jones	34,056	D. J. Shepherd	2174	A. Jones	52
Gloucestershire	W. R. Hammond	33,664	C. W. L. Parker	3170	W. R. Hammond	113
Hampshire	C. P. Mead	48,892	D. Shackleton	2669	C. P. Mead	138
Kent	F. E. Woolley	47,868	A. P. Freeman	3340	F. E. Woolley	122
Lancashire	E. Tyldesley	34,222	J. B. Statham	1816	E. Tyldesley	90
Leicestershire	L. G. Berry	30,143	W. E. Astill	2130	L. G. Berry	45
Middlesex	E. H. Hendren	40,302	F. J. Titmus	2361	E. H. Hendren	119
Northamptonshire	D. Brookes	28,980	E. W. Clark	1097	D. Brookes	67
Nottinghamshire	G. Gunn	31,592	T. G. Wass	1653	J. Hardstaff Jnr	65
Somerset	H. Gimblett	21,142	J. C. White	2166	H. Gimblett	49
Surrey	J. B. Hobbs	43,554	T. Richardson	1775	J. B. Hobbs	144
Sussex	John Langridge	34,152	M. W. Tate	2211	John Langridge	76
Warwickshire	D. L. Amiss	35,146	W. E. Hollies	2201	D. L. Amiss	78
Worcestershire	D. Kenyon	33,490	R. T. D. Perks	2143	G. M. Turner	72
Yorkshire	H. Sutcliffe	38,561	W. Rhodes	3608	H. Sutcliffe	112

APPENDIX 7

Most times 1000 runs, 100 wickets and the 'double' for the county

	Most times 1000 runs		Most times 100 wickets		Most times* 100 wickets/ 1000 runs	
Derbyshire	D. Smith	12	C. Gladwin	12		
Essex	K. W. R. Fletcher	19	M. S. Nichols	11	M. S. Nichols	8
Glamorgan	A. Jones	20	D. J. Shepherd	12		
Gloucestershire	W. R. Hammond	17	T. Goddard/C. Parker	16		
Hampshire	C. P. Mead	27	D. Shackleton	19	J. A. Newman	5
Kent	F. E. Woolley	27	A. P. Freeman	17	F. E. Woolley	6
Lancashire	J. T. Tyldesley	19	J. Briggs	11		
Leicestershire	L. G. Berry	18	G. Geary	9	W. E. Astill	5
Middlesex	E. H. Hendren	20	F. J. Titmus	11	F. A. Tarrant	6
Northamptonshire	D. Brookes	17	G. E. Tribe	8	G. E. Tribe	7
Nottinghamshire	G. Gunn	20	T. G. Wass	10		
Somerset	H. Gimblett	12	J. C. White	14		
Surrey	J. B. Hobbs	24	T. Richardson	10		
Sussex	James Langridge	20	M. W. Tate	13	M. W. Tate	7
Warwickshire	W. Quaife/D. L. Amiss	20	W. E. Hollies	14		
Worcestershire	D. Kenyon	19	R. T. D. Perks	15		
Yorkshire	H. Sutcliffe	21	W. Rhodes	22	W. Rhodes	12

* Minimum five times

APPENDIX 8

Most wicket-keeping victims and most catches in the field for the county

	Wicket-keeping victims		Most catches	
Derbyshire	R. W. Taylor	1304	D. C. Morgan	563
Essex	B. Taylor	1205	K. W. R. Fletcher	519
Glamorgan	E. W. Jones	933*	P. M. Walker	656
Gloucestershire	J. H. Board	1016	C. A. Milton	719
Hampshire	N. McCorkell	688	C. P. Mead	629
Kent	F. H. Huish	1253	F. E. Woolley	773
Lancashire	G. Duckworth	922	K. J. Grieves	555
Leicestershire	R. W. Tolchard	903*	M. R. Hallam	427
Middlesex	J. T. Murray	1223	E. H. Hendren	562
Northamptonshire	K. V. Andrew	810	D. S. Steele	469
Nottinghamshire	T. W. Oates	958	A. O. Jones	466
Somerset	H. W. Stephenson	1007	J. C. White	381
Surrey	H. Strudwick	1223	M. J. Stewart	604
Sussex	H. R. Butt	1176	John Langridge	779
Warwickshire	E. J. Smith	800	M. J. K. Smith	422
Worcestershire	R. Booth	1015	D. W. Richardson	412
Yorkshire	D. Hunter	1189	J. Tunnicliffe	665

* Includes catches as a fielder

APPENDIX 9

Most appearances for each county; longest-serving county captains

	Appearances		Captaincy
Derbyshire	D. C. Morgan 1950–69	540	K. J. Barnett 1983–91
Essex	K. W. R. Fletcher 1962–88	575	J. W. H. T. Douglas 1911–28
Glamorgan	D. J. Shepherd 1950–72	647	M. J. Turnbull 1930–39
Gloucestershire	C. W. L. Parker 1903–35	602	W. G. Grace 1870–93
Hampshire	C. P. Mead 1905–36	700	Hon. L. H./Lord Tennyson 1919–33
Kent	F. E. Woolley 1906–38	764	Lord Harris 1871–89
Lancashire	E. Tyldesley 1909–36	573	A. N. Hornby 1880–91; 1892–93 (shared); 1897–98
Leicestershire	W. E. Astill 1906–39	628	C. E. de Trafford 1894–1906
Middlesex	F. J. Titmus 1949–82	642	A. J. Webbe 1885–98 (1898 shared)
Northamptonshire	D. Brookes 1934–59	492	G. Cook 1981–89
Nottinghamshire	G. Gunn 1902–32	583	W. Clarke 1835–55
Somerset	B. A. Langford 1953–74	504	S. M. J. Woods 1894–1906
Surrey	J. B. Hobbs 1905–34	598	P. G. H. Fender 1921–31
Sussex	James Langridge 1924–53	622	E. Napper 1847–62
Warwickshire	W. G. Quaife 1894–1928	665	F. S. G. Calthorpe 1920–29
Worcestershire	D. Kenyon 1946–67	589	H. K. Foster 1901–10; N. Gifford 1971–80
Yorkshire	W. Rhodes 1898–1930	881	Hon. M. B./Lord Hawke 1883–1910

Index

(This index covers the text and captions to the illustrated material in Parts 1 and 2. It does not cover any of the names in the Appendices)